FOOD AND EATING EXPERIENCES
OF OLDER WOMEN
IN A RETIREMENT COMMUNITY

FOOD AND EATING EXPERIENCES OF OLDER WOMEN IN A RETIREMENT COMMUNITY

A Sociological Study

Lisa Curch

The Edwin Mellen Press
Lewiston•Queenston•Lampeter

Library of Congress Cataloging-in-Publication Data

Curch, Lisa.
  Food and eating experiences of older women in a retirement community : a sociological
study / Lisa Curch.
    p. cm.
  Includes bibliographical references and index.
  ISBN 0-7734-5920-0
  I. Title.

hors série.

A CIP catalog record for this book is available from the British Library.

Copyright © 2005 Lisa Curch

The Edwin Mellen Press   The Edwin Mellen Press
        Box 450   Box 67
   Lewiston, New York   Queenston, Ontario
   USA 14092-0450   CANADA L0S 1L0

            The Edwin Mellen Press, Ltd.
            Lampeter, Ceredigion, Wales
            UNITED KINGDOM SA48 8LT

        Printed in the United States of America

For my parents, Terry and Toni Crowder

Table of Contents

List of Illustrations

Foreword

I was not as a child a big fan of asparagus, but individual culinary preferences didn't matter much in our family. At dinner one Sunday my grandmother, in response to the endless vegetable re-arrangement on my plate, told me to finish my asparagus because people were starving in India. With logic unbecoming of me at any age, I casually suggested that we send the food to India where it would do some good. My father suggested something else. I finished the asparagus. And I was sure that people in India, unaware of my physical discomfort on their behalf, suffered little from my failed efforts to help.

One of my doctoral students recently held her first advisory committee meeting. Upon entering the conference room we were greeted by a beautifully decorated table covered with food: fresh fruit and vegetables; clam dip; cheeses; crackers; and cookies to die for. Flabbergasted might be an adequate word to describe the initial reaction of the committee members. (I should add here that such a spread is *not* standard protocol in our program for anything other than the occasional party, reception, or birthday pot-luck lunch.) But the student made clear her intent by saying "You've got to remember that I'm from a strong church-going family, and food is at the middle of everything we do. So put up with it!"

And finally, an old friend and his bride-to-be invited my wife and I to dinner a number of years ago. We happily accepted, and on the appointed evening we joined them in the dining room of their retirement community. Of course we were not invited simply to fuel our bodies, although our hosts made it immediately clear that "their" dietician and chef built every menu around healthy eating. Our time together was spent in lively conversation on such topics as their health, the lives of their families and neighbors, steamy gossip surrounding the facility's staff, and recent and planned travels. It also became quite clear by the end of the evening that the invitation was a chance for our old friend to introduce and show off his 'young' friends to his betrothed and to other residents of the community.

I doubt these personal anecdotes are unusual; everyone is sure to have many memorable experiences—pleasant and unpleasant—associated with meals and food. I offer a sampling of my own stories to illustrate a familiar yet essential reality that serves as a conceptual basis for this book; the act of eating nourishes the body, while significant actions and meanings *associated with* eating nourish the mind and the spirit. These two forms of nourishment are distinct, yet they are entwined in ways that significantly and differentially affect people, and especially as people age.

I also offer my stories to evoke thought of the complexities and dynamics of our food practices. We develop, early in life, certain food preferences and dietary behaviors that follow us in subtle ways through adulthood and old age. I was brought up in the farm county of the north-central United States, with parents who were children of the Great Depression. My dietary heritage stems from a household of limited means and a dominant yet limited variety of meat and starch, with fresh seasonal vegetables and fruits from a garden at best, and from a can on normal occasions. My wife, on the other hand, was raised near coastal Norway and in eastern Africa, with parents who were children of World War II. My spouse learned early in life to eat and enjoy virtually anything: seafood and wild game served fresh, dried, or pickled, and vegetables and fruits gathered from the highlands of Scandinavia and the veldt of Kenya and surrounding areas. As adults, we both feel compelled to clean our plates. My food preferences have been dramatically expanded because of marriage, while both of our actual food choices and consumption behaviors have been modified to support work and exercise schedules and accommodate normal age related changes in nutritional requirements. Although what and how my wife and I eat, and indeed what and how most people eat, is strongly influenced by early life experiences, our dietary preferences and behaviors are continually supplemented and reshaped as we acquire new experiences and make decisions in light of evolving situations and anticipated futures.

Lisa Curch's research over at least the past five years has sought to develop a better understanding of why we eat what we do in the ways we do and the meanings derived from food and eating. At least two significant phenomena underscore the urgency and importance of her work. First is the current pandemic of obesity. Rapidly increasing numbers *and percentages* of Americans are eating more, exercising less, and gaining significant weight. And the health repercussions already are pronounced, with conditions relating to high body mass index now ranking among leading causes of morbidity and mortality. From an epidemiological perspective, what is going on in terms of obesity seems fairly clear. To be blunt, we are gaining in girth because of dramatic social changes associated with complex interactions between at least new technologies, service-based economies, income disparities, shifting gender roles and role expectations, geographic location and context, and a food industry responding without remorse to consumer demands. Substantial research already exists, and more is ongoing, that seeks to unravel and explain the complex dynamics leading to obesity.

A second phenomenon is the aging of America's population. Again the number and percentage of older adults are growing, and with the post-World War II Baby Boom approaching retirement we can surely expect unprecedented growth in the near future. Proper diet becomes increasingly important with age, especially as body systems become less capable of compensating for and recovering from the physical insults of under-nutrition and malnutrition. Interestingly, health statistics indicate that problems of obesity are just barely creeping into today's elderly population. But this, I am certain, will change.

Curch's research, therefore, could not be more timely. What you will read in the pages that follow has direct bearing on the pressing social issues of obesity and aging, and the beauty of this book lies in its integrative, holistic, and highly individualized tenor that explicitly addresses the complexities surrounding food and food practices in the lives of older American women. You will *not* encounter the usual trappings of statistically based research. Despite her quantitative proficiency, Curch wisely chose an ethnographic approach centered on in-depth narrative life course interviews with 18 older women that include extensive participant observation in which she became immersed in the community lives, food activities, and cultures of her women. By the end of this book you will know these women; you will see how their lives have unfolded over the years, learn how to make some of their favorite foods, share many of their joys and heartaches, and hear what they have to say about the place of food and food behaviors in their lives.

But these women's stories are only the beginning of a compelling journey in scholarship. By employing a multidisciplinary survey of both theoretical and applied scientific literature, Curch is able to situate the stories of her individual women within a much larger field of knowledge, thus allowing her to suggest explanations of *why* older women have come to view food and food practices the way they do, and *how* such things represent an ongoing and, at times, extremely important influence in life.

Food is much more than something to be categorized into basic groups and prioritized within a geometric form. Food preparation and dietary behaviors cannot and should not be viewed simply from the perspectives of the FDA and social etiquette experts. The proof of this is in the pudding, so to speak, as I welcome you into this book. I have no doubt that Lisa Curch's work will evoke your own food-related memories, and will challenge you to consider the consequences—both good and bad—of what and how we eat as we age through the later stages of life.

John F. Watkins

Dr. John F. Watkins is Professor of Gerontology and Health Behavior, in the College of Public Health, at the University of Kentucky.

Acknowledgements

I would like to thank my friends and colleagues in the Sociology Department of the State University of New York – College at Oneonta for their support and encouragement throughout the time I worked on this book. I am thankful to the staff at the Milne Library and the Teaching, Learning, and Technology Center of SUNY-Oneonta for all of their help. I am exceedingly grateful to John Watkins, for his time and effort put into writing the foreword and for his support and guidance. My appreciation goes to the reviewers for this book: Graham Rowles, Janice Plahuta, and those anonymous. I would like to thank my mentors and guides at the University of Kentucky for their support and expertise in the development of the dissertation upon which this book is based. I am indebted to my brother, Brian Crowder, who gave generously of his computer and artistic expertise and his time, including the development of the physical layout graphics. I also thank the staff and editors at *Geographica Helvetica*, especially Veronika Frei and Rita Schneider-Sliwa, for their assistance.

I am very grateful to the research participants, who literally made this book possible.

I thank my family and friends who have kept me in their thoughts and prayers throughout the entire project. I thank my parents, my grandmothers and great-aunt, my brother and his wife, and my extended family who have supported me over the years. Finally, special thanks and endless gratitude to my husband, Chris Curch, who I really cannot thank enough, as his support, help, and love have been indispensable to me and the writing of this book.

Introduction

Colonial Square (a pseudonym) is an independent living retirement housing community in the heart of Kentucky and the residence of about two hundred older people, who all have a wealth of personal experiences and unique life stories from which much can be learned. Eighteen women who make a home in the physical place called Colonial Square opened up their lives to me and allowed me to explore the sociocultural place of food and eating in their lives. I probed social contexts and influences on their dietary actions of the past, present and future, and examined how daily life at a retirement community structures current dietary behavior. One theme in their stories was magnificently apparent: Food and eating are much more than bodily nourishment.

This insight in and of itself is not a profound revelation. What the general public has long known, and scholars have also more recently recognized, is that food practices contain multiple sociocultural meanings, functions, and implications – food and eating are about more than just bodily nourishment. Lupton (1996) suggests that a social science perspective on food and eating considers the meaning of food and eating in the context of a culture, and argues that the practices surrounding the foodways of people (food acquisition, preparation and consumption) may be governed by biological needs, but "these practices are then elaborated according to cultural mores" (p. 7). Dietary behavior, therefore, is much more complex than traditional nutritional or biological perspectives might portray.

It is this very nature of the social aspects of dietary behavior that renders it so fascinating a topic for study. Personally, I have greatly enjoyed food for as long as I can remember. One of my early memories is a happy one of my grandparents, my parents, and myself at a Red Lobster restaurant, and I recall the extremely satisfying taste sensation of Alaskan snow crabmeat dunked in melted butter. I have vague impressions of the setting - dimmed lighting, dark wood furniture, and a candle in a red holder are about all I can conjure up - but the delight in that crabmeat is clear, as is the attention that my zealous love for seafood brought upon me. As the story goes, a pound of crab legs were ordered for me, and, to the astonishment of my grandparents, as a three-year-old girl, I ate every bite, cleaning those leg shells out (and I still love seafood).

Fast forward to almost twenty years later, and as a new bride, I am dismayed at my new husband's lack of food safety awareness. How could he possibly use the same cutting board for cutting up raw chicken and chopping vegetables, without *fully* sterilizing the board in between - not just running some water over it? Was he crazy? He thought I was after the fuss I made. I became aware that not everyone learned the same food safety practices as I did growing up and that apparently having two parents who were in the medical field produced a heightened consciousness of bacteria lurking in foodstuffs. My husband is now very careful, particularly with raw meat, though he may be just as motivated to avoid my consternation as he is to practice food safety.

Years later, and knowing firsthand the impact of early life experiences and life transitions such as marriage on foodways, I found myself in the midst of this research, attempting to more fully understand social impacts on dietary behavior across the life course. Appreciating that the female gender traditionally is responsible for providing nourishment for others, I talked with older women about their past and present experiences, seeking to address three main questions:

1. How does the social milieu shape dietary behaviors, affecting the development and maintenance of behaviors throughout life among elderly women?

2. How do life course transitions, such as changes in residence and familial states, modify dietary behaviors?

3. How does the retirement community environment shape current

dietary behaviors of older female residents? These questions guided the in-depth life history narratives (including food history narratives) that I collected from the eighteen older women at Colonial Square. These narratives and participant observation notes provided the data for my qualitative analysis. Qualitative methodology was used because it has the capacity to elicit issues of context and meaning and to gain the perspectives of the women, in their own voices.

From the stories of the women, important perceived influences on their dietary experiences and the nature of their current dietary experiences surfaced. Themes regarding the women's relationships to food and eating emerged, and their approaches are broadly categorized as dietary morality, dietary wellness, dietary sociability, and dietary duty. I primarily utilized a life course framework to understand current and past influences on dietary behaviors of older women, but also integrated symbolic interactionism and drew from social cognitive theory, social support perspectives, and ecological models. I developed a conceptual model of influences on dietary behavior of older women out of the research findings, which furthers understanding of how social theories and perspectives can inform theorizing about health behavior in general and dietary behavior in particular. A more holistic picture of dietary behavior of older women was pieced together through illumination of meaning, context and sociocultural mechanisms of influence.

The following sections address reasons for the study of health behavior, and especially dietary behavior, of older adults and of social influences on health behavior over the life course. Included also is a short section on theoretical needs and possible outcomes of such research. Finally, a few words about the methodology used for this research concludes the chapter.

Health Behavior, Dietary Practices and Aging

The study of the health behavior of older adults is a relatively recent area of research, although the last few decades have seen a steady increase in our basic knowledge (Ory, Abeles, & Lipman, 1992). It is an important area for research because of the significant impact that a host of behaviors and habits exert on health and well-being. According to the U.S. Department of Health and Human Services (2000), behavioral and environmental factors are responsible for 70 percent of all premature deaths in the United States. Many of the leading causes of death (e.g., heart disease, cancer, stroke, and diabetes) and other chronic illnesses affecting older adults (e.g., hypertension and osteoporosis) can be attributed, at least partially, to health-related behaviors such as smoking, dietary and exercise practices. Prior to the late 1980s, however, it was thought that behavioral factors did not matter in later life and that changes in later life could not reverse any damage that had already been done (Kaplan & Strawbridge, 1994).

Recent research has shown that altering behaviors and maintaining healthy behaviors can influence morbidity and mortality even into advanced ages (Fries, 2000; Kaplan, 1992). The U.S. Department of Health and Human Services (2000) noted significant health benefits for older adults who improve health behaviors and strongly encouraged such improvement. According to Wilcox and King (1999, p. 287), the bulk of evidence shows that appropriate health behaviors "can prevent or control many chronic diseases and can reduce functional disabilities that increase with age. These behaviors also can lead to significant enhancement of the quality of life and general well-being of older adults." The International Longevity Center (2000) reported that it is never too late to improve health through a healthy lifestyle and the risks involved with unhealthy behaviors cannot be out-lived. Evans and Cyr-Campbell (1997) even suggested that some physical age changes (e.g., reduced muscle mass) are not age-related at all, but the result of health behaviors (e.g., amounts and levels of physical activity).

Despite the shift in thinking about older adults and health behavior, there remains a relative lack of basic knowledge about the health behaviors of older adults. Older adults in general appear to follow healthier lifestyles. In Berkman and Breslow's (1983) Alameda County study, more people age 75 and older reported practicing all seven of the positive health behaviors studied (concerning diet, physical activity, sleeping, alcohol use, and smoking) than in any other age group. However, various patterns of health behavior practices of older adults have been found, e.g., Rakowski, Julius, Hickey, & Halter (1987) and Walker, Volkan, Sechrist, & Pender (1988). Walker (1997) observed that the heterogeneity of older adults extends to their health behavior practices, and although many follow healthy lifestyles, many do not.

Kaplan and Strawbridge (1994) remarked that the heterogeneity of the older adult population supports the importance of behavioral and social factors as they influence health in later life, as they explained:

> In the case of genetic factors, the behavioral and social environment provides the context that determines the expression of these factors. Even more importantly, behavioral and social factors may dynamically interact with biological processes to determine the health of the elderly. (p. 59)

Genetic and biological factors certainly play a role in the health of an elder, but behavioral and social processes are critical.

Also lacking is knowledge about the meanings associated with behaviors, social contexts of behaviors, and factors that determine, stabilize and change behaviors over time. Much research and theory on health behaviors of adults in general has focused on cognitive and psychological processes, such as motivation, beliefs, efficacy, and locus of control (Bennett & Murphy, 1997). This tendency is further evident in studies of older adults' health behaviors. The sociocultural and temporal aspects of health behavior in later life have not been adequately addressed.

Detailed examinations of actual health behaviors of older adults, and the foundations of such behaviors, are needed. Furthermore, situating the health practices of older adults within social and historical contexts, as well as the individual's personal and family histories, may reveal a more holistic view of the behaviors studied. As mentioned, constructs such as self-efficacy, locus of control and beliefs are commonly found in the literature (e.g., Grembowksi et al., 1993;

Huck & Armer, 1996; Rakowski & Hickey, 1980). Yet Nowicki's (1996) demonstration of the effects of the Depression on one older woman's dietary behavior, and O'Brien Cousins' (2000) illustration of the effects of marital and societal contexts on elder women's physical activity, both confirm the existence of a more complex picture regarding factors affecting the health behaviors of older adults.

As for specific health behaviors, research has implicated dietary behaviors as relevant for physical well-being of older adults. The physiological benefits of a nutritious diet seem to be well known to both the scientific community and the American public. Diet affects longevity; a low-quality diet has been shown to increase mortality risk and, alternatively, a healthy diet can lower mortality risk (de Groot, Verheijden, de Henauw, Schroll, & van Staveren, 2004; Kant, Graubard, & Schatzkin, 2004; Michels & Wolk, 2002). Diet is a factor associated with five of the ten leading causes of death: coronary heart disease, atherosclerosis, stroke, diabetes, and some types of cancer (Institute of Medicine, 2000; Wilcox & King, 1999). Eating habits are also a factor associated with some chronic diseases, such as osteoporosis (Institute of Medicine, 2000; White & Ham, 1999). Obesity is a common nutritional problem that affects older adults, but nutritional deficiencies are also of much concern (Institute of Medicine, 2000; White & Ham, 1999). In a review of research on nutrition, aging, and disease, Yu (2002) concluded that there is strong evidence in the scientific literature for using nutritional interventions in promoting longevity and preventing or attenuating various diseases.

There is further evidence that dietary behaviors contribute to psychosocial well-being. Positive health behaviors in general can help maintain physical functioning, prevent morbidity and disability, and ameliorate the effects of disease, and thus become a strategy for an older adult to preserve his/her independence (Evans & Cyr-Campbell, 1997). Good nutrition and dietary behaviors can also greatly affect an elder's quality of life (Amarantos, Martinez, & Dwyer, 2001; Drewnowski & Evans, 2001; Wilcox & King, 1999). Research commonly attempts to evaluate dietary practices, interventions, and programs in terms of the classic biomedical endpoints: mortality and morbidity. The goals of dietary change therefore emphasize the lowering of mortality rates and reducing the risk of disease and illness. Certainly this is important, especially reducing morbidity, since even a small change in morbidity can have a large impact on quality of life. As Morley (1993, p. 63) pointed out, the "impact on quality of life of a 95-year-old who does not fracture a hip when falling because of nutritional (calcium and vitamin D) and exercise interventions is immeasurable."

Yet, as Amarantos et al. (2001) alternatively pointed out in their work, quality of life is more than mortality rates and goes beyond reducing morbidity and optimizing function; they contended that quality of life also involves life satisfaction and mental well-being. They also called attention to a gap in quality of life research, in that nutrition and dietary practices have not been included among domains of influence on quality of life. Drewnowski and Evans (2001, p. 89) asserted that "such factors as perceived mastery and control, enjoyment of the diet or satisfaction with exercise programs may be as important to quality of life as is reduced plasma cholesterol or increased grip strength." Indeed, some researchers, in discussing disease prevention and health promotion as related to diet, have warned that certain dietary changes may not be worth considering because they offer relatively little benefit and may do more damage to the older adult if the change renders eating and meals less enjoyable, which in turn could lead to nutritional repercussions (Morley, 1993).

The potential for economic consequences is another consideration. Though not thoroughly tested, it has been proposed that improved nutritional status and healthy dietary practices could ultimately save a substantial amount of money for consumers, the government, and health care organizations, in terms of reduced health care costs (Frazão, 1999; Leigh & Fries, 1992; Stearns et al., 2000).

Social Aspects of Health and Dietary Behavior

Investigation of social contexts, such as family and gender, is needed in health behavior and aging research. Family experiences and family life transitions have been shown to affect dietary behavior (Backett & Davison, 1995). But such experiences and transitions have neither been examined in depth, nor have they been studied in later life or as earlier determinants of dietary behavior in later life. There is relatively little work, for example, examining the impact of widowhood or caregiving in later life on dietary behavior, or how experiences in childhood may have been carried throughout life. Of the work that has been conducted specifically on the influences of life transitions, with some exceptions (e.g., Rosenbloom & Whittington, 1999), such research has much more often focused on transitions in early adulthood (about ages 18 to 40).

Several researchers have demonstrated that changes in family status might cause health behavior change for younger adult age groups (Backett & Davison, 1995; Kremmer, Anderson, & Marshall, 1998; Umberson, 1987). Some investigations have compared different family stages from young to old (such as Louk, Schafer, Schafer, & Keith, 1999), but such research does not adequately address possible cohort effects, alternative family structures, nor possible reasons for why being in a different family stage should result in altered behaviors. Nor do such life stage approaches consider how experiences and preferences extend and are modified across the life span in terms of gender. Women comprise the majority of the older adult population, have more chronic illnesses, and generally attend to the health, and dietary, matters of their families. Differences in health behavior practices among men and women begin to appear at young ages, and there may be differences in meaning associated with health behaviors (Leventhal, 2000). Women also have been subject to certain societal expectations and stereotypes regarding particular health behaviors (O'Brien Cousins, 2000; Verbrugge, 1990).

More research is needed to explore everyday life in contemporary retirement communities. This particular residential setting comes in various forms, and has become a burgeoning sphere of economic and housing development. Real estate developers see potential for profit as baby boomers approach retirement age, and economic planners see the potential for stimulating stagnant economies of local and regional areas. As older adults increasingly move into these communities, it becomes important to understand the impact that this new social and physical environment exerts on its inhabitants and their behaviors. Additionally, a number of these communities offer food and dining services, and thus affect the food and eating behaviors and experiences of the residents.

Though the social aspects of dietary behaviors are less frequently discussed in the health literature, they might have powerful meanings associated with them and be very important for psychosocial quality of life for older adults. For example, Sidenvall, Nydahl, and Fjellstrom (2000) interviewed older women about the meaning of food and cooking. Being able to cook for someone else and to give meals and food as gifts were acts associated with feelings of comfort, intimacy and joy. If the gift giving aspect was lost, as it often was for the widows who lived alone, the researchers found that the meaning of cooking also disappeared, and "thereby a risk of lost self-esteem as well as declining nutritional intake arose due to meal skipping" (Sidenvall et al., 2000, p. 421). As illustrated by the authors, social aspects of food are related to personal meaning and other intrapersonal dimensions, such as self-esteem. One can easily argue that the inclusion of social aspects of dietary practices is very relevant and important for both physical health outcomes and psychosocial quality of life.

Theory and Outcomes

Gochman (1997) stated that basic research in health behavior which establishes sound theoretical foundations would improve the effectiveness of health promotion and education efforts. Prohaska, Peters, and Warren (2000) have similarly contended that health care professionals need to have appropriate theory and information available to them, in order for intervention strategies to be most effective when used with heterogeneous and diverse groups, such as older adults.

In addition to improving health promotion and education, basic research might also provide health care practitioners with more insight into their clients' actions and circumstances surrounding behaviors and therefore might be able to provide more person-centered and tailored care and recommendations for their clients.

While there are policy initiatives addressing the nutrition and dietary behavior of the nation (McGinnis & Meyers, 1995), health policy and government efforts could be better informed by a more contextual understanding of sociocultural influences on health behaviors, particularly policy that is concerned with health promotion, health education/training and preventive health care. But there are other policy implications, particularly in terms of economics and costs. As previously mentioned, some evidence suggests that positive health behaviors (e.g. healthy eating habits) can lead to decreased costs in medical care and treatment, while negative behaviors (e.g. smoking) can increase expenditures (Stearns et al., 2000).

As discussed earlier, much of the discourse on outcomes of dietary behavior centers on such physical health-focused results. Economic savings to the government and consumers are sometimes invoked, but more often the biomedical endpoints of morbidity and mortality are discussed, in terms of delaying mortality and reducing morbidity. Nutritionists, clinicians and other health professionals seek to intervene in individuals' health behavior performance and modify habits for the sake of physical health. This is a worthy intent to be sure, as good physical health can prolong independence and participation in activities. But such a goal falls short because quality of life and psychosocial well-being extend beyond what good physical health can do for us.

Research Methodology

The overall design for this study utilized a qualitative research framework, based mainly on in-depth narrative interviews with a small sample of older women. The interviews served as the basis for exploring life experiences as related to individual development of dietary behaviors and the construction of meaningful themes.

In Chapter Two, I more fully describe the research setting and the participants in my study, thus providing a context for the findings and discussion. I recruited participants from and conducted my research at a retirement community, Colonial Square. The retirement community as a research site offered the opportunity to explore in-depth particular aspects of environmental and structural factors as related to dietary practices, and to more closely examine daily life, food, and eating in such communities.

All the participants were living independently, although two of them did receive some assistance for personal physical care. None of the participants reported or exhibited any cognitive impairment. The sample consisted entirely of older women. My intention was that sampling would be purposive, and that the participants, at a minimum, vary by age and familial situations, operationalized as different current marital statuses.

I used in-depth narrative interviewing as the main method of collecting data, because of the capacity of this method for collecting histories and eliciting aspects of context, meaning and process in the responses of the participants. The entire interview process was essentially comprised of two parts. At the first meeting, I began a general life history interview with the participant, using a life history interview guide that I developed for this study. Leininger (1985) and Rybarczyk and Bellg (1997) contributed to the development of the life history interview guide.

Following the review of a participant's general life history, I began a "food history" interview with the participant, in which I elicited details about their food and eating experiences over their lifetimes. I also used an interview guide for these interviews, which was created for this purpose (see Appendix A). Carol Devine and colleagues had shared an interview guide they used for research on food choice with me (Devine, Connors, Bisogni, & Sobal, 1998); it was of much assistance and contributed to the development of my food history interview guide.

The initial food history interview session began with discussion of the participant's favorite recipe(s); the recipes were a way to get us talking about food and eating, but they also drew out interesting information, for example, on the participant's view of cooking (see Appendix D for a compilation of recipes collected from the participants). From there, the food history interviews progressed in a variety of ways. Throughout the entire interviewing process, participants were allowed to use certain techniques, specifically visual cues, to assist in recall of past experiences and events. For example, a few participants referred to photographs and framed pictures in their apartment.

I also used participant observation methods. This included taking meals in the Dining Room, attending a food committee meeting, informal conversations with staff and residents, and picture taking. Participant observation made it possible to collect different kinds of data, gathering information from sources other than the participants and interviews.

The bulk of the data used for analysis consisted of interview transcripts, field notes, and recipes. However, there are a few other items collected that were referred to for analysis and writing. These items include: copies of weekly and daily menus, a blank dining room comment card, a copy of one month's worth of resident comments from comments cards, a copy of the resident handbook, marketing materials, leasing materials, physical layout sketches, and photographs.

There were three ways in which I processed the data to organize and prepare it for analysis: 1) use of descriptive statistics; 2) development of life course timelines; and 3) content coding. Basic descriptive statistical techniques were applied to produce frequencies, averages, medians and modes for several characteristics of each participant. This provided a descriptive overview of the sample and a snapshot of each participant, useful for contextualizing comments made by a particular participant. A different type of snapshot was the life course timeline. Based on notes and transcripts, I developed a general outline for each participant of major life events and transitions, following the general trajectories for family life, education, career, and residence. These life course timelines illustrated the variety of life experiences of the participants, and again were useful for contextualizing comments made in the interviews. Coding of the data is a process that prepares the data for analysis, but is also a type of analysis itself. Both open and focused coding processes generated an exhaustive list of themes that guided analysis, interpretation and writing.

Thematic analysis was used to extract meaningful themes, patterns and topics (Luborsky, 1994). The generation of meaning from analysis involved clustering techniques and making contrasts and comparisons (Miles & Huberman, 1994). Recurring themes were identified, and pieces of text were categorized (i.e. clustered) that related to various themes. The clustering process groups phenomena according to common meanings (themes), and then conceptualizes "objects" (e.g. events, acts, individuals, processes, settings/ locales, sites or cases as a whole) that have similar identified patterns or characteristics. Making comparisons and contrasts, on the other hand, highlighted points at which there were concrete and conceptual differences in the data. Identifying differences in data (data that cannot be clustered and grouped, or is a single instance of a theme) sharpened understandings and helped make sense of what appeared to be going on in the lives of the participants. Additionally, comparisons were made with relevant literature findings, in order to get a sense of how the data related to previous research and further identify relevant factors in the narratives that were collected.

The findings that emerged from this analysis are reported in Chapters Three and Four. Before getting to the results, however, background literature (on dietary behavior and theoretical frameworks) and a detailed description of the retirement community setting and participants will provide the context that the reader needs to more fully appreciate the findings of this research.

Chapter One

Background: Social Contexts & Theoretical Foundations

Research on health and dietary behaviors comes from varied and sometimes rather disparate literatures, for example, the areas of gerontology, health promotion and health education, nutritional sciences, biomedical sciences (including nursing, public health, and medicine), psychology, geography, anthropology, and sociology. This background review attempts to pull together research from these varied areas, focusing on literature that pertains to aging and older adults, although some research regarding earlier stages of life are included as required by the life course nature of this study. The background provided is not exhaustive; for example, it does not address specifically physiological issues of nutrition and food for older adults (e.g., the impact of age-related physical changes) or go into much depth regarding psychological issues (e.g., attitudes and beliefs). The focus here is more on particular social issues and contexts, including review of older adults' general food and eating practices and theoretical issues affecting this research.

Finally, it should be noted that for the purpose of this review, material is limited to Western cultures, though there are certainly important cultural differences even among Western societies that can render some comparisons a bit inconclusive. But overall there are enough similarities to make research on various Western populations useful when pulled together.

Dietary Behavior in Later Life

The literature on dietary behaviors of older adults is modest, but has been developing since the late 1970s. Wilcox and King (1999, p. 300) observed "more is known about the health benefits of good nutrition and the nutritional needs of older adults than is known about actual dietary behaviors...," an observation echoed by Elsner (2002), who noted that although there are some good general resources on eating behavior, "none exist which address nonpathological changes in eating behaviors that typically occur in later life" (p. 16). Elsner (2002) further noted the difficulty involved in examining relations between dietary behavior and aging:

> The complexity of the issue makes attempts at research difficult, as there are so many factors to examine that few definite conclusions can be made. Changes in physiology can affect eating behavior, and what is eaten can affect the physiology. Add in the changes in the body associated with aging, the prevalence of pharmaceutical use of older persons, and psychosocial considerations, and the complications increase. (p. 33)

As Elsner indicated, eating is an intricate, multidimensional process that may be further complicated by issues unique to aging and older adults. Research in the social sciences on food, eating, and aging has been more limited in scope than coverage of other issues of food and eating. The rest of this section will review findings regarding older adults in the areas of food acquisition, food preparation, and food consumption, including two more contemporary issues of eating out and dietary supplementation.

Food Acquisition

Read and Schlenker (1993, p. 298) remarked, "Food shopping can be a recreational or leisure time activity for the healthy older person with available transportation or a problem for the physically disadvantaged." Shopping for food can be an enjoyable activity for older adults (Bonnel, 1999), and it has been noted that shopping trips can be an important avenue for social contact (Read & Schlenker, 1993), though some older adults simply view shopping as a task that must be accomplished (Bonnel, 1999). For those whose physical capacities are not what they once were, such as frail elders or the oldest-old, shopping can be problematic. Problems when shopping include having to lift heavy items, difficulty reaching items on high or low shelves, difficulty reading labels, and difficulty pushing a cart (Read & Schlenker, 1993). Some no longer shop for groceries themselves, and have come to rely on others to purchase what they need (Bonnel, 1999). When functional limitations lead to food-related difficulties, it can result in nutritional deficiencies (Bartali et al., 2003).

Another aspect of shopping that can create problems is getting to the store in the first place. For older adults who no longer drive, access to grocery shopping means reliance on others (neighbors, friends, family, paid help), dependence on public transit and transportation services, and/or walking, each of which poses possible difficulties (Read & Schlenker, 1993). If an older person relies on others, they are limited in when, where, and how much to buy. The same limitations occur when transportation services are used and when walking.

Sidenvall, Nydahl, and Fjellstrom (2001) studied the experiences of older Swedish women, aged 64 and older, in managing food shopping. Their analysis revealed some differences among age groups and family situations, although in general all the women shopped according to familiar routines. Women who shopped with their husbands were more flexible in going to different stores, but the oldest women, who lived alone, preferred their usual local store. One of the shopping problems expressed by the oldest participants was a loss of strength. Economically speaking, the women balanced food expenditures against their capacities for preparing food items. Schlettwein and Barclay (1995) found that food budgeting problems of older European adults were associated with increased shopping problems, along with decreased dietary intake and poor self-perceived health.

Another way for older adults to acquire food is through food sharing and receiving gifts of food. Quandt, Arcury, Bell, McDonald, and Vitolins (2001) examined the meaning of food sharing among rural older adults and how giving and receiving food gifts can be a mechanism by which nutritional well-being of rural older adults is enhanced. The researchers found that these elders believed that receiving food gifts contributed to their food security, alleviating food shortages and preventing hunger. The food gift received most often was garden produce, which contained some of the nutrients in which the older adults' diets were deficient. For these older adults, the gifts tide them over when times get lean. However, not all older adults in the study received food gifts, the amount of food received varied greatly, and sometimes the gift was not something the elder could or would eat. Additionally, Quandt et al. found it more realistic to view food sharing as a process of redistribution within the community that eliminates potential food waste, than to see it as a means to alleviate hunger. Nevertheless, adult children who stock an elder's home with groceries or neighbors who share the bounty of their garden sometimes provide the means by which older adults acquire food in addition to, or instead of, their own shopping, and "may augment a diet limited by income and functional status" (Quandt et al., 2001, p. 145).

Food Preparation

What few studies there are about food preparation show that older adults use a wide array of strategies and approaches, some of which are different from those used by younger age groups. Sometimes, older adults purchase pre-made foods to reduce the amount of preparation work or use cooking strategies that primarily involve familiar routines (Sidenvall et al., 2001).

Bonnel (1999) investigated older women's perceived challenges and strategies for meal management, which includes meal preparation or making alternative arrangements for meals. She identified types of meal management transitions, some of which related to cooking strategies and described various approaches to fixing meals (Bonnel, 1999):

> Some women still cooked because they enjoyed it, it kept them busy and they liked to share. Others wanted to cook but had to make modifications because of pain or weakness. For others cooking was very difficult and done only when Meals on Wheels did not deliver. (p. 44)

The participants used strategies generally to make cooking easier, advising the preparation of extra food and freezing it, the use of frozen vegetables, and the use of microwave ovens (although this was felt by some to be a poor substitute for cooking). A functional environment for meal preparation was important to the women, who made their kitchen spaces as functional as possible, for example, by leaving out frequently used cooking equipment. Gustafsson, Andersson, Andersson, Fjellstrom, and Sidenvall (2003) found that the Swedish older women in their study highly valued independence, as it made food-related work easier and also meant that they continued to perform an important function of being a housewife (i.e., cooking) and thus maintain a female role that they have held for many years.

Brombach (2001a) reported on the meal patterns of older women in Germany. She discovered that some of the women, who were not originally from the town where the research was conducted, continued to prepare and eat certain dishes from their region of Germany, indicating some stability in the life course regarding food preparation and consumption. Her findings indicated that social and cultural factors influence the kinds of foods prepared and eaten as well as the timing of meals, and function then as a part of an individual's regional and cultural identity. Additionally, Brombach's study suggested that meals have an important role for structuring the day; Gustafsson et al. (2003) also reported that elder Swedish women created order in their everyday lives through food-related work.

Food Consumption

A number of studies have been conducted to understand older adults' beliefs and attitudes regarding food and eating and the effects on food selection and consumption (e.g., Cluskey, 2001b; International Food Information Council, 2001; Matheson, Woolcott, Matthews, & Roth, 1991; Rainey, Mayo, Haley-Zitlin, Kemper, & Cason, 2000; Schlettwein & Barclay, 1995; Sharpe & Mezoff, 1995; Yen, 1995). The International Food Information Council (2001) suggested that the most common values used by older adults to make food selections are sensory perception, convenience, social considerations, and physical well-being. They additionally noted that health concerns and medical conditions have a greater impact on food choices as people get older. Rainey et al. (2000) also found that health conditions influenced food choices; other themes in their research included food preferences based on taste and childhood familiarity. Similarly, Holmes and Gates (2003) reported that older men indicated health crises to be an influence on their eating behaviors.

McKie, MacInnes, Hendry, Donald, and Peace (2000) investigated beliefs and practices of Scottish elders and found a disparity between stated beliefs and actual consumption behavior, as practices were affected by social factors such as access to food and the cost and quality of foods. They additionally investigated attitudes specifically toward nutrition information and advice, uncovering high levels of skepticism regarding the reliability of nutrition information and advice; the older adults in the study often contrasted changing and conflicting advice with personal experiences (of themselves and others they knew).

Wakimoto and Block (2001, p. 75) concluded that cross-sectional studies on food patterns of older adults in general show "that older people are less likely to consume red meat, whole milk, and other fatty foods than younger people, and are more likely to consume fruits and vegetables than are younger people." They felt this contention was also supported by longitudinal data and stated "it appears that these changes in desirable directions may be larger among older than younger persons, and are larger and more consistent among older women than older men" (Wakimoto & Block, 2001, p. 75). More recent research supports the continuation of such trends, for example, research on preferences for red meat and meatless meals found that the older respondents "preferred more meatless meals and less red meat" (Rimal, 2002, p. 41).

However, there is variation among older adults, and an evaluation of rural older adults' quality of their diets showed that recommended levels of most food groups were not being met (except for fruits and vegetables) and that there were racial/ethnic differences in food consumption patterns (Vitolins, Quandt, Bell, Arcury, & Case, 2002). This suggested to the researchers that nutrition messages might not be reaching rural elders, particularly minorities. Similarly, rural residents in Sharpe, Huston, and Finke's (2003) research on single older women also had lower levels of nutritional adequacy in their diets.

As seen, some studies have focused on consumption of specific foods and food groups, as well as Fischer, Johnson, Poon, and Martin (1995), Holmes and Gates (2003), Patterson, Block, Rosenberger, Pee, and Kahle (1990), and Spangler and Pettit (2003). Johnson et al. (1998) examined fruit and vegetable consumption among older adults in the United Kingdom. Predictors of higher fruit consumption were higher social engagement, not smoking, being female, and a higher social class, while predictors for higher vegetable consumption were younger age and not smoking. Lancaster (2004) investigated influences on fruit, vegetable, and low-fat diary product consumption by hypertensive older adults. Lancaster's findings were congruent with Johnson et al.'s results. Women and those who had more social interaction had higher daily intake of all three food types. Higher daily intake of fruits and vegetables was also found among those with a higher education (and presumably a higher social class) and who were older, whereas higher daily intake of dairy products was found among whites and those with other positive health behaviors.

Food consumption of older adults has also been studied in terms of meal patterns. The most common pattern for older adults is to eat three meals a day: breakfast, lunch, and dinner (Read & Schlenker, 1993). Breakfast is a particularly popular meal with older adults (Read & Schlenker, 1993), and some researchers have found that it plays an important role in dietary quality and even mental abilities (Morgan, Zabik, & Stampley, 1986; Smith, 1998).

Some research has been conducted regarding fluid intake and the consumption of beverages. Adams (1988) compared fluid intake of institutionalized and noninstitutionalized older adults, finding that patterns of intake were similar for both groups, with almost no intake at night and the highest intake in the afternoon. However, the noninstitutionalized elders had a higher mean daily fluid intake and water made up a higher percentage of their daily intake. Fetto (2000) discussed patterns of beverage consumption among Americans, finding that in general, consumption rates of many beverages decreased with age. However, those aged 50 years and older drank more than twice as much hot coffee or tea than those aged 18-24 years.

Eating Out

Eating out (i.e., consuming food away from home) is a way to acquire and consume food without the work of preparing the food. Eating out has become a standard foodway for many Americans; older adults consume their share of food outside of the home as well, although research indicates that they are less likely to eat out than the rest of the American population. According to Wakimoto and Block (2001):

> ...calories from foods obtained and eaten away from home are highest among those aged 20 to 29 years (approximately 37% of energy for men and 34% for women), and lowest among those aged 70 years and older (approximately 16% for men and 11% for women). (p. 74-75)

Although these figures could also have included food and meals eaten at the homes of friends and family, it still suggests that older adults are much less likely to eat out or purchase/consume meals way from home. Paulin's (2000) results also indicated that adults aged 65 and older were less likely to buy meals away from home.

The fast food phenomenon has become a symbol of American culture, and although they may be less likely to patronize fast food restaurants, older adults will go to such establishments. Read and Schlenker (1993) cited research indicating that fast food businesses are increasingly attracting an older market. Reynolds, Kenyon, and Kniatt (1998) reported on factors that influence older adults to eat fast food, finding that older men were more likely to go to fast food restaurants than older women and lunch was the preferred primary meal purchased. Factors that were most influential included convenience, speed of service, low cost, price promotions/coupons, and lack of time to prepare meals.

Cheang's (2002) ethnographic study of elders who regularly congregated at a fast food restaurant found that the social aspects of their gatherings were important; the opportunity for social interaction beyond family or work, in which older adults gathered with friends for fun and laughter, provided a significant social outlet for these older adults. This was not a "support" group, but rather a meaningful leisure activity for these elders.

Vitamin and Mineral Supplementation

One particular dietary practice that has gained attention in recent years is the use of dietary supplements. Although the effects of supplementation in later life are somewhat inconclusive (Dangour, Sibson, & Fletcher, 2004), many elders take vitamins, minerals, and/or herbs on a regular basis, as studies of supplementation and complementary and alternative medicine use by older adults indicate (Barnes, Powell-Griner, McFann, & Nahin, 2004; Brownie & Myers, 2003; Hogan, Maxwell, & Elby, 2003; King & Pettigrew, 2004; Weng, Raab, Georgiou, & Dunton, 2004). In fact, a larger proportion of older adults than younger people consume supplements (Subar & Block, 1990; Slesinki, Subar, & Kahle, 1995). Chernoff (2001, p. 49) stated that vitamin and mineral supplementation by older adults "is generally self-prescribed and is frequently not associated with any medical conditions," but is begun by older adults because of the desire to prevent disease and to be responsible for their own health care. This desire was also found in McKenzie and Keller's (2003) study of Canadian elders. However, 67 percent of the vitamin/mineral users in Weng et al.'s (2004) study reported that their doctor advised them to take supplements.

Daniel, Houston, and Johnson (1996) reviewed studies published between 1980 and 1994 and made several conclusions regarding dietary supplementation among older adults. The studies indicated that about 30 percent of older adults used supplements daily and 60 percent had used supplements in the past two years. The use of supplements was associated with high socioeconomic status and residence in the western United States. Vitamin and mineral supplement use seemed to be most prevalent among affluent older adults who practice a wide variety of health behaviors. A recent study of older adults in the western United States (Oregon) found that 87% of 277 elders took a vitamin and/or mineral supplement regularly or occasionally (Weng et al., 2004). This is consistent with previous findings of higher use on the West coast, but could also indicate overall increased usage among older adults. Although the economic status of the study participants was not indicated, they did reside in a retirement community, suggesting that they likely had higher incomes, and thus the findings would also be consistent with studies indicating use is more prevalent among more affluent elders.

Additional characteristics include sex and race. Women are more likely to take supplements than men (Daniel et al., 1996; Houston, Daniel, Johnson, & Poon, 1998; Weng et al., 2004). Whites are more likely to use supplements than African-Americans and Hispanics (Houston et al., 1998; Morley, 1993).

Social Aspects of Dietary and Health Behavior

Overall, influences on the foodways of older adults have been put into three main categories: physiological, psychological, and sociocultural (Briley, 1994; Read & Schlenker, 1993). Physiological factors include aging changes that affect nutrition in late life, physical activity, and food intolerances. Psychological influences include beliefs, values, and attitudes, as well as self-esteem, knowledge, loneliness, bereavement, mental alertness, food preferences, food faddism, stress, and symbolism of food. Social factors involve dimensions such as age, socioeconomic status, education, daily schedules, leisure time, issues of access, and others mentioned in the previous chapter. As noted by Douglas (1984):

> Many of the important questions about food habits are moral and social. How many people come to your table? How regularly? Why those names and not others? There is a range of social intercourse which is based on food... (p. 11)

The social factors which this section addresses includes some of the above, but specifically focuses on gender, family, later life transitions, social support, living arrangements, environment, and morality.

Gender as a Life Course Context

It has been well established that, as compared to men, women have higher rates of morbidity, women live longer, and women use health services more (Coreil, Bryant, & Henderson, 2001; Leventhal, 2000; Rieker & Bird, 2000). Verbrugge (1990) has asserted that the health disparities found between men and women largely reflect psychosocial factors, suggesting that "controlling for a wide array of social factors makes sex differences in health narrow and often vanish statistically" (p. 175). Courtenay (2000) has also asserted that social factors and health behaviors contribute to the health-related differences between genders and suggested that health beliefs and behaviors are a means of demonstrating masculinities and femininities and health behaviors in daily interactions structure gender and power.

There is evidence that gender differences in health behavior develop at young ages (O'Brien & Bush, 1997). For example, among a sample of nine- to ten-year-old children, girls reported a higher number of health behaviors than boys (Farrand & Cox, 1993). According to Cohen, Brownell, and Felix (1990), school age girls more often reported choosing healthful foods than boys, although girls also reported more smoking and less exercise than boys. In adolescence and early adulthood, girls often use various dietary practices as a means for attaining or maintaining thinness, while many boys use exercise and increased caloric intake as a means of bulking up (Leventhal, 2000; Trowbridge & Collins, 1993). Gender differences in behavior among adolescents might also be associated with gendered behavior in the family. Wickrama, Conger, Wallace, and Elder's (1999) study of adolescents' and their parents' health risk behaviors revealed gender moderating effects on health-risk lifestyles within the family. Their analysis indicated that the father's health-risk lifestyle affected only sons' health-risk lifestyles whereas the mother's health-risk lifestyle only affected daughters' health- risk lifestyle.

These early influences, combined with societal factors, could continue to the other end of the life span, in late adulthood. Leventhal (2000) had suggested that adolescent dietary practices related to appearance might persist throughout life, especially for women, though Waldron (1997) cited data indicating that there are smaller gender differences in dieting (to lose weight) among older adults and proposed that health motivations related to dietary practices are more important in later life than appearance motivations. However, cases of older women with anorexia nervosa have been documented,[1] and though these women usually have histories of anorexia, for some, it is a first time occurrence (Morley, 1993). Clarke's (2002) investigation of Canadian older women's perceptions regarding body weight found that health was viewed as a reason for losing weight, but appearance was recognized by many to be a key motivation; however, consumer culture was not considered an impetus for their concern about weight loss, but mothers and siblings were cited as sources for learning about dieting. These findings among older women provide support for the notion that it is important to understand women's worlds and perceptions when studying health behaviors.

Social and gender roles can be influential in the development and shaping of health behaviors. Waldron (1997) contended that some health behaviors actually can be seen as part of gender roles in that the behaviors are more common and socially acceptable for one gender than for the other. For example, dieting might be part of the female role for young women in some social groups, reflecting concern for appearance and society's contemporary beauty ideal.

Devine and Olson (1992) found that women described their work role as a major barrier to healthy eating because of the demands on their time and energy. Devine and Sandström (1996) investigated associations among women's social

---

[1] Anorexia nervosa is a psychologically-based disorder that is different from what has been called age-related anorexia, anorexia of aging, or geriatric anorexia, although it is considered a potential factor in geriatric anorexia – see Donini, Savina, and Cannella (2003) or Elsner (2002).

roles, their nutrition beliefs, and dietary fat avoidance practices among Danish women, interpreting their findings as evidence that the social roles themselves did not influence fat avoidance behaviors, but the nutrition beliefs associated with particular roles did have an influence. They found that employment was positively associated with fat avoidance, but only among women who perceived few barriers to healthy eating.

Increased labor force participation is an example of how roles for women have changed over historical time; such change can affect behavior. Bowers (2000) stated:

> One of the most important developments affecting America's eating habits in the past 100 years has been the evolution of new roles for women (and men), as more women have entered the workforce and families have become smaller. New technologies and changes in gender relationships have both played a role. (p. 23)

Haines (1996) specified perceived social roles as a major factor affecting the eating patterns of women, referring to how conflicting role expectations might influence dietary behavior (for example, behaviors arising from conflicts between the role of working woman and "the good mother"). Findings from studies led Haines (1996) to deduce:

> Because women would prepare and consume a different mix of foods if they were not balancing multiple roles, this suggests that some level of role confluence may be needed if women are to be expected to successfully consume a healthy personal diet and also meet family needs and expectations. (p. 110)

Lewin (1943) developed the concept of the gatekeeper role in his channel theory of how and why food gets to the table in the home. Food gets to the table through various channels, such as the store, the garden, and the refrigerator; the woman as gatekeeper controls the selection of channels and the foods that go through them. McIntosh and Zey (1998) agreed that there is an impression that women control food within a household, but critiqued Lewin's work based on a "seeming disjunction between the expectation that women control food decisions and the limited reality of such control" (p.131). McIntosh and Zey reviewed research on particular elements of domestic roles that they believe ensure men ultimately control food decisions, including men's control over family finances, women's obligations to produce a harmonious family life, and women's deference toward men's food preferences.

Mennell, Murcott, and van Otterloo (1992) addressed the place of food in the division of labor in the home and remarked that men do cook at home, but this is something men can decide to do, whereas women generally have no option. Men assist or fill in when the woman is unable to cook (due to illness, for example), but no matter how competent the man may be as a cook, he does not often take over preparation of the main meals. Schafer and Schafer (1989) also examined gender roles as related to food roles and tasks in families, by interviewing couples in various family life stages (young families to retirement families). They found that the couples, in all stages, generally agreed that food selection and preparation should be under the woman's purview, with little to no marital conflict over the equity of role expectations and performance as related to food. Husbands in the younger life stages did do slightly more cooking than those in later stages, but were not more involved in food selection. Additionally, the younger wives thought that the husbands should be more involved in food-related chores. The authors felt that this might "reflect a sensitivity by younger families to changing gender-roles of women and the need for husbands to share more of the responsibilities of household tasks," or alternatively it could "reflect the bargaining of couples who have been married longer, by which adjustments have been made in various role behaviors to produce equity" (Schafer & Schafer, 1989, p. 123).

However, husbands in the older retired families tended to be more involved in food shopping and food purchase and budget decisions. Schafer and Schafer (1989) speculated that this was due to greater time availability of retired men for household and food-related tasks. Yet, their findings on older families could also suggest that either: 1) there are gender role changes associated with a retirement transition in contemporary older families, 2) the older couples are reflecting some societal change in gender roles, and/or 3) some food-related tasks are perceived as more female than others (shopping and food purchase decisions are related to finances and therefore are perhaps considered to be less feminine activities). Simply because the older men had more time does not mean they would perform the tasks if they truly believed that such chores were "women's work." They would likely need to believe that these are acceptable things for men to do. Or this is another example of how beliefs are not always associated with actual practices.

Finally, Gustafsson et al. (2003) asserted that, since the role of the woman in the home was closely associated with food-related work, it was protected as much as possible in later years through maintenance of independent living and avoiding dependence. This was exemplified in strategies that participants in their research developed to manage their food-related work when disability and disease encroached on their abilities to function completely independently.

Social Relationships and Transitions Across the Life Course

As seen in the studies of the previous section, family relationships and other social relationships have an important role in food and eating experiences. Mennell, Murcott, and van Otterloo (1992) stated:

> As food is used to create and maintain social relationships, it plays a very important role in primary groups of family and household in which individuals pass through their life cycle. The consequences of social positions in family and household for the production, distribution, preparation and consumption of food and meals form an important topic of research. (p. 91)

There is a significant body of research on food, dietary practices, and social relationships in the health behavior literature, but also in the broader anthropological and sociological literatures.[2] The focus is commonly on the

---

[2] It is well beyond the scope of this review to exhaustively examine all the literatures on social relations in food and eating, but those who are interested can find it summarized in works such as Beardsworth and Keil (1997) and Mennell et al. (1992). Classic and oft-cited works on social aspects of food and eating, especially regarding the family, can be found in Charles and Kerr (1988), DeVault (1991), Douglas and Isherwood (1979), Levenstein (2003), Mennell (1996), Murcott (1982), Lévi-Strauss (1970), Lupton (1996), and Warde and Hetherington (1994). For thoughtful review of research on food and families, consult Coveney (2002).

family, typically conceived of as a nuclear family with children, also noted by Coveney (2002), and on practices at home, although some research on children has examined practices at school. Valentine's (1999, p.42) assessment of the evidence of such research is that "food plays an important part in the production of 'family' identities and in the negotiation of gender relationships within the homes." Beardsworth and Keil (1997, p. 96) reflected that research on food and families has shown that "while eating patterns reflect family processes, at the same time, family relationships and family boundaries are expressed and reinforced by the day-to-day routines of provisioning, preparation and consumption."

Charles and Kerr's (1988) research on food and families in England is one of the most widely referenced studies on the subject. One of their key findings was the emphasis on the concept and importance of a "proper meal," one based on freshly cooked meat with potatoes and vegetables and eaten together as a family. Charles and Kerr proposed that this concept is fundamental to the identity of the family and its well-being and represents the family as a cohesive social unit, a "proper family." Another key finding was the deference of the women when cooking to the tastes and preferences of their husbands, even over the children. Charles and Kerr concluded that women have responsibility without authority in relation to food and food preparation, given the economic dominance of their husbands and their prioritizing of their husbands' preferences. This supports McIntosh and Zey's (1998) contentions regarding the power of women in families related to the gatekeeper role for food.

Research on families in the United States by DeVault (1991) produced findings similar to Charles and Kerr. DeVault interviewed households in and around Chicago, also finding that women bore almost all of the responsibility for food work and that Americans also have a notion of a proper meal. DeVault also supports McIntosh and Zey (1998), as she viewed the seeming autonomy of women in household operations as obscuring the fact that they essentially do what they perceive will please and accommodate others in the family. However,

Coveney pointed out that DeVault additionally observed that "women were not coerced by despotic husbands, but actively took part in, and indeed took pleasure from, the role of caring for others" (cited in Coveney, 2002, p. 116).

Coveney (2002) provided a review of research on food and families, in an effort "to shed light on the social dynamics that influence eating patterns of family members" (p. 113) and raised the following points:

> Firstly, the reciprocal relationships that are played out in family life have major implications for food and eating. Most research suggests that women play a major role as food providers. While earlier research suggested that men (as husbands or partners) exerted an influence over what food is actually provided, more recent research has indicated that the part played by children, when present, should not be underestimated...Secondly, social position and privilege have, not surprisingly, an important influence over family food choice...Lastly, the stage of family life itself influences food choice and dietary patterns...That is to say, the arrangements and relationships that develop between people, with or without children, have an impact on the choice of diet. (p. 117)

Coveney concluded that overall, research examining food in a family context is lacking and postulated that instead, "Many have examined specific variables (e.g. children's food preferences) within a laboratory-type setting and have tried to extrapolate results into a social milieu" (2002, p. 118). The solution, according to Coveney, is to conduct more research in "realistic and appropriate social settings" (2002, p. 118).

As indicated in Coveney's review, family life is subject to changes over time. Baranowksi (1997, p. 200) pointed out, noting societal changes in family structure and family relationships, "What can be said about families and diet at one time may not be true of them at another." The composition and structure of a family can take many forms and go through changes over an individual's lifetime. These family transitions are critical periods that usually instigate or are accompanied by other changes in an individual's life. Thus, the familial milieu for health behavior changes over time, and so there may be differential influences of family on behavior, depending on the change and/or the behavior. Rimal and Flora (1998) discussed how family roles and position in the family structure may affect health behaviors, giving the example of how the health behaviors of a 19-year-old living in a household as a child will be different from those of a 19-year-old living in a household as a parent.

Family provides an important and fundamental context for children in which behaviors are learned, established, and developed (or are not learned or developed), with parental influence as a major factor in the process (e.g., Wickrama et al., 1999). For children and adolescents, parents generally are assumed to be the predominant family members of influence and much of the research on familial influence of health behavior in childhood and youth focuses on the parents. Little work seems to have addressed other family members, or even fictive kin, as influences on health behavior and experiences. In an exception, Lau, Quadrel, and Hartman's (1990) study of influences on young people's health behaviors defined family to include siblings as well as parents. Lupton's (1994) work on adult memories of childhood food-related experiences clearly indicated that other family members besides the parents may be influential. For example, grandparents and other older relatives were remembered as indulging their young grandchildren, nieces, and nephews with treats (usually sweets) that the children were not normally allowed to eat. These treats became associated with special times and kindness from the older family members.

Health behaviors continue to develop in adolescence. During this time, peers begin to gain ground as important influences on health behavior (Hover & Gaffney, 1988), but parents still retain a prime position as an influence on their children's health behaviors. Cowell and Marks (1997) noted that family nutritional behavior has traditionally been considered one of the most important external variables to consider in explaining adolescent dietary patterns.

The transition from adolescence to adulthood presents opportunity for change in health behaviors. Pavis, Cunningham-Burley, and Amos (1998) interviewed young people in Scotland who were beginning the transition from school to employment, training, or further education. The researchers noted that their respondents explained changes in health-related behaviors by emphasizing their new social positions and other changes taking place in their lives. The behaviors were strongly associated with the behaviors of friends, the use of leisure time, and changes in disposable income.

Lau et al. (1990) used a longitudinal data set to explore sources of stability and change in American young adults' health beliefs and behaviors concerning alcohol use, diet, exercise, and wearing seat belts. They found that there is substantial change in health behaviors during the first three years of college and peers have a strong impact on the degree of that change, consistent with Pavis et al. (1998). But they also found family socialization to still be very important for young adults, much more important than peers as sources of influence. The researchers asserted that their data, along with previous analyses in their program of research, suggest a gradually increasing parental influence on their children's health behavior while the children are living at home and the persistence of that influence at least through the college years.

Through analysis of childhood memories of food of college students,[3] Lupton (1994) found that such memories were strongly linked to family relationships and characterized by emotional themes of control, disappointment, security, happiness, and belonging/not belonging. The parent-child relationship in many of the memories was typified by a power struggle related to the eating habits of the child. This struggle often centered on the discourse of "good" food versus "bad" food, in which the parents defined good food as vegetables, meat, and milk and bad food as sweets and junk food. Lupton (1994, p. 681) noted, however, that "'Bad' food was associated not with bad feelings, but with feelings of being indulged and loved" and with special events, such as birthday parties. "Good" food was often problematic for the participants and associated with

---

[3] The students ranged in age from early twenties to middle-aged, though Lupton does not indicate a specific age range or an upper age grouping to give an approximation of what constituted middle-aged.

conflict and feelings of physical revulsion. For Lupton, this food morality explains why bad food habits persist despite the efforts of health educators, who usually use a rational, common sense approach to health educating. Lupton (1996) later contended that childhood patterns of dietary preferences and practices never completely disappear; childhood experiences are always reacted to, consciously or not, and often lead to the acceptance or rejection of certain foods, based on those experiences.

During young adulthood is when individuals typically make transitions in their family life course, such as marrying and becoming parents. Kremmer et al. (1998) examined the changes that took place in the eating habits and food-related activities of young Scottish couples when they made the transition from single to married or cohabitating. In general, there was much negotiation and adaptation in food choice and eating patterns after marriage/cohabitation, but the researchers did not identify any significant gendering of power in food choice among the couples studied. However, more often women influenced men and it was in the context of taking care of her husband/partner as well as herself and so she took on the traditional role of nurturer in the relationship. Sobal, Bove, and Rauschenbach (2002) found that commensality (i.e., eating together) had been an important component of dating for couples, but in the transition to marriage, it became primary, though varied across daily and weekly schedules. The researchers concluded that for married couples, commensality was a significant aspect of "doing" marriage.

Olson (2005) conducted a prospective study of pregnant women, following them until two years after giving birth, to examine food choice patterns during the transition to motherhood. Olson found that for some food selection behaviors, especially fruit and vegetable intake and breakfast consumption, positive changes were linked to the transition to motherhood. As families become established, Umberson (1987, 1992) has suggested that family roles promote the social control of health behaviors, but family solidarity has also been explored as a mechanism of influence. Grzywacz and Marks (1999) examined family solidarity, gender, and various health behaviors (including body mass [diet indicator]). Though they found that some dimensions of family solidarity had positive effects on some health behaviors and negative effects on others, in general, higher levels of family solidarity were associated with a greater likelihood of engaging in positive health behaviors, and men's health behaviors were positively influenced by family solidarity more so than women's health behaviors.

Regarding factors that affect married couples' dietary practices, Lupton (2000) conducted a qualitative study of food preferences and habits of rural Australian couples, with and without children living at home. The findings indicated that their approaches to food are rather conservative, emphasizing a traditional meat and vegetable main meal, though pasta and stir-fry meals had been widely adopted. Lupton suggested that region of residence, social class, and education contribute to a conservative approach. Health and balance were also valued and influenced food choices. Parents saw themselves as responsible for their children eating healthy foods and having a healthy diet. According to Lupton, these findings illustrated how eating healthy meals were an important aspect of living as a couple or a family.

Paisley, Sheeshka, and Daly (2001) specifically investigated vegetable and fruit consumption of Canadian couples, with and without children, and two overarching themes emerged from the interviews. The first theme was the emergence of a fruit and vegetable morality that the researchers called the "should syndrome," as participants often spoke of what they should and should not do regarding eating fruits and vegetables. The second overarching theme was the creation of couple gastronomies. In their lives as a couple, the participants constructed shared gastronomies consisting of rules, norms, practices, and meanings concerning food. These were different from the gastronomies of childhood and when they were single. The researchers found these couple gastronomies had been constructed primarily through commensality, choice, and balance, which was a guiding principle for food choices.

Schone and Weinick (1998) investigated the relationship between marital status and health behaviors among older adults. Married older adults were more likely to practice healthy behaviors (such as regular physical activity, eating breakfast, wearing seat belts and not smoking), though these effects tended to be larger for men than for women. Because age had an effect on health behaviors, they suggest that the propensity to engage in health behaviors changes over the life course, even for older adults. The researchers concluded that the benefits of marriage for health, which has been seen in younger populations, continue into later life. In another example of this, a study of the diets of Finnish elderly persons over a 16-year period found that women and married persons had the healthiest diets (Sulander, Helakorpi, Rahkonen, Nissinen, & Uutela, 2003).

Schafer and Keith (1982) used a social-psychological approach to study dietary quality of married older adults and single older women who lived alone. They found that the single women made food decisions independent of others and had a significantly better diet than the married couples (which was due in part to the lower diet quality scores of the married men). For the married women, a significant relationship was found between household role dissatisfaction and diet quality, where greater dissatisfaction was related to poorer diets. For the single women, there was a negative relationship between age and diet quality, where the older they were, the poorer their diet quality. The researchers speculated that such findings suggest marriage might diminish negative effects of age on diet quality of older adults or that it might be due to the fact that the sample included single elderly women who were older than the married elderly women.

Horwath (1989) examined the interaction of living arrangements, marital status, and dietary patterns among older Australians. Her analysis of self-completed questionnaires revealed that older men living with a spouse generally had better diets than older men who lived alone. Older women living alone, however, had fairly similar dietary patterns to the married women and nutrient intakes equal to or better than the women who lived with a spouse, similar to Schafer and Keith (1982). Horwath asserted that the findings indicate that the relationship between living arrangements, marital status, and dietary patterns is contingent on gender.

In a study that focused specifically on single, older men, Russell and Porter (2003) collected and analyzed narratives of everyday life for these men. An everyday activity such as eating was found to be imbued with social meaning, as many of the men categorized eating as a primarily social activity. Callen and Wells (2003) found that social connectedness was a major factor in aiding nutritional health, as it "enabled these old-old people to continue to live independently in their own hones or apartments long after they might otherwise have needed to have moved to an assisted living situation" (p. 259). For these elders, assistance from family and friends was most often the primary aid to maintaining their nutritional health; assistance included everything from doing the older adult's grocery shopping and physically stocking cupboards to sometimes sharing a dish.

Family and friends are important, but other social relationships might also play a role in our eating behavior. Holmes and Gates (2003) examined influences on older men's intakes of fruits, vegetables, and grains, finding that wives did influence eating habits, as supported by other studies, but health professionals emerged as persons of influence as well.

Connors, Bisogni, Sobal, and Devine (2001) determined that social relationships play a key role in how adults manage their personal food values and resulting behavior:

> People frequently faced situations where they wanted to accommodate the needs of other people in their social circles, and placed the management of their social relationships above all of their other food specific values. Often women were more accommodating than men, placing social relationships first when faced with conflicting food-choice values...Some people mentioned that they would eat what was served to them even if they disliked it or it did not meet their other values, in order to avoid creating a food incident and disrupting social relationships. This desire for pleasant mealtimes increased the salience of the

value of managing social relationships for these participants. (p. 195)

Thus, the consideration of others significant to an individual (and their particular food-related preferences) and the quality of social interaction at mealtimes were important factors influencing eating practices, especially for women.

Later Life Transitions: Retirement, Widowhood, and Caregiving

Transitions often associated with later life, such as retirement, widowhood, and caregiving, might impact the health behavior of individuals experiencing such transitions. Regarding dietary behavior, Hendricks, Calasanti, and Turner (1988, p. 77) stated, "Loss of spouse and retirement are two roles...portending a change in eating habits. The alterations in living situations and contexts of eating that both these transitions imply can have an important influence on nutrition." The same can be said of caregiving as well.

Lauque et al. (1995) investigated the effects of retirement on the dietary behavior of French men and women. The researchers observed few changes overall, but did find that retirees take more time for meals, ate more often at restaurants or friends' homes, and had guests over to eat more often. Vitamin and mineral supplement use did increase after retirement, with some subjects beginning supplement use after retirement. From their findings, the researchers concluded that retirement does not bring about major modifications in eating habits during the first year of retirement. Although the researchers understood their findings as indication that there is no significant change in nutritional intake, the lifestyle changes and social changes related to eating could be significant to those who have instituted such changes in their lives and the leisurely enjoyment of meals and friends could perhaps contribute to overall quality of life.

A limited amount of research has addressed the life course transition of widowhood and possible effects on health behavior, with few attempts to investigate a relationship between widowhood and dietary behavior. Sidenvall et al. (2000) interviewed single and co-residing Swedish older women about the meaning of preparing, cooking, and serving meals. For widows, however, and particularly those who had recently lost their spouse, the meaning of cooking and eating was lost; they felt there was no purpose in cooking for only one person. The researchers concluded that these women might be at nutritional risk, as meal skipping was common, as well as some psychological risk from a loss in self-esteem.

Rosenbloom and Whittington (1993) compared the eating practices of recently widowed elders to same-age adults whose spouses were still living. They found that widowhood triggered disorganization and changes in daily routines associated with food preparation and consumption. The widows in the study reported a loss of appetite, lack of enjoyment of meals, unintentional weight loss, and less use of vitamin and mineral supplements; on the whole, they experienced a decline in nutritional quality. All the participants had the means to purchase and prepare foods, which suggested to the researchers that social activities surrounding eating were stronger contributors to changes in dietary behavior and nutrient intake. Shahar, Schultz, Shahar, and Wing (2001) similarly investigated the effects of widowhood on weight, food intake, and dietary behavior among recently widowed older adults, comparing them to married older adults. Weight loss was significantly higher among widowed elders. They enjoyed their eating less, and ate more meals alone, more commercial meals, and fewer snacks. They lacked interest in activities related to food and eating, such as cooking and grocery shopping. These findings are consistent with Rosenbloom and Whittington's findings.

Howarth (1993) focused on the food consumption patterns of widowed English people over the age of 75, also finding that the organization of dietary activities could be completely changed by widowhood. Howarth's research suggested that as older widowed people "attempt to maintain continuity of food consumption, both men and women strive to retain familiar practices" (1993, p. 77), but this striving for continuity, however, was more difficult for the men. Most of the widowers were inclined to use convenience foods and technology that made cooking less threatening. Some men reported that their daughters cooked for them or that they were part of a reciprocal arrangement with neighbors who were widows.

Based on research examining nutritional risk among recently bereaved older adults, Johnson (2002) suggested bereavement counseling should address food and nutrition. Johnson found that there were a number of dietary issues facing bereaved older adults, similar to findings in the previously mentioned studies, such as difficulties with preparation, consumption, and the time and place of meals. Callen and Wells (2003) also found among their widowed oldest-old participants that a transition to eating alone was accompanied by difficulties regarding cooking and eating, such as learning to cook for one and eating less-balanced meals. The lack of mealtime companionship was cited as a negative change by the widowed participants and resulted in a lack of motivation for them. Some responded to the loneliness by making themselves be with others, taking anti-depressants, and putting a TV in their kitchen.

Quandt, McDonald, Arcury, Bell, and Vitolins' (2000) data from in-depth interviews with widowed women revealed that there are varied responses to widowhood, some of which had a positive impact on their nutritional strategies, such as following their own dietary needs. But most responses resulted in a negative impact, such as meal skipping, reduced home food production, and decreased dietary variety. McDonald, Quandt, Arcury, and Vitolins (2000) also interviewed older widowers about their dietary behavior, illustrating a variety of means used by the widowers to create a reliable nutritional strategy after becoming widowed, such as self-care, informal support, formal programs, or some combination of these. Many of the widowers cared for their ailing wives before widowhood, and the researchers speculated that they had reason therefore to become more self-sufficient, including in food-related tasks.

Relatively little is known about the effects of caregiving on the health behavior of the caregivers; what is known seems to indicate a generally negative trend, although this may depend on the specific behavior and on the caregiver's gender (Burton, Schulz, German, Hirsch, & Mittlemark, 1994; Connell & Schulenberg, 1990). Sisk (2000) investigated the relation of caregiver burden and health behaviors, with results suggesting that caregivers with lower subjective burden scores practiced more health-promoting behaviors (e.g., eating nutritiously) than those perceiving higher subjective burden. Connell (1994) found that after beginning caregiving, about 32 percent of the caregivers in the study ate less nutritiously, 32 percent decreased exercise, and 43 percent increased their smoking. The negative direction of the behaviors seemed to be attempts to reduce stress, however, as caregivers reported finding comfort in food and reduced tension and anxiety from smoking. Prohaska and Clark (1997) speculated that the reasons for caregivers' low rates of positive health behaviors are most likely role overload and possibly some denial that they are even at risk.

Social Support

Social support is another mechanism through which social relationships might influence the health behaviors of individuals. Numerous studies have linked social support, health, and dietary behaviors for specific conditions, for example, cardiovascular disease (Bovbjerg et al., 1995; Ford, Ahluwalia, & Galuska, 2000), chronic renal failure (Hitchcock, Brantley, Jones, & McKnight, 1992; Oka & Chaboyer, 1999), diabetes (Brown et al., 2000; Wdowik, Kendall, & Harris, 1997), hypertension (Cohen et al., 1991; Wilson & Ampey-Thornhill, 2001), obesity (Hayaki & Brownell, 1996; Wadden et al., 1990), and even phenylketonuria, generally referred to as PKU (Waisbren, Rokni, Bailey, Brown, & Warner-Rogers, 1997). Positive associations between social support, weight loss, and weight management have also been established (e.g., Parham, 1993; Wing & Jeffrey, 1999), as well as identification of social support as a strategy for maintaining healthy eating and exercise habits (Greaney, Lees, Greene, & Clark, 2004). However, there is some complexity to a relationship between social support and positive health behavior. For example, in Devine and Sandström's (1996) study of Danish women, perceived social support for healthy eating was positively associated with fat avoidance among women who were not employed, although no such association was found with women who were employed.

Kelsey, Earp, and Kirkley (1997) reviewed literature from the early 1980s to mid-1990s in the area of social support and dietary change, in order to answer whether social support is beneficial for dietary change. The authors stated that relationships have several support-related aspects, including the provision of: "models for lifestyle change; controls and constraints on behavior (i.e., peers may support healthy or unhealthy eating habits); access to information; and a sense of meaning and purpose to life that can make healthy lifestyle changes seem more attainable" and "resources to directly assist individuals who are trying to make changes in their diets" (Kelsey et al., 1997, p. 71). They noted that support could come from family, friends, co-workers, professional sources (e.g., health care providers, therapists, and social workers), community affiliations, religious activities, and organized self-help groups. Kelsey et al. remarked that there can be a negative dimension to relationships that should be considered when looking at the effects of social support on behavior change; sabotaging, nagging, or family conflicts or demands around food can have a negative impact on dietary change.

Kelsely et al.'s (1997) review found several studies that showed gender differences regarding the effect of social support on dietary change. They suggested that social support might operate differently for men and women, based on research that indicated women's social networks might support healthy eating and health behaviors, whereas in men's social networks, support for less healthy behaviors might be more the norm.

Studies have shown the benefit of social support regarding the maintenance of health behavior for older adults (Riffle, Yoho, & Sams, 1989; Seigley, 1998). Social support is generally thought to positively affect food intake and dietary quality among older adults, although this is not always a consistent finding in the literature. Conn and Armer (1995) found social support to be important in their study of older spouses. Significant correlations between husband and wife were identified for exercise, nutrition, interpersonal support, self-actualization and health responsibility. Pierce, Sheehan, and Ferris (2001) discovered that older women received substantial support from friends, but also were more likely to receive support from others if a physician prescribed a diet; this suggested to the researchers that physicians may mobilize social support and perhaps sanction the acceptance of offers of help. In their development and testing of a model of dietary change and social support, Silverman, Hecht, and McMillan (2002) similarly observed that one of the most significant positive support factors, for both male and female elder participants, was a physician's recommendation for dietary change. Elders also receive and use different types of social support related to food and eating, as in Pierce, Sheehan, and Ferris' research, in which the older women described instrumental support for food acquisition activities and emotional and informational support for dietary changes.

Schoenberg (1998) found inconclusive evidence for a relationship between perceived social support and adherence to dietary regimens in a study of older African Americans with hypertension. However, Schoenberg offered reasons for the apparent lack of an association that included the identification of supportive others who did not fit standard definitions of supportive others (e.g., supernatural sources of support) and a gradual approach in diet modification, based on a philosophy of moderation and balance, whereby dietary changes entailed an incremental process that did not require much social support, as opposed to a radical change in diet that disrupts an individual's way of life.

Schoenberg (1998) also did not find an association between living arrangements and perceived social support, despite that the majority of participants lived with their children and/or grandchildren. Studies often presume a direct relationship between social support and living with others, and therefore those who live alone might have less social support and smaller social networks. As Schoenberg's results indicated, this may be an erroneous presumption to make. However, McIntosh and Shifflett (1984) had examined the influence of social support systems on dietary intake of older adults and concluded that living alone did have a negative effect on dietary quality.

Environmental and Spatial Factors

Living arrangements as an environmental factor have received some limited attention as related to dietary and health behavior. The use of space within the home for food and eating is a factor that has not been commonly addressed, but is very much influenced by social issues. Another environmental factor is residential setting; for elders this includes the context of age-segregated residential communities, such as nursing homes, assisted living facilities, independent living retirement communities, and continuing care retirement communities.

There has been inconsistent evidence regarding the effects of living situations, particularly on dietary behavior. As mentioned, McIntosh and Shifflett (1984) found living alone had a negative effect on dietary quality for elders, as did Niewind, Krondl, and Lau (1988) in terms of food variety, but Horwath (1989) found that the effects of living arrangements were contingent on gender, uncovering an adverse effect for men living alone, but not for women living alone. Similarly, Schlettwein and Barclay (1995) found that European women living alone did not differ from women living with others in dietary intake and nutritional status. Doyle (1994) explored the experience of living alone among Canadian older women, finding that almost two-thirds of them conceived of living alone as a choice, although they expressed a dislike of the necessity of cooking for one and eating alone.

Davis, Murphy, and Neuhaus (1988) examined associations between living arrangements and various dietary behaviors, using data from the Nationwide Food Consumption Survey 1977-1978, finding evidence that the eating behaviors of older adults living alone, especially men, were different from the behaviors of older adults living with a spouse. They suggested, as did McIntosh and Shifflett (1984) and Horwath (1989), that it is not just merely living with someone else that was influential, but living with a spouse had added significance and influence. What is unknown, and generally not considered in such studies, is the number of years the person has lived alone and adjustment to the living situation. The practices of a recently widowed woman living alone, for example, might be different from a woman who has never been married and has always lived alone.

Practices might also vary according to an elder's physical environment. Percival (2002) investigated how older adults in England use their domestic spaces for everyday living. Routines for eating and meals depended in part on the amount of space within the home. Many expressed a preference for eating in a kitchen or a dining room, and did so if they had large enough kitchens for a table or who had dining rooms. But almost half of the elders ate meals in their living room. For some this was because of lack of suitable alternative space for eating, but for others it was either because they liked to watch television while they ate or because the living room had become for them a "centre of operations" (Percival, 2002, p. 732), where many of their daily activities occurred and they could eat in a favorite chair, with easy access to television, phones, newspapers, etc.

Participants in Percival's (2002) study additionally discussed issues of space for sharing meals when family and friends visited. Some no longer entertained due to their age and physical limitations, but others did not due to a lack of adequate space. Having a large kitchen or a dining room was seen as important for entertaining purposes, as these more formal arrangements were preferred when guests came to eat with them. As Percival (2002, p. 734) noted, "When there is no designated eating room, whether kitchen or dining room, older people may feel not only the loss of space but also of a personally meaningful role, that of being a host to the family" and if the older person's home is a "non-family-friendly environment," then there are negative implications for the older person's "morale and sense of self-determination." For Percival, the findings illustrated "the importance to older people of self-determination in and the environmental congruity of their eating routines" (2002, p. 734) and both the need for and benefit from having "adequate spaces that facilitate eating routines" (2002, p. 746).

46

Research has fairly recently begun to examine dietary and health behavior of older adults in specific residential settings, scrutinizing behaviors in the context of age-segregated communities. Over the last twenty years, a number of studies have addressed food and eating in nursing homes.[4] Studies of assisted living facilities and other retirement communities have indicated that food and dining services are important factors in quality of life issues for residents (Ball et al., 2000; Gilani, 1995; Harper, 2000; Mitchell, 1999; Raynes, 1998). Cluskey (2001a, 2001b) researched dining and food intake of residents in continuing care retirement communities. Cluskey (2001b) reported that residents in the community site ate fairly well, even the oldest old, who had similar or better intakes compared with other studies of older adults. The residents surveyed did not believe their intakes had changed as a result of residing in the community.

A few ethnographies of communities in which elders reside have been conducted, though they were conducted in the 1970s. Gubrium's (1975/1997) ethnographic study of a nursing and residential home considered the aspect of dining and eating at the facility. He observed that residents divided the day into three parts, according to mealtimes, and that a great deal of the residents' discussions centered on dining and food, often involving judgments of the food. Jacobs (1975), in his description of a high-rise retirement complex, noted the importance of food and food-related activities. Residents devoted a good portion of their leisure time to food-related activities, such as shopping, looking for bargains, clipping coupons, exchanging recipes, and discussing the day's menu

---

[4] Research has examined dining experiences and interventions (Beattie, Algase, & Song, 2004; Marken, 2004; Stinnett & Adams, 1995), the role of nursing staff at mealtimes (Pearson, Fitzgerald, & Nay, 2002), the attitudes and practices of the food services staff (Evans & Crogan, 2005; Matthews, 1987), residents' perspectives of food and food services (Alford, 1986; Evans, Crogan, & Shultz, 2003, 2005; Yen, 1995), the effects of nursing home regulations on residents' autonomy, including dietary practices (Cohen, Werner, Weinfield, Braun, & Kraft, 1995), dining interventions for and factors influencing residents with dementia (Altus, Engleman, & Mathews, 2002; Amella, 1999; McDaniel, Hunt, Hackes, & Pope, 2001; Nolan & Matthews, 2004), and identity production, social interaction, and organizational structure as reflected in dining and dietary experiences (Beck & Ovensen, 2003; Douglas-Steele, 1995). Kayser-Jones has conducted studies on food and eating in nursing homes, investigating the social, cultural, psychological, environmental, and clinical factors that influence residents' eating (Kayser-Jones, 1996, 2000; Kayser-Jones & Schell, 1997).

with neighbors. Food was frequently a topic of conversation, but it also was an incentive when social events were planned; the promise of food did more than anything else to draw residents to organized social activities of the complex.

Keith Ross (1977) described food-related activities in her study of the French retirement community Les Floralies, particularly the social organizational aspects of the dining room. Because all members of the community were required to eat the noon meal in the dining room, it was the one place where each resident at least daily saw all the other residents. It is in the dining room that new residents met people, often moving to a table with established residents within a few days, although usually the new resident would move around to different tables during the first month before settling into a permanent spot. This also made the resident's progress toward their attachment to a social network a public process.

Moral Meanings

The final aspect of dietary and health behavior considered in this chapter is the social construction of moral meanings associated with food and eating. In the quote from Douglas (1984) earlier, she noted that the important questions about food habits are not only social, but also moral. Health behavior can be imbued with moral meaning, and dietary behavior in particular has been laden with moral undertones. As previously discussed, Lupton (1994) and Paisley et al. (2001) illustrated how moral meaning emerges in discussions of dietary practices.

Manton (1999, p. 83) suggested that food and eating can be viewed as a morality play, asking, "Is eating the oldest sin?" Manton discussed issues of dieting, self-control, trust, gluttony, and changing moral meanings of food. Manton (1999) wrote:

> Food consumption consistently has had negative meaning throughout the twentieth century; however, the specific negative message given has changed over time. For an earlier-twentieth century American, food guilt may have meant illicitly eating meat on Fridays or failing to achieve membership in the "clean plate club." (p. 83)

Manton purported that there is almost no aspect of food that has not inspired a feeling of guilt at some level. But she suggested that for many people, the first linking of food with guilt began in childhood with exhortations to think of the poor, starving children in some far-off foreign country, in order to urge children to finish eating what was on their plates.

Lupton (1996) has also commented on the moral nature of food and eating. She proposed that eating practices in the family involve positive emotions and family bonding, but are also characterized by power struggles and feelings of frustration, unhappiness, and hostility that accompany such struggles. Lupton (1996) also addressed the concept of "good" and "bad" foods:

> 'Good' food is often described as nourishing and 'good for you,' but is also indicative of self-control and concern for one's health, while 'bad' food is bad for one's health and on a deeper level of meaning is a sign of moral weakness. (p. 27)

Alternatively then, eating "good" food can be a sign of moral strength, as indicated in Paisley et al.'s (2001) work. Lupton noted that foods can have aspects of both being good and bad, with meat as an example of a food having conflicting meanings in Western societies. Healthy diets are often described in terms of a balanced diet and eating foods in moderation (i.e., not too much bad food, and not too much good food).

Conceptual and Theoretical Foundations

Theory development in health behavior has had a primary focus on intrapersonal processes; in other words, much conceptualization has focused on the role of psychological issues such as beliefs, attitudes, values, locus of control, and self-efficacy. The relevance of these processes is not in dispute, but the superficial treatment of social and temporal issues in many frameworks of health behavior are challenged. Furthermore, older adults and issues of age have not been considered adequately in conceptualization; Hendricks et al. (1988, p. 61) contended that "a conceptual framework for a sociologically meaningful analysis of nutrition in later life does not exist." The point is still valid almost two decades later, and although the focus of this research is not nutrition per se, the aim is to bring to the forefront the social issues of dietary behavior, particularly for elders.

Major Models and Theories of Health Behavior

Table 1.1 provides an overview of oft-used, current theories of health behavior.[5] These models have been studied and applied both separately (in basic and modified forms) and in various combinations. Recently research has used traditional health behavior models in the study of older adults' health behaviors, e.g., Bell, Quandt, Arcury, McDonald, and Vitolins (2002), Clark, Nigg, Greene, Reibe, and Saunders (2002), Padula et al. (2003), Sjoberg, Kim, and Reicks (2004) and Yoon and Home (2004). The field of psychology has been and continues to be a strong contributor to health behavior theory, and as would be expected, there is a strong emphasis on the psychological processes of the individual as mediators of health behavior. A few other currently used theories include Social Cognitive Theory, Social Networks & Social Support, and Ecological models; these address some relevant social processes and are briefly reviewed later in the chapter because of insights they offer.

The individual and his/her intrapersonal processes (e.g., cognition, motivation, and beliefs) cannot be discounted, for such factors certainly affect health behavior, but focusing primarily on such factors is over-psychologizing the issue. To better understand health behavior, particularly dietary behavior, social processes that affect health behavior need to be as well understood as psychological processes. Two theories that have much potential for such purposes are the life course perspective and symbolic interactionism. Both are frameworks that have been infrequently applied to health behavior, but have much potential to address social processes that are missing from the traditional theories.

---

[5] This overview does not include theories and models that address health behavior interventions, health behavior at the level of groups, communities and organizations, or use of health services. The table is based on information from Glanz, Lewis, and Rimer (1997) and Gochman (1997).

Table 1.1: Major Theories and Models of Health Behavior

Theory/Model	Discipline/ Field	Defining Features	Key Components, Concepts, Constructs & Principles
Health Belief Model	Social Psychology, Public Health	Focus on beliefs and perceptions	*Individual perceptions*: perceived susceptibility and perceived severity *Modifying factors*: cues to action, perceived threat, and other variables (e.g. age, gender, ethnicity, SES) *Likelihood of action*: perceived benefits minus perceived barriers *Self-efficacy*
Health Locus of Control Theory	Psychology	Personal control beliefs	*Internals*: people who believe that their health is under their own control *Externals*: people who believe that external factors, such as luck, determine their health
Transtheoretical Model or Stages of Change Model	Psychology	Temporal aspect and processes of change	*Stages of change*: precontemplation, contemplation, preparation, action, maintenance *Processes of change*: consciousness raising, dramatic relief, self re-evaluation, environmental re-evaluation, self liberation, helping relationships, counter conditioning, contingency management, stimulus control, social liberation *Decisional balance*: Pros & cons *Self-efficacy*: confidence & temptation
Protection Motivation Theory	Psychology	Fear appeals and persuasion, motivations	*Sources of information*: environmental and intrapersonal *Cognitive mediating processes*: threat appraisal, coping appraisal, maladaptive response, adaptive *Coping modes*: Adaptive coping, maladaptive coping
Theory of Reasoned Action/ Theory of Planned Behavior	Psychology	Focus on intentions and motivations	*Behavioral intention* *Attitude*: behavioral belief, evaluation *Subjective norm*: normative belief, motivation to comply *Perceived behavioral control*: control belief, perceived power (Theory of Planned Behavior only)

The Life Course Perspective

Bengtson, Burgess, and Parrott (1997, p. S79) described the life course perspective as a framework "about processes at both macro- and micro-social levels of analysis for both populations and individuals over time," although as Hatch (2000) pointed out, families have been used as the unit of analysis also. Elder (1995, p. 103) asserted that a life course perspective emphasizes "the social pathways of human lives, their sequence of events, transitions and social roles."

Elder (1985) identified life trajectories, transitions, and events as three key concepts in the life course perspective. A trajectory (also called a pathway or career) is the course of an individual's experiences in a particular domain, for example, family, work, education, residence) over time. Trajectories involve sequences of events and transitions. A transition is a change in one's state of existence, such as from married to widowed. An event is a discrete happening that often initiates a transition (e.g., marriage is the event, but the change in marital status from single to married is the transition). Transitions and events contribute to the uniqueness of individual trajectories.

Giele and Elder (1998) identified four central constructs of the life course perspective: location in time and place, linked lives, human agency, and timing of lives. Location in time and place refers to historical context and sociocultural background, including both the social and physical environments. Linked lives signify the role of social relationships and social integration in human lives. Human agency refers to the role of the individual in meeting needs/goals and of self-regulation in development. The timing of lives involves several dimensions of time: historical time, social timing, the synchrony of individual and significant others' timing, and life stage.[6]

Variation and interdependence are key features of the perspective (Elder, 1985, 1995). Although a birth cohort may be exposed to similar societal contexts, differences in place, timing, choices, and structural constraints will cause

---

[6] For further explanation of these aspects of timing, refer to Elder (1995) and Giele and Elder (1998).

members of a cohort to have varied experiences. Interdependence is a feature of lives and trajectories. Changes in one person's life influences the life of another (e.g., a parent who takes a new job in another state means a change in school and friends for a child), and changes in one trajectory might lead to changes in another trajectory (e.g., becoming widowed might mean moving to a smaller home).

The Life Course Perspective and Health Behavior

Wethington (2005), in an overview of the life course perspective and its implications for health and nutrition, illustrated the value of using a life course perspective and stated:

> The major theoretical innovation of the life course perspective for health is that it integrates disparate explanations for individual and group differences in health, including personality factors, current influences on health and health behavior, life history, and the collective life history of different social groups. (p. 115)

A number of studies have examined various health issues using a life course perspective.[7] But few studies have focused on health behavior, or specifically dietary behavior, using a life course perspective. For Devine (2005), applying a life course perspective to food choice behavior not only assists in explaining differences but also change:

> It is this attention to individual development in changing contexts that makes a life course perspective so rich for understanding food choices because of the multiple ways in which foods, the individuals choosing them, and food choice environments are changing. (p. 121)

Some have used a similar approach, the life cycle concept, which according to O'Rand and Krecker (1990, p. 258), when "most precisely defined, requires explicit treatment of stages (phases), maturation (development), and generation (reproduction)." O'Rand and Krecker asserted that the concept is relevant for examining notions of social order, identified common states, and equilibrium

---

[7] For example, Clipp, Elder, George, and Pieper (1998), Elder, Shanahan, and Clipp (1994), Ferraro, Farmer, and Wybraniec (1997), Moen, Dempster-McClain, and Williams (1992), Lynch, Kaplan, and Salonen (1997), Rahkonen, Lahelma, and Huuhka (1997), Rose (1991), and Wadsworth (1997).

processes, and therefore is limited in examining heterogeneity and change. The concept as applied to the family assumes typical passage (for individuals or families) through successive stages (e.g., for families, beginning with courtship and ending with widowhood).

Schafer and Keith (1981) studied influences on food decisions across the family life cycle, focusing on the nuclear family. They found that changes and unique events at each life cycle stage have a bearing on the family's food patterns and what influences are important to the family, demonstrating that family members have significant influence over time. Medeiros et al. (1993) also used a life cycle orientation and found stage differences, which they referred to as age-related differences, even though their study was cross-sectional. They also found a potential cohort difference (although they did not refer to it as such), noting that the over-60 adult group in their study seemed less secure in their nutrition information; the authors hypothesized that it may be a function of how recently research-based information has become available to that group and that older adults might not have had the same opportunity to learn newer information as the younger age groups have had.

There are other possible explanations that the researchers neglected to offer. First is that older adults have more experience with changing and sometimes seemingly conflicting nutritional information. While the youngest age group may have just learned the latest recommendations, older adults have likely been exposed to earlier recommendations as well. Older adults may be insecure in their knowledge because either they do not know the latest information (and are certain there is a latest recommendation out there) or are unsure as to the certainty of the latest information (knowing that it was different in the past and may change again). Another possible explanation is that older adults are more firmly ensconced in habit and therefore are less likely to respond to new information without direct experience.

There are some researchers who use a life span approach, which focuses on human development stages, from birth to death. Devine and Olson (1991) used what they refer to as a life stage framework to examine influences on women's motives for preventive dietary behavior, citing life span developmental psychology research in their background. They concluded that motives vary with life stage, due to altered perceptions of health status, body weight, and social roles. They noted the possibility of a cohort effect, as women in younger cohorts may have a different orientation to personal nutrition than the women in the older cohort, which may be related to the timing and influence of new public information about diet and health.

The concepts of life cycle and life span do recognize the importance of considering temporal aspects and transitions and the need to view phenomena in the context of the entire span of life and an individual's personal history. But all of these concepts generally lack the life course perspective's consideration of complexity within the life course, such as variation, multiple and interactive contexts, timing, and influence of cohort and period effects.

Existing life course research on dietary behavior has considered aspects of the life course such as transitions, for example, Pavis et al. (1998) and Olson (2005). Others have attempted to involve multiple aspects of the life course perspective in their research. Furst, Connors, Bisogni, Sobal, and Falk (1996) developed a model of food choice for adults, in which they determined an individual's life course to be a primary factor that creates a whole set of various influences on food choice. They conceived of the life course as "the personal roles and the social, cultural and physical environments to which a person has been and is exposed" (Furst et al., 1996, p. 250) and included historical events as well as personal experience. The influences included ideals, personal factors, resources, social framework, and food context. The researchers concluded that their "data indicate that the role of the life course must be explicitly considered when conceptualizing food choice" (Furst et al., 1996, p. 261).

Using a life course perspective, Devine et al. (1998) conducted qualitative interviews to investigate influences on the fruit and vegetable choices of adults. Their analysis showed that past life course events and experiences were strong influences on present systems for fruit and vegetable choices. Key influences on fruit and vegetable dietary trajectories included food upbringing, roles, health, ethnic traditions, resources, location, and the food system. Early life food experiences were a prominent factor in shaping fruit and vegetable trajectories, creating lasting "food roots" (Devine et al., 1998, p. 364). While having favorable early experiences with fruits and vegetables resulted in more positive trajectories of higher fruit and vegetable consumption, the opposite was also true, as negative or non-existent experiences resulted in lifelong dislike or non-incorporation of fruits and vegetables into personal food systems and practices.

Although rooted in experiences with long-lasting effects, food choice patterns can change over time and with exposure to new environments. Devine et al.'s (1998) results suggested that life course transitions are times when food choice systems may undergo change (and, according to the authors, offer opportunities for intervention). The study also provided support for the importance of role transitions and social status, especially familial. Role and family transitions, such as childbearing, marriage, divorce, employment, empty nest, and return nesters, affected fruit and vegetable trajectories. For example, new parents increased the serving and eating of vegetables for their children's sake, and for newlyweds, it took some adjustment to mesh a personal food system with the system of a new spouse. Devine, Wolfe, Frongillo, and Bisogni (1999) further demonstrated that life course events and experiences differed by ethnicity (specifically African Americans, Hispanics, and whites) and differentially affected fruit and vegetable consumption.

Edstrom and Devine (2001) conducted a study to understand women's perceptions of stability and change in their orientation to food and nutrition during a time of physical, social, and psychological transitions. Using a life course perspective as a conceptual guide, the researchers found that most of the women described consistent orientations to food and nutrition, with little to no perceived change during the ten-year period, despite changes in health, social environment, and roles. Three of the women perceived noteworthy changes in their orientations and attributed the changes to debilitating disease and transitions in family and work roles. Edstrom and Devine therefore concluded that the women's perceptions of consistency in food and nutrition orientations are evidence of stable trajectories, which influence their responses to nutrition education and approaches to dietary changes.

Brombach (2001b) used a life course approach in an investigation of biographical factors that shape current eating behavior of older German women. Brombach identified four different eating types, which changed only in certain cases, such as marriage to a partner of another eating type, illness, or fear of health implications. Quandt, Vitolins, Dewalt, and Roos (1997) used a life course approach for understanding the meal patterns of rural older adults. The elder respondents in their study indicated that as they have grown older, they have experienced changes in their meal and food consumption patterns, e.g., smaller meals and more frequent cold meals. They perceived processes that affected their current eating patterns, such as changes in work patterns, family life stage, health, and health awareness. The experiences of men and women were somewhat different; for example, cooking for others had meaning for many of these women. The authors posited that these older adults' recollections reveal that food has social meanings that relate to the family and to gender and family roles. Life course changes in these roles brought about changes in meal patterns (e.g., the loss of a spouse, followed by fewer cooked meals), and older adults recognized these changes and their influence on the social meanings of food and meals.

Symbolic Interactionism

LaRossa and Reitzes (1993) identified three central themes of symbolic interactionism. The first theme involves the importance of meanings for human behavior. The second theme concentrates on the development and importance of self-concept. Once self-concepts have been developed, they provide important motivation for behavior. The third theme deals with assumptions about society. Individual behavior is affected by societal norms and values. This theme also emphasizes the dynamic nature of social structure; people work out the details of social structure through social interaction in everyday situations.

Key concepts of symbolic interactionism include symbols, identities, roles, interactions, and contexts (LaRossa and Reitzes, 1993). Each concept is closely linked to each other. Symbols are anything that socially has come to stand for something else; we use symbols to mentally represent the world and to communicate with others about the world. Symbols can take many forms including verbal and written words, gestures, and objects (e.g., food). A second key concept is the identity. Identities refer to self-meanings in a role. A third key concept is the role, which are shared norms regarding social positions. The fourth concept is interactions, for as LaRossa and Reitzes (1993, p. 149) stated, "it is through social interaction that individuals apply broad shared symbols and actively create the specific meanings of self, others and situations." A final concept is contexts, the backdrops and circumstances in which identities are formed, roles are occupied, and interactions occur.

Symbolic interactionism is interested in how behavior is shaped by culture and how culture is shaped by behavior (LaRossa and Reitzes, 1993). The perspective recognizes various levels of contexts, from the micro and immediate structural properties to the macro and larger, societal level aspects.

Symbolic Interactionism and Health Behavior

Symbolic interactionism is no stranger to health research; however, similar to the life course perspective, symbolic interactionism is not a commonly applied in the study of health behavior. In the area of health-related behavior, studies have focused more on illness behavior, such as symptom response, care seeking, and medical-related behavior (Alonzo & Reynolds, 1994; Burton & Hudson, 2001; Frazier & Garvin, 1996; Geersten, 1997; Sigman, 1985). Little research has used symbolic interactionism to understand those actions related to wellness and health prevention/promotion (exceptions include Glik and Kronenfeld, 1989, Pezza, 1990-1991, and Duncan, Travis, and McAuley, 1995).

It is not a stretch to see how symbolic interactionism could illuminate roles, rituals, and meanings associated with food and eating experiences throughout life, and to a small extent, researchers have applied symbolic interactionism to such experiences. Some have approached the American fast food phenomena from a symbolic interactionist perspective, as well as eating out in general (Finkelstein, 1985; Law, 1984; Shelton, 1993). Others have studied such diverse dietary topics as written instructions for the preparation of food, commitment to natural foods, anorexia, weight issues, and drinking patterns and sociability in an African American outdoor drinking place (Pestello, 1995; Roebuck, 1986; Sobal & Maurer, 2000; Taub & McLorb, 2001; Tomlinson, 1986). Yet neither everyday dietary practices nor behaviors throughout life have been explored from this perspective.

Integrating the Life Course Perspective and Symbolic Interactionism

Symbolic interactionist insights seem to mesh well with a life course perspective. Hatch (2000) noted that the life course perspective can benefit from integration with symbolic interactionism, pointing out that a symbolic interactionist perspective is implicit in many life course studies and some contemporary life course researchers explicitly use symbolic interactionism in their work. The life course perspective and symbolic interactionism share early roots, particularly in the Chicago school of sociology in the earlier part of the 20th century, rendering their incorporation historically and theoretically consistent.

Both perspectives take a dynamic, process point of reference, but a life course perspective also highlights a temporal element that is absent in symbolic interactionism. The life course perspective's inclusion of environment fits within symbolic interactionism's concept of contexts, but adds an emphasis on place that is not as well defined in symbolic interactionism. Symbolic interactionism strengthens a life course perspective in terms of emphasis on meaning and social interaction. A focus on subjective interpretations complements the biographical component in a life course perspective, as the interpretive process mediates the impact and experience of events and transitions on an individual as much as the timing of those events and transitions. The interplay of social relations and the content of social interaction in symbolic interactionism more fully expresses the social relations concept and mechanisms of influence in the life course perspective. Thus, an integration of the two perspectives is not only doable, but also of theoretical value in the study of social influences on individual behavior.

Other Theoretical Considerations

Social Cognitive Theory, Heaney and Isreal's model of Social Networks and Social Support, and Ecological models incorporate social, cultural, and other environmental factors that affect individuals, more so than the major theories and models of health behavior referenced earlier. Therefore, they provide theoretical considerations and insights that are in line with a focus on social and life course influences on dietary behavior.

Social Cognitive Theory (SCT) is defined by a focus on the interaction between the person, environment (all factors physically external to the person), and behavior (Bandura, 1986). It is assumed that all three affect one another, referred to as reciprocal determinism. There are a number of other key principles and constructs of SCT that affect this interaction.[8] One problem with how SCT has been used is that single aspects of the theory are used in its name (Baranowski, Perry, & Parcel, 1997). The most-applied single aspect of SCT is the self-efficacy component (e.g., Conn, 1997; Duncan et al., 1995; Grembowski et al., 1993; Strecher, DeVellis, Becker, & Rosenstock, 1986). This might partly have to do with the disciplines utilizing the construct; after all, the theory was developed by a social psychologist. Its popularity also might reflect that an emphasis on changing individuals' actions is easier than trying to change social

---

[8] According to Bandura (1986), one such principle is the situation, which is the person's perception of the environment. Other components are the expectations and expectancies (values) of the person, self-efficacy, self-control, and emotional coping responses. Behavioral capability, observational learning, and reinforcement (positive and negative) are concepts that involve what and how behaviors are learned and performed by the individual.

and structural factors. SCT tries to situate behavior in social as well as personal spheres of influence more so than the other current theories. SCT does heavily focus on intrapersonal processes though, and lacks with regard to a temporal perspective, meaning, and social structural factors.

The social environment takes a prominent place in the conceptual model of the relationship of social networks and social support to health as presented by Heaney and Israel (1997). The terms "social network" and "social support" are concepts that describe aspects of social relationships, and though they are not theories per se, there is empirical evidence to show that the concepts play an important role in health and health behavior, such as Potts, Hurwicz, Goldstein, and Berkanovic (1992) and Trippet (1991). In this model, different pathways affect health (physical, mental, and social) directly and indirectly through stressors, individual coping resources, organizational and community resources, and health behaviors. Several of these paths entail reciprocal influence. The model lacks in a couple of areas, perhaps due to the focus on the role of stress in this particular web of relations. It is interesting that no relationship is indicated in the model between stress and health behaviors. However, social context is clearly included as a major component of influence on health and health behaviors, and therefore makes an important contribution to health behavior theory.

In their review of ecological models of health behavior, Sallis and Owen (1997) noted that social cognitive theory shares some features with ecological models, such as an emphasis on relationships between behavior and personal and environmental factors. According to Sallis and Owen (1997, p. 404), ecological models propose that "behaviors are influenced by intrapersonal, social and cultural, and physical environment variables; posit that these variables are likely to interact; and describe multiple levels of social and cultural and physical environment variables." Unlike many other theories that include the environment as a factor, ecological models assume that environments directly influence behavior and there is no mediation through cognitive processes.

Summary

This chapter illustrates the significance of and need for research on the dietary behavior of older adults, particularly women, guided by theoretical frameworks that highlight social issues. This chapter further demonstrated the importance of social issues related to dietary and health behavior, such as the consideration of gender as it affects health and behavior through roles and societal expectations, the impact of social relationships, statuses and concomitant roles, and life course transitions on the development and progression of health behavior, and environmental situations that impact behavior and the social milieu for behavior. This social focus also included reference to moral discourse on dietary behavior, based upon the proposition that moral orientations regarding health behavior are socially constructed and shaped.

The chapter turned to theoretical considerations, illuminating deficiencies in commonly used theories of health behavior and strengths in theories not often applied to the study of health behavior, especially the life course perspective and symbolic interactionism. Deficiencies of popular theories include an extreme focus on psychological processes that neglects wider social factors, while strengths of the life course perspective and symbolic interactionism involve temporal, social, structural, and interpretive processes, though the frameworks do not preclude the function and operation of intrapersonal factors.

Chapter Two

The Setting & Participant Characteristics

This chapter describes the physical and social environments of Colonial Square and sociodemographic characteristics of the participants in the study. The setting of the retirement community is important to know and understand; it is within this multi-layered environment that the participants live and act. In turn, it is important to gain familiarity with the women who shared their stories for this research. Though similar in many ways, each woman expresses a unique life history. Together, the setting and life characteristics of each woman constitute significant contexts within which to situate their stories of food and eating.

The description of the setting is divided into four sections. The first section discusses a brief historical background of the place and the physical locale, locating Colonial Square in time and space relative to the larger community of Lexington, Kentucky. The second section describes the structure itself and physical layout of the complex. The third section delves into the activities, amenities, and services offered to residents, detailing the dining services particularly, and includes ways in which residents provide input into operations of the community. The fourth section addresses the social environment, including general characteristics of the resident population, social interaction, and community participation. Finally, a description of participant characteristics completes the chapter.

The Setting: Historical and Physical Location

Kentucky was a part of the 1980s retirement community boom, which included the opening of several retirement communities in the Lexington metropolitan area. Colonial Square was one of three retirement communities in town when it began operations in the mid-1980s. Within a month of its opening, the first two residents, a married couple, moved into an apartment, and in the next five months, residents occupied fifteen apartments. Throughout the 1980s, the building continued to fill with new occupants. Two years after Colonial Square opened, the Retirement Housing Company (RHC)[1] bought the community and took over management operations. Founded in 1978, RHC is a publicly traded company on the New York Stock Exchange (since 1997) that also owns or provides services for more than 50 communities in 16 states. The various RHC communities provide a range of care levels and services, including independent living, personal care/assisted living, skilled nursing, and Alzheimer's care; any one community might have a combination of levels of care. The company's focus is on large upscale congregate and continuing care retirement communities, both for-profit and not-for-profit.

By the late 1990s, occupancy rates at Colonial Square were consistently in the upper 90th percentiles. Being put on a waiting list became the normal routine for anyone wishing to secure an apartment ($250 to get on the list), and a future's list had even been developed. The future's list is a step below the waiting list, designed for those interested, but not quite ready to make a firm commitment (it does require a $100 deposit, of course transferable, if one decides to go to the wait list).

There have been changes in the community over the years, and there has been expansion on the property of Colonial Square during the past three years. It is now a campus that includes a personal care facility, Oak Ridge Manor, and a care facility for those in the early stages of Alzheimer's disease, the Meadows.[2] Despite such growth, Colonial Square has had some marketing struggles in the early 2000s. In addition to some residents of Colonial Square making their way

---

[1] A pseudonym, for purposes of confidentiality
[2] Oak Ridge Manor and the Meadows are also pseudonyms, for purposes of confidentiality.

over to Oak Ridge Manor and the Meadows, there is increased competition. Colonial Square is now one of about six retirement communities in the Lexington area. The latest community to be developed is almost identical to Colonial Square in its service and amenity offerings, and only 10 to 15 minutes away. Occupancy rates at Colonial Square have fallen somewhat, although not precipitously.

Colonial Square is situated on 20 acres of land in the Lexington, Kentucky metropolitan area. The location, long used for farming and agriculture, had become engulfed by urban expansion, resulting in the shift to residential and commercial land use along the area's main transportation corridor. The complex is on the north-northeastern corner of an intersection on this major road, putting it on a local bus route. It is not quite five minutes from shopping, banking, restaurants, and entertainment (movie theaters) and about 15 minutes from downtown businesses, government offices, and cultural centers. Colonial Square is surrounded to the north and northeast by a middle class neighborhood, consisting of apartments, townhouses and single-family dwellings. To the west and south are commercial developments, comprised of building clusters that house offices and facilities for health care, business, and industry. To the east are some woods, and then an industrial area. About 100 yards away from the main structure is Oak Ridge Manor, the three-story personal care facility, and adjacent to Oak Ridge is the Meadows, a one-story Alzheimer's care facility.

The Setting: The Physical Structure

Colonial Square's main physical structure is a mid-rise apartment complex, consisting of three above ground levels and a basement. Colonial Square contains 178 private apartments, several public spaces and common areas, and offices and staff work areas.

The building is laid out in a U-shape, with the parking lot creating an asphalt U around the building. Along the outer edges of the parking lot are carports, which are for residents only. Certain spaces nearer to the front of the building are designated for visitors, although sometimes visitors park in open resident spaces due all the visitor spots being occupied. Generally, this does not pose a problem for residents or visitors. Visitors have to enter the building through the main doors in the front, as other entries to the building are locked (residents carry keys to the building). Occasionally if visitors are expected, a resident will meet them at the doorway closest to their apartment and let them in, particularly if the apartment is in the back of the building. Visitors are also supposed to sign-in at the front desk, although this is not strictly enforced. After 9:00 p.m., the front doors are locked, and a phone at the front may be used to call security to allow entry.

The First Floor

Through the main entrance is a small lobby. During the day, the receptionist sits to the right, behind a long white counter; when the receptionist is not there, a nurse, nursing assistant, or someone from activities will staff the front desk. In the evenings, a security officer sits behind the counter. Directly ahead in the lobby is an elevator. There is a board on an easel to the left of the doors that states the manager on duty and activities for the day. Most illumination in the lobby during the day comes from a large window behind the receptionist's desk. At night there is soft lighting from lamps and an overhead light.

There are two corridors off the lobby, one to the right and one to the left. These lead to resident apartments, but also to administrative offices and service facilities. Most public spaces are on the first floor. Following the left corridor, the first public space encountered is the computer lab and library. The computer lab is a small room with about six personal computers set up for resident use. Connected to the lab through a wide, open doorway is the library, another small room that contains books, magazines, and newspapers, and in which there is a table and a few chairs for residents who choose to peruse materials in the library. There is also a separate entrance to the library off the corridor.

Figure 2.1: First Floor of Colonial Square[3]

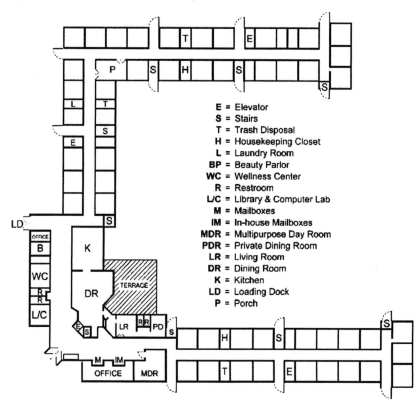

E = Elevator
S = Stairs
T = Trash Disposal
H = Housekeeping Closet
L = Laundry Room
BP = Beauty Parlor
WC = Wellness Center
R = Restroom
L/C = Library & Computer Lab
M = Mailboxes
IM = In-house Mailboxes
MDR = Multipurpose Day Room
PDR = Private Dining Room
LR = Living Room
DR = Dining Room
K = Kitchen
LD = Loading Dock
P = Porch

Along this corridor there are also public restrooms (with a water fountain and a place to hang coats just outside of them), the Wellness Center, and the beauty salon. The smell of hair care and treatment products is strong as one passes the salon, particularly if the door is open. Also on the left corridor, before one gets to the apartments, are the loading dock and an entrance to the kitchen, which further leads to the office of the director of dining services.

The kitchen has a commercial appearance, such as one would see in a

---

[3] Figure is not to scale. Source: Curch, L. M. (2004). Food, eating and social dynamics in the retirement community. *Geographica Helvetica, 59*(4), 282. Draft: L.M. Curch; Concept: B. Crowder; Cartography: L. Baumann.

restaurant or hotel, with abundant stainless steel counters and appliances. The director's office is a very small room at the back of the kitchen, brightly lit by overhead fluorescent lights, and with a window that looks out into the kitchen. The office was formerly located across the hall from the kitchen, but the director has recently moved into this space to allow greater involvement with and accessibility to the kitchen staff. Much further down the left corridor, after passing about six resident apartments, double doors lead outside to a covered concrete porch area.

Moving from the main entrance along the right corridor brings one to the main administrative offices, where the executive director, resident services coordinator, staff development manager, and marketing director all have offices. The resident mailboxes are located here, and bulletin boards for community news and communications are in the mailbox station. A sign above the mailboxes indicates whether the mail has been delivered yet that day or not. Post-it notes stuck on the outside of some mailboxes indicate that a package is waiting, which can be picked up at any time from a bookshelf in the main administrative office area. Next are the in-house boxes; these are rows upon rows of dark brown cubbyholes used for delivery of flyers, newsletters, memos, and other information from the management. Personal communications between residents can also be delivered this way. Across the hall from the in-house mailboxes is the entrance to the Living Room and Dining Room.

A sign at the entrance of the Living Room states the featured soups and entrees for the next meal to be served. Residents go through the Living Room to get into the Dining Room. There are actually two parts to the Living Room: a large room, which is the main seating area, and then a smaller room known as the fireplace room (due to the presence of a gas log fireplace). The Living Room areas are elegantly appointed, with dark wood furniture and fabrics in pastel and neutral colors; the furnishings are arranged in groupings.

Figure 2.2: The Dining Room and Living Room Areas of Colonial Square[4]

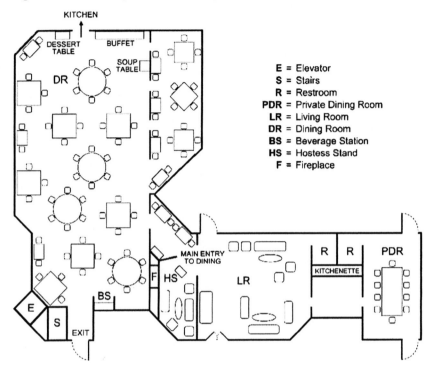

E = Elevator
S = Stairs
R = Restroom
PDR = Private Dining Room
LR = Living Room
DR = Dining Room
BS = Beverage Station
HS = Hostess Stand
F = Fireplace

The fireplace room is an area connecting the main Living Room and the Dining Room, and is the current location of the hostess station, which is a small, rectangular table of dark cherry wood with brass drawer pulls. It is at the hostess station where each resident must stop to have their community card scanned before a meal. Beyond the hostess station, one moves through a small room, with two dining tables (each seats four) and a sideboard, and into the main dining area, in which there are about 20 tables and the buffet.

The Dining Room is a well-lit area, with ornate wrought iron chandeliers (painted a cream color) and small lanterns hanging from the ceiling. The walls are

___

[4] Figure is not to scale. Source: Curch, L. M. (2004). Food, eating and social dynamics in the retirement community. *Geographica Helvetica, 59*(4), 283. Draft: L.M. Curch; Concept: B. Crowder; Cartography: L. Baumann.

painted beige or are covered in pinkish-gray brick, with gold-accented decorations (mirrors and prints), and brown carpeting with a dark blue grid pattern. The chairs all have armrests and wheels and are upholstered in coral, green, and beige stripes. Tables seat various numbers of residents; there are two-tops, four-tops and six-tops (tables that seat two, four and six, respectively). A white tablecloth covers each table, which is set with cloth napkins, silver utensils (a salad fork, a dinner fork, a knife, a soup spoon and a tea spoon), water goblets, cups and saucers, and bread plates. Each table also has a salt and pepper set, a small white container with packets of sugar and artificial sweeteners, comment cards, and pencils. Tables that seat six will have two sets of the condiments, cards, and pencils.

At dinner, a menu is placed at each setting. Residents in wheelchairs can be accommodated in the Dining Room, but limited space between most tables generally makes navigation difficult. The wall separating the main dining area from the hallway and lobby is lined with multi- paned windows at chair rail height; there are no window treatments. The buffet at the end of the room, where there is a doorway to the kitchen, is used only during lunch and the continental breakfast, as table service is provided for the evening meal. At dinner, the buffet holds water pitchers and coffee carafes for the servers.

To the right side of this area is another room, sometimes referred to as the garden room. Although part of the main dining area, several gray brick, faux columns against short walls create wide doorways, and essentially separate the garden room, giving it the feel of being a different room. There are large windows along the outer wall of the garden room and from which white sheer draperies are hung. One can also get to a private dining room from the Living Room, through a doorway on the side of Living Room opposite of the doorway to the fireplace room and Dining Room. The private dining room also has a separate entrance down the hall. Across the hall from the private dining room, before the resident apartments, is a multipurpose day room. Interspersed among the apartments of both wings are laundry rooms (there are free washers and dryers on each floor for the residents' use), trash disposal rooms, housekeeping closets, stairwells (a total of six) and elevators (a total of four; only the central elevator services the basement). Two years ago, management contracted for the remodeling of the hallways and common areas on each floor. The residents of each hallway voted on final color schemes and patterns, which resulted in each hallway being a little different from the others. The preferences of the residents' were for light, soft colors, with various shades of blue, beige, mauve, and green prevailing.

There are 51 apartment homes on the first floor. They range in size from about 480 to 1064 square feet, vary in layout from a studio to a two-bedroom/two-bath plan, vary in location, whether on the first, second or third floor, and vary in views, with or without a balcony or courtyard view. Residents are able to make minor cosmetic changes to their apartments, such as in decor and painting/wallpapering, but any major changes need the approval of management.

All apartments are carpeted, and have fully equipped kitchens (all electric appliances), individual climate control, drapes and washer and dryer hook-ups. The apartments have some features to assist elders and those with disabilities, such as wheelchair-accessible sinks and grab bars in the showers. In general, however, maneuvering room for someone in a wheelchair is limited through existing doorways, hallways, and many of the kitchens. Apartments also come equipped with emergency pull cords (generally in the bedroom), and an electronic check-in system in the bathroom.

The Second Floor

The second floor consists of mostly apartments; there are 61 apartments on this level. Just as on the first floor, there are laundry rooms, trash disposal rooms, housekeeping closets, stairwells and elevators intermittently stationed on each wing. There is also a public restroom, and a conference room that is used for both staff and resident meetings. As one faces the central elevator, on the right side are about half a dozen square tables, with four high-back chairs around each. On the left side of the elevator are chairs and a television. Directly in front of the central elevator is a coffee table, which is surrounded by a loveseat and a couple of chairs. On the coffee table are magazines, mostly related to travel. Behind this grouping are double doors that lead out to a second floor balcony that is just above the main entrance. On the opposite side, behind the elevator, is a large balcony overlooking the back of the property. Just as on the first floor, there are also other elevators located at various intervals on each wing. These are helpful of course, but it is still a very long walk to the Dining Room, mailboxes, etc. on the first floor from the far ends of the building, regardless of floor or elevator location. Occasionally one sees a mobie or two parked in an alcove or lounge area (mobie is the nickname used for electric mobile chair).

Figure 2.3: Second Floor of Colonial Square[5]

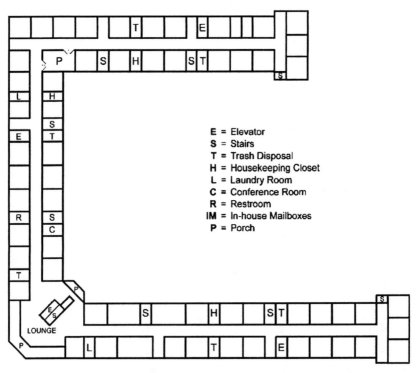

E = Elevator
S = Stairs
T = Trash Disposal
H = Housekeeping Closet
L = Laundry Room
C = Conference Room
R = Restroom
IM = In-house Mailboxes
P = Porch

---

[5] Figure is not to scale. Graphic by Brian Crowder.

Anyone interested in the history of Colonial Square can go down the right corridor to a small side alcove. Here one can peruse the Residents' Archives, designated as such by a handwritten paper sign. A dark brown three-shelf bookcase and a filing cabinet contain records that sketch the history of Colonial Square. The archives include photo albums, videos, association meeting minutes, newsletters, resident rosters, alumni lists, entries made by the archivist on events and happenings, and the history of an outdoor memorial park area.

The Third Floor

The third floor, with 66 apartments, is basically the same as the second floor. One difference is in how the open (lounge) spaces on this level are used. To the left of the central elevator is a lounge area is arranged for serious TV viewing; there are several rows of chairs facing a large television, which is set on a stand high enough so that nobody's head will be in anyone else's way. The other open space, to the right of the elevator, is set up as a gaming area with billiards and about three or four poker tables. The jewel tone colors and dark wood is reminiscent of a pool hall. A long, pub-like lamp hangs over the billiard table, casting a yellowish light. An impressionistic mural of a horse racing event covers the entire right wall. Another feature of the third floor is the guest apartment for overnight visitors.

The Basement

Finally, there is the basement, a fairly stark and sterile area with bright fluorescent lights and off-white concrete walls. The basement is mostly staff territory dominated by offices, such as those for activities, housekeeping, maintenance, and the home health agency. The employee break room is also located in the basement. There are three areas for residents in the basement: a workshop for residents inclined to woodworking, a shuffleboard court, and limited storage space for residents' use. Neither the workshop nor shuffleboard court is used very much.

The Grounds

The grounds of Colonial Square are a point of pride for both residents and staff. The landscaping is professional and meticulously maintained, with many trees and plenty of flowers in the spring and summer. Residents are allowed to do some landscaping and outdoor decorating just outside their apartments. There are many birdfeeders, window boxes, and even some metal sculptures of animals and insects. Outside of the building, behind the Living Room and Dining Room, is a large, uncovered concrete and brick terrace. Beyond the terrace, is a very large courtyard area, in which paved walking paths (lit at night) meander throughout to the eastern area of the property. Outdoor recreational facilities include shuffleboard courts, a putting green, a swimming pool and tennis courts. There is an herb garden among the walking paths, which has suffered from some neglect since the passing of the resident who began it. The raised garden boxes and garden plots in the northeastern area of the property are popular with residents. Also to the eastern side of the property is Memory Hill. Memory Hill is not really much of a hill, but it is a grassy area, with a small bridge walk and trees, that was developed from funds donated in memory of deceased residents. There is a plaque in the ground designating the area as such.

The Setting: Activities, Amenities, and Services

Residents need to have some level of financial security to live at Colonial Square. In fact, each potential resident is subjected to a financial screening before moving in to assure the management that the resident will be able to meet the monthly financial obligation for years to come. Monthly fees range from $1550.00 for a basic studio, to $3140.00 for two people living in a two-bedroom/two-bath apartment on the first floor that opens out to the courtyard (there is a $400.00 double occupancy fee). These monthly fees do include a number of services and amenities, such as dining services, weekly housekeeping, maintenance, washers and dryers, all utilities (except phone and cable), wellness services, activities (some events have an extra cost), transportation, and safety and security systems. Many residents feel that all the services and amenities justify the monthly cost. The services that are often a consideration in decisions to move to Colonial Square, and which seem to be quite appreciated, are the dining services.

Dining Services

The director of dining services has the following staff under his supervision: the chef, cooks, hosts, servers, and bus people. The majority of the food and dining services staff tends to be young; most all of the hosts, servers, and bus people are high school and college students. The food and dining services at Colonial Square also include preparation of the meals for Oak Ridge Manor and the Meadows, sending the food across the parking lot via a mobile hot/cold unit (it looks like an oversize golf cart with a big refrigerator on it). They also cater any activities or special events as requested by other staff.

There is a free continental breakfast available in the Dining Room on weekday mornings from 8:30 a.m. to 9:30 a.m. This breakfast includes baked goods (e.g., muffins), breads, pastries, dry cereals, hot oatmeal, fresh fruit, coffee, tea, milk, and juice. On Saturdays, complimentary coffee and doughnuts are served from 9:00 a.m. to 11:00 a.m. on the second floor in the elevator lobby area. This is referred to as the "Coffee Klatch."

One meal a day is included in the monthly fee, and residents may choose to take either lunch or dinner. Which meal a resident chooses can change from day to day. Lunch is served from 11:30 a.m. to 1:00 p.m. on weekdays; a lunchtime meal is not served on Saturdays. Lunch meals are buffet-style, and include breads, soup, salads, two or three entrees, three or four sides, relish/garnish items, and desserts. A server brings beverages to the table. Friday lunches are brunches, as they include breakfast foods, such as scrambled eggs, sausage, bacon, hash browns, and biscuits and gravy.

76

Figure 2.4: Sample Dinner Menu

SOUP DU JOUR

SALADS
House Garden Salad*
Spinach Salad
Sugar Free Jell-O*

Salad is served with your choice of 1000 Island, Low Fat Ranch, Blue Cheese,
Low Fat Italian, Honey Mustard, French or Oil & Vinegar

ENTREES
Grilled Chicken
Breast of chicken grilled

Hot Browns
Turkey, ham and bacon served on toast and topped with a cream sauce

Fried Oysters
Fresh Oysters deep fried to perfection

ACCOMPANIMENTS
| Onion Rings | Mixed Vegetables |
| Broccoli | Cauliflower |

ALTERNATIVES
Fresh Seasonal Fruit Plate*
Served with your choice of cottage cheese, tuna or chicken salad

Grilled Chicken Breast

DESSERTS
Ice cream flavors include Vanilla, Chocolate, Low Fat Frozen Yogurt along with
a Featured Flavor.

For Sugar Free selections and Daily Features...Please Ask Your Server.

* DENOTES NO ADDED SUGAR OR SALT

Dinner is served from 3:30 p.m. to 7:00 p.m., Monday through Saturday. Sunday dinner is served from 11:00 a.m. to 1:30 p.m., and there is no evening meal. Weekly abbreviated menus are sent out to residents that list featured salads, entrees and sides for dinner each night. Dinner meals are provided by table service. There is a menu for the evening meal at each place setting on the tables (see Figure 2.4 for a sample menu and Appendix B for sample weekly menus).

A young man or woman takes the resident's order and brings the food and beverages to the tables. Twice a week, on Thursdays and Saturdays, wine is served; red and white wine carafes are on the table and diners may help themselves. Dinners include breads, soup, salads, three choices of entrees (one is usually chosen), four choices of sides (two are usually chosen, although three is acceptable), and desserts. There is a daily feature salad, in addition to a house salad and Jell-O. There are alternative entrees that are always available, if none of the main entrees are appealing. One can choose from: a fresh fruit plate with choice of cottage cheese, chicken salad, or tuna salad; a grilled chicken breast; or a grilled ham steak. Interestingly, the grilled chicken breast is listed on the menu as an alternative even on the evenings that grilled chicken breast is a main entree item. There is a featured dessert each day (e.g., bread pudding, apple pie, or chocolate cake), and there are standard desserts that are always available: ice cream, sherbet, and frozen yogurt. Some low-sodium and sugar-free items are available. Menus will designate if an item has no added sugar or salt. While there is no dietician on staff, occasionally a consulting dietician comes by the facility to assist in maintaining nutrition standards.

A resident may have as much as they like of any item at all meals. However, there are no doggie bags; leftover food may not be taken back to the resident's apartment, because the policy is that no food is allowed to leave the Dining Room. The only exception is that one serving of a dessert may be taken home, as long as the resident provides a container, and the resident has not already eaten a dessert. Another corporate regulation for the Dining Room is a no tipping policy, which applies to all employees, not just the dining staff.

As far as accounting for meals, each resident is assigned a bar code. The code is kept at the hostess stand. The resident also has the code imprinted on a Colonial Square charge card (often hung on a key ring). As the resident enters the dining room, the code is scanned, electronically recording the meal for the resident. Periodically, a report is available at the hostess stand giving the number of meals already served during the month for each resident. At the end of the month, the totals are sent to the business office for billing purposes. Meals not taken by the end of the month are lost; they cannot be saved and used later, although residents do receive a small refund for meals not taken. Meals not taken also cannot be used for guests or any other residents; the only exception is when the other resident is a second person in the same apartment. A resident can pre-order extra meals if that option has been written into his/her lease. A resident can also have a lunch-only meal package.

The bar code scanning is a recent development and was instituted a few years ago. Previously, residents were each issued a month's worth of meal tickets, which were redeemed when taking a meal. Each resident was additionally issued five extra lunch tickets per month. They used their allotments as they saw fit, and many used the extra tickets for guests.

The Resident Council (and not the corporate administration) developed a Dining Room dress code for residents and guests. It is suggested that for lunch, women wear dresses, pant suits, walking shorts, or skirts, and men wear a casual suit, slacks or walking shorts (no jacket is required). For dinner, the Sunday meal, and special events, women should wear dresses or pant suits and men should wear dress shirts, slacks, a tie, and a jacket. The jacket is required and is defined as a sport coat or suit coat. On Saturdays, the dress code for dinner is more relaxed and follows the same guidelines as weekday lunch. No one will be barred from going into the Dining Room if they do not follow the code, but others may frown upon them if they are not dressed according to the guidelines and the mental and physical wellness of that resident may be questioned.

Guests are welcome to dine at Colonial Square, if accompanied by a resident or staff member. Residents are charged a guest meal rate for their visitors; dinner and lunch for an adult costs $11.00 and $6.00, respectively, and for children ages 5 to 11, the prices are $5.50 and $3.00. Children under the age of five may eat free. Residents can reserve tables for guests, as a few tables are set aside each evening for reservations, either made for 4:15 to 4:45 p.m. or 6:15 to 6:45 p.m. Residents, of course, do not need reservations, and are seated and served on a first-come, first-served basis during the designated dining hours. If there must be a wait for a table, then the host or hostess will start a wait list. Although there is not a set rule, the resident handbook asks that residents and guests limit their time in the Dining Room to no more than one hour and thirty minutes.

Room service is available for an extra fee. The delivery charge for a meal tray is $3.25, and each additional tray to the same apartment is $1.75. Regular meal deliveries count as though they were meals consumed in the Dining Room, and are billed as such (the resident's bar code is scanned before the meal is delivered). Up to five complimentary deliveries can be made to residents returning from a hospital admission or outpatient surgery, based on the approval of the wellness nurse. Such meals count as meals consumed and are billed to the resident, but there is no delivery charge. Take-out meals can also be prepared for pick-up. Again, take-out meals are counted as meals consumed, and there is an extra fee of $1.75 per take-out meal.

Two miscellaneous food and dining services are offered for residents' personal functions. A catering service is available, and residents can request catering for any private celebrations or special occasions that they are hosting on the premises. The cost will depend on the items selected and quantity prepared. Residents can also reserve the private dining room for personal use, e.g., a dinner with family. Staff may use the private dining room for official business, e.g., a marketing luncheon.

Other Services and Amenities

There are a number of other services and amenities provided for residents. These include wellness services, safety systems, maintenance, housekeeping, transportation, social activities programs, and other recreational activities and facilities.

The Wellness Center provides health information, health education programs, basic drugstore-type items at a small cost (such as toiletries, pain relievers, and digestive aids) and health services administered by the wellness nurse, such as blood pressure checks (very popular with residents, particularly after breakfast on open clinic days) and shots/ injections. Podiatrists, dentists, and massage therapists have hours in the clinic and residents can schedule appointments for their services. Residents can also contract for private duty services through the on-site home health agency.

The emergency response system is under the aegis of wellness services. Emergency pull cords are located in a convenient place in resident apartments, often in a bedroom area. There is a staff person available 24 hours a day to respond to emergencies. A call-first response was established due to the frequency of false alarms. Therefore, the front desk staff person calls the apartment at the sounding of the alarm, before a staff member goes to the apartment. Another system in place to monitor residents' status involves a check-in procedure. A button in the main bathroom begins flashing around 5:00 a.m., and residents must push the button by 11:00 a.m. (which makes it stop flashing), to let a computer know that they are okay. In the evening, security and/or a nurse will get a printout from the computer and check on any residents who did not push their button; they are aware of residents who may be on vacation or an extended leave.

Routine maintenance and housekeeping services are included in the monthly rental fee, although extra services can be acquired, with the charges appearing on the monthly bill. Routine services offered by maintenance include work on appliances and permanent fixtures, preventive maintenance on air conditioning and heating units, and painting of apartments as needed.

Housekeeping is provided on a weekly basis and includes cleaning bathrooms and the kitchen (including floors, countertops, and outside of appliances), vacuuming, dusting, and bed linen changes. There are also annual services that include window washing, carpet cleaning, cabinet cleaning, and thorough cleaning of the refrigerator.

The Activities Department of Colonial Square oversees transportation, social programs, and use of recreational facilities. Colonial Square has a bus, van, and car for transportation purposes. On Wednesdays and Saturdays, twice a day, the bus does a shopping circuit, called the Loop. The morning circuit is different from the afternoon circuit. There are several stops on these routes, including discount stores, drugstores, a mall and grocery stores. The resident is dropped off at one of these places and the bus will return later at a designated time to pick them up. Many residents do their grocery shopping this way. Residents can schedule transportation for personal reasons, such as shopping or medical appointments, although medical appointments take priority. On Sunday mornings, church service runs are made to particular churches. Colonial Square transportation is also provided to select fine arts, cultural, and entertainment programs and events in Lexington; these trips are set up by the Activities Department.

In addition to such trips, the Activities Department organizes a number of social programs and activities, as well as coordinates the use of indoor and outdoor facilities for leisure and recreational pursuits. Social programs may be holiday parties, games (Bridge and Bingo are popular), special entertainment, educational speakers, and movie showings. The Activities Department also sponsors a Social Hour each Wednesday from 4:00 p.m. to 5:00 p.m. in the multipurpose day room. It is essentially a cocktail hour, where residents can have a glass of wine and some hors d'oeuvres before dinner. An activities staff member generally plays the role of bartender. Hard liquor is not served, but residents can bring their own if they want.

Another activity, called the Dinner Club, involves a monthly outing to a local restaurant. Sometimes, longer trips are planned to go to a special restaurant out of town. During warmer times of the year, cookouts are held, and a luau has become an annual tradition at Colonial Square. Events and activities are often advertised with the qualifier that refreshments will be provided, or sometimes, more specifically, that hot dogs and popcorn will be sold for $1.00. Activities staff have noted that at certain events, if a nominal fee is not charged, too many people will come for the free food. They have also noted that an event or activity is much more popular if food is available, even if there is a small cost.

Additional activities provided include exercise classes and vesper services. The Activities Department coordinates use of certain areas inside, such as the common areas on the second and third floors, the conference room, and multipurpose day room, and areas outside, such as the garden areas and raised box gardens.

Special Activities and Events

There are also special activities and events that occur, sometimes organized only by the Activities Department and sometimes in conjunction with other departments. For example, banking services are a special activity. About once a week, a representative from a bank will be in the Living Room on Friday mornings. Residents can actually conduct business with the bank at those times. A different bank representative will be there during different weeks.

A special event put on by Dining Services, and supported by Activities, is held once a month on a Friday night. "Friday Night Out" involves a special meal served that evening in the Dining Room (e.g., prime rib, stuffed flounder). In the Living Room, wine and hors d'oeuvres (cheeses, fruits and crackers) are served, and live musical entertainment plays, to enjoy before and/or after the meal.

The annual fall bazaar is a special event completely organized by the residents. Residents donate items to be sold at the bazaar, from secondhand things, such as furniture and cookware, to handcrafted items, such as wreaths and homemade baked goods, including cakes, muffins, pies, and cookies. Money raised by the sale is donated to the Employee Appreciation Fund. This is a fund built up all year by donations and sales such as the fall bazaar, and then divided among hourly employees, based on the number of hours they have worked. Because there is a no tipping policy, residents can show their appreciation to the employees through this fund.

Resident Involvement in Community Operations

Although residents do not own any part of Colonial Square, there are mechanisms in place for resident involvement in how the community is operated. Management and staff make efforts to try to keep lines of communication open with the residents. Residents, of course, may talk directly with employees. There is also a suggestion box, through which residents can bring up issues. A major avenue of involvement for residents is through the Residents Association, to which all residents automatically belong upon moving in. It is governed by Resident Council, for which the officers and at-large Council members are elected by the entire membership. There are various standing and special committees (e.g., food services committee, activities committee), which have chairs who are appointed by the Council. The relevant managers and directors attend committee meetings; for example, the director of dining services attends the food services committee meeting and the executive director attends Council and Association meetings. In this way, residents play an active role in the running of the community, by airing complaints, reinforcing positive aspects, making suggestions, and working through issues.

Management recognizes that dining experiences are an important part of the lives of residents, and that providing a means of communication about their experiences is a valuable tool. In addition to verbal communication, residents may also submit their views of their dining experiences in writing via the comment cards mentioned earlier (see Figure 2.5).

Residents are welcome to comment on their meals and the service, extolling the good and lamenting the bad. Residents are required to sign their names to the card, however, because otherwise management will not consider their comments. Each month, the director of dining services compiles and types up all comments for the previous month. He brings this report to the food services committee, which meets the first Wednesday of the month, and distributes a copy to each committee member. Each comment is reviewed and addressed by the director, the chef (who also attends) and the committee members. Committee members may shed more light on a comment, reinforce a comment, or they may refute a comment, dismissing it (e.g., "She thinks everything is too salty!").

Figure 2.5: Dining Room Comment Card

| Date: _____ | | | Lunch ❏ |
| | | | Dinner ❏ |

COMMENT CARD

	Excellent	Good	Fair	Poor
Quality of Service	___	___	___	___
Quantity of Food Sufficient	___	___	___	___
Quality of Food	___	___	___	___

Comments: _____

_____

_____

Were you greeted pleasantly at door? Yes ____ No ____

Suggestions: _____

_____

_____

_____

Server's Name: _____

Resident's Name: _____

The Setting: The Social Milieu

Resident Characteristics

There are about 200 to 205 residents of Colonial Square. The residents are overwhelmingly white, and most are well educated and fairly affluent. Many had professional careers, but some come from trade and agricultural backgrounds, and many women were full-time homemakers. The women outnumber the men, although in the past year or two, a slight surge in the number of men, particularly unmarried men, has been noted. As similar as they are in certain demographic characteristics, residents do come from all over the United States (e.g., Massachusetts, Michigan, and Texas) and bring regional distinctions with them. Despite these geographically diverse origins, many of the residents are from Kentucky. The state to contribute the second largest number of residents is Florida; typically, they had moved to Florida from somewhere else first, planning to permanently retire there, but then moved to Colonial Square.

Social Organization and Community Participation

Many residents speak well of the general community of adults that have gathered at Colonial Square. The friendliness of the people who live there is often mentioned as a strength of the community, and some residents mentioned it as a positive point that helped sell them on the idea of Colonial Square. A few remarked that there are certain residents they will avoid, often people who are perceived as negative and complaining. Although the openness and acceptance of others is brought up as an asset of the community, the residents are not without at least a loose social organization. There are definitely groups of residents, some of which are apparently quite tight and "cliquish." There are also some residents who are perceived by others to be the elites of Colonial Square. These resident elites are active people, involved in leadership roles and governance at Colonial Square, and often participate in organizations and volunteer roles in Lexington. They maintain a high level of social engagement, but usually had been as socially active before moving to Colonial Square.

Residents, of course, can be as involved or not involved as they like in the Colonial Square community activities. Some residents involve themselves through the Residents Association, serving as an officer or on a committee. Others take tasks upon themselves. For example, the resident archives are mostly the work of one resident who was a professional archivist before his retirement; when he died though, the driving force behind the archives faded. It has not been kept well up-to-date since then. The herb garden in the middle of walking paths in the back of the property was planted by a botanically minded resident, who has also since passed away. It fell into some neglect for a while, but has now been taken under wing by another resident, who will attempt to revitalize it. Some are only involved in community activities, some only in activities outside the retirement community, and others are involved in activities both within and outside the community.

Places of Social Interaction and Activity

Different public areas of Colonial Square are used and occupied in different ways and at different times. This often seems to depend on what is happening or about to happen, and the centrality of the place, physically and socially. For example, in the lobby, there tends to be a moderate amount of traffic, because for those who live on the left side of the building, it is necessary to go through the lobby to get to a variety of other places, such as the mailboxes, administrative offices, and the day room. There are also a number of functions that the front desk serves for residents, including paperwork to make routine maintenance requests and schedule transportation. Traffic becomes particularly heavy around meal times and just before the bus is ready to leave for a recreational trip or a shopping circuit. Often, there are one or two people who sit in one of the wing chairs, either waiting for someone or just to pass the time. Frequently, after they have had dinner, a small group of women (five or six) will occupy the lobby, chatting about various topics, including the dinner itself.

The Living Room is generally an area where much waiting occurs, such as for lunch or dinner. It is also a meeting place, where residents will arrange to join up with each other or guests before going into the Dining Room. The fireplace alcove is mainly used for waiting before meals. Sometimes, there is a card or two sitting out on a table, in view of those passing through; these are either sympathy cards for grieving residents or get well cards for sick residents, and anyone can sign them. Sometimes special events and activities will occur in the Living Room, such as speakers and banking services, which liven up the place. Friday Night Out, for example is very popular, as many residents and guests go to dinner that evening. A wait list becomes necessary because the Dining Room cannot accommodate everyone at the same time. On these nights, it is lively and crowded in the Living Room. Otherwise, unless it is a bank day, Friday Night Out, before mealtime, or during a special activity, the Living Room is a rather quiet place.

In the Dining Room, dinner is the most crowded mealtime, with roughly two rounds of diners; there is a wave of diners around 4:30-5:00 p.m. and another wave around 5:30-6:00 p.m. There are some who do eat as early as 3:30 p.m., when the Dining Room opens for dinner. Lunch is not as well attended, for it seems most people chose to use their one meal a day at dinner. The continental breakfast attracts about 30 regulars. Sometimes staff will get lunch from the Dining Room, but do not often eat there. Occasionally, there will be an administrative lunch meeting in the Dining Room. During the months of October and April, lunchtime on Fridays is especially sparsely attended, due to the local horse racing events that are held on those days.

Down the hall, the Multipurpose Day Room is frequently an active place, as a number of planned activities, such as crafts, exercise classes, dances, television events (local sports are important), and parties enliven the area. Meetings and luncheons will also be held there, such as resident committee meetings or staff luncheons. The conference room on the second floor is also used for meetings, both staff and resident, and for social activities, such as Bible study on Tuesday afternoons.

In the second and third floor lounge/common areas, the tables are used for serious and not-so-serious card playing, mainly bridge, and mainly in afternoons and evenings. Otherwise, during the day it can be fairly quiet in the common areas and throughout the floors, though occasionally one hears the sound of a television from an apartment. A few people will pass through going from their apartment to the first floor and vice versa. On the second floor, there is one woman who regularly leaves her apartment door wide open. She does not make much noise, although sometimes music will be softly playing. She often can be seen sitting in her living room, doing some sort of handiwork, such as cross-stitching. In the evenings, it might become a little livelier on these upper floors, with games and other social activities, such as movies and television viewing, taking place in the lounge areas.

Outside, the terrace is used during the warmer months for informal gatherings and planned events, such as cookouts. Walking paths may be used during all times of the year, whenever the weather is accommodating. Quite a few residents walk about at various times during the day and evening hours. The outside shuffleboard courts, the putting green and swimming pool (open from Memorial Day to Labor Day) are all well used in good weather, but the tennis courts are not often used, and look neglected.

The gardening areas are popular among residents. In years past, a lottery would be held annually to assign gardening spaces; however, demand for the beds has been down in recent years and a lottery has not been necessary. It is speculated by the Activities staff that there are fewer residents who are interested or, more importantly, who are able to garden. It seems the avid gardeners of the past are not as physically capable of keeping up a garden plot or box, and so have given them up.

Participant Characteristics and Life Overviews

The previous description of the setting presents a general portrait of the physical and social aspects of the community as whole at Colonial Square. It is within this setting that the participants of this research live and act out the daily routines of life. It is the place where a good number of their current dietary behaviors are performed and dietary preferences are enacted. While Colonial Square itself encompasses central physical and social contexts for the participants' dietary behavior, the residents themselves have a number of personal and social characteristics that also provide a context for their food- and eating-related practices. This section offers an overview of particular characteristics of the participants and their lives, to further contextualize and situate the stories they told.

The eighteen participants in this study were, of course, all residents of Colonial Square. Their geographic characteristics are summarized in Table 2.1. Most participants (11 women or 61%) were already living in Lexington when they moved to Colonial Square. Two others moved from elsewhere in the state; one from an urban area and the other from a rural area. Four women came from other states of the South Census region, and one came from the Southwest region (she also had retired there).

Table 2.1: Residential and Mobility Characteristics of Participants[6]

Spatial Feature	Lexington	Kentucky	South	Midwest	Southwest	North-east
Place moved from[7]	11	2	4	0	1	0
Place of birth	2	6	3	4	0	3

All but two of the women were born outside of Lexington, and over half (10 women) were born in states other than Kentucky, mainly the Northeast, Midwest and South. One woman who moved to Colonial Square from the Southwest was originally from the Midwest, where she was born and lived during young adulthood and middle age. Those who moved to Colonial Square from Florida (three women, in the category of those who moved from the South) were originally from the Midwest, Northeast and Kentucky.

As seen in Table 2.2, the participants' length of time in residence at Colonial Square ranged from one year to eighteen years, with an average of five

---

[6] Each column value represents the number of participants for the category.
[7] The place where the participant was residing before moving to Colonial Square.

90

years. Thus, newcomers, long-time residents, and those in between are all represented in the participant mix.

Participants ranged in age from 72 to 94 years, with most them (12 women or 67%) in their eighties. The majority of participants, 10 out of 18 women (56%) were widowed and one had twice experienced widowhood. On average, the widowed women lived without husbands for just over 15 years, and with a range of 3 to 38 years. One third of the participants were married and, at the time of the study, lived with their husbands. Even though one participant was in her second marriage, all of the couples had been together from 33 to 63 years. One participant had been divorced for 21 years (it was a second marriage and had been a widow from her first marriage), and another participant was single and had never been married.

Table 2.2: Select Socio-demographic Characteristics of the Participants

Characteristics	Average	Median	Mode	Minimum	Maximum
Time in residence (in years)[8]	5	3	1	1	18
Age (in years)	85	86	86	72	94
Married (in years)	54	56.5	NA	33	63
Widowed (in years)	15.2	15.5	3	3	38
# of children	2.3	2	2	0	5

All but two of the participants had children. Of those with children, all but one had grandchildren and several had great-grandchildren. Complex family histories were illustrated by the inclusion of step-children and step-grandchildren. Most participants had at least one child residing in or within an hour of Lexington.

On the whole, the participants were well educated. All of the women were

---

[8] Amount of time the participant has been a resident of Colonial Square.

at least high school graduates. Most of them, 14 out of 18 women, pursued education beyond high school, whether it was professional business school and/or college. Four women had some college (2-3 years) or an associate degree. Eight women had bachelor degrees and two women had master degrees. A few of the college graduates had non-typical collegiate experiences, as a couple of the women worked on their bachelor degrees over the course of quite a few years (one woman went summers and weekends for 20 plus years) and another woman attended college in her forties. For some, their education was a platform for their future career(s), but for others it was not. The two women with their master's and some of the women with their bachelor's worked in the field of their degree, but several of the participants never used their advanced education, or at least did so only very briefly. This was often due to marrying soon after their schooling, if not upon graduation, and becoming full-time wives and mothers.

All of the participants were retired and none were employed at the time of the study. The women who worked in the past had traditional female employment in office/clerical positions and in education (teachers, librarians, and the state department of education). Three of the women worked for their husbands, managing the office and bookkeeping for their husband's business (two of these businesses were out of their home, and these women were at the same time raising their family and caring for ill parents). Another woman, who had initially retired from an office position, took over her husband's work when he became too ill to do it himself. Six of the participants were full-time homemakers, yet only four women were homemakers from the start. The others worked at least a few years before getting married. A few of these homemakers also took on some paid work later in life. And then there was the army wife, who although technically a homemaker, could be said to have had a career as an army wife, as she worked hard to fulfill all the duties expected of a military wife.

The husbands of the participants, who had been or were married, worked in a variety of fields. They were city and state government employees, engineers, store and business owners, contractors, stockbrokers, farmers, army officers, professors, human resources employees, office workers, and truck drivers. The savings and retirement income from these various occupations no doubt contributed to the state of financial well-being that most of these women enjoyed, in addition, of course, to any retirement income they themselves brought in, as several had pensions from their own careers.

Although fairly financially secure now, most of the women did not come from well-to-do families. Many remembered difficult times during the Depression, although more so for the women whose families did not farm. Most of the mothers of these women did not work and were full-time homemakers (a few did part time work here and there, such as sewing or substitute teaching). Only three participants had mothers who worked full-time. About a third of the participants' fathers worked in agriculture, about a third were employed in blue-collar jobs, and a third were employed in white-collar professions (sales, government, business owners).

Most of the participants' parents had stable marital histories; only one had parents who divorced. Three of the women had a parent die when they were young, either as a teen or young adult. Some of the women came from large families, with four of the women having 6 to 8 siblings. Another eight women had medium-sized families, with 2 to 4 siblings. Four participants had only one sibling. Two participants were only children, although one had uncles who were only a few years older and they were like brothers to her. Most of the women were at one extreme of the birth order spectrum. In other words, half of them were the oldest, and another four were the youngest. Two, of course, had no siblings and the other three women were somewhere in the middle.

For many of the women, religion was an important part of family life growing up and continued to be an important aspect of their lives today, although in different ways than when they were younger. For the women who were of the same religious denomination as their family while growing up, this was almost a point of pride for them, for example, that they were a fourth-generation Methodist. However, some of the participants claimed religious denominations different from the ones they grew up in, usually due to adopting their husband's religious tradition upon marriage. All but one of the women, who were or had been married, were coupled with men of Protestant backgrounds, and so those who switched still remained within the Protestant tradition. One participant married a Jewish man, however, he and his family did not follow Jewish dietary regulations (they ate pork and pork products), and he simply did not attend church with her.

At the time of the study, the participants claimed various religious denominations, although all were Protestant. Just over a third of them were Methodist (7 out of 18 women), and not quite a third were Presbyterian (5 out of 18 women). Three considered themselves a part of the Disciples of Christ tradition, and two women attended an Episcopalian church. One participant said she went to a Christian church. A few of them were attending the same church in Lexington as they had before moving to Colonial Square.

Church and service attendance sometimes depended on transportation (for those who no longer drove) and desire. Some women had various ways of getting to church: Colonial Square transportation, a church bus (that goes to Colonial Square to pick up parishioners) or friends and neighbors. This to some extent also influenced what particular church they went to. A few women no longer attended church services, due to either the physical difficulty of attending or a personal choice. However, these women participated in informal and private religious practices, such as watching religious programming, reading religious materials, Bible study, devotions, and private prayer. A few attended the Sunday vespers and mid-week Bible study that was held at Colonial Square.

Another aspect of family mentioned by some participants involved their ethnic heritage. For those who were aware of their ancestry, especially those not many generations removed from family members who migrated to the United States (one woman's father was an immigrant), a European legacy was predominant. Those women who were of German, English, and Scottish stock particularly made their genealogy known. I think a few participants would have been tempted to claim "Southern" as their ethnic heritage, having a family line that has been firmly established in the American South. Many did not claim an ethnic tradition, and it did not seem to be a relevant aspect of their lives to them, in the past or present.

Finally, the participants rated their health as fair to good. A few had conditions in which their diet played a role in its management, such as diabetes, diverticulosis, high blood pressure, and high cholesterol. The two women who had diabetes were both insulin-dependent. Several participants had osteoporosis, and were taking calcium supplements and/or medication to treat it. Some have had falls and/or broken hips and had gone through, or were going through, physical therapy. One woman was permanently in a wheelchair. Some women underwent surgeries and/or treatment for serious illnesses, including two women who had hip replacements, two women who had a colostomy, two women who were afflicted with cancer, and one woman who was having difficulties with congestive heart failure. Several participants had other chronic conditions, such as arthritis and hearing loss (a few had hearing aids). Of the women who no longer drove, health declines were the reason given (12 out of the 18 participants). Yet most counted themselves as fortunate health-wise and felt they were doing pretty well either for their age or as compared to others.

These eighteen women were very similar in some respects and very different in others. They brought to this study a minimum of seven decades of life experience, and the stories to show it. An overview of each participant's life course, including various life course trajectories (family, education, career, and place) can be found in Appendix C.

Chapter Three

Past and Present Influences on Dietary Practices: Experiences of Older Women Residing in a Retirement Community

This chapter explores past and present influences on the dietary practices of the women of this study. Some of these influences originated earlier in the women's lives, even childhood, but continued to be felt in the present. Other influences related specifically to the retirement community environment in which the participants resided and spent much of their time.

The first section addresses influences categorized as personal factors, representing psychological and physiological processes perceived as affecting dietary behavior. The next section concentrates on interpersonal relationships, illustrating the importance of social relationships such as family and the effect of interactions with other residents and employees of Colonial Square on dietary practices. The third section considers social roles and statuses as a category of influence, specifically how the women's past and/or present statuses as parent and spouse were an influence on their dietary experiences. The fourth section reviews contexts of the participants' dietary practices, focusing on contexts of meal patterns and food preparation, community policy, and political economic forces. All of these factors shape participants' dietary practices, interacting to create both common patterns and unique experiences.

Personal Factors

Several women referred to personal characteristics and experiences as affecting their dietary patterns. Two of the participants believed that simply their own preferences and tastes (what they liked and disliked eating) influenced them, and did not necessarily view their preferences as having ever been influenced by others. Mrs. Michaels[1] took a very psychological approach towards interpreting how and why she eats, as she shared that she was somewhat affected by her moods, attitudes, and overall the way she felt. She admitted to sometimes eating when she was bored or lonely.

Physical aging, especially as related to energy, strength, and ambulation, affected the women in terms of shopping for food, getting to meals, and social stigma. Shopping could be a difficult chore, even for the women who were still able to do so on their own. For example, Mrs. Michaels had broken her hip, and a friend and her son were picking up items from the store for her. Before that, she used Colonial Square transportation to get to the store, riding on the Loop (the shopping circuit that the Colonial Square bus runs on Wednesdays and Saturdays). But that did not solve all of her shopping problems:

> And the grocery store was so big. I feel like I'd lean on that old thing [grocery cart] and try to get around. It took forever. And then another thing - they've got the milk and the bread in the far back of the store, so that you'll go through all these other parts, and buy something else. Sometimes just all you need is milk. And you have to go way back there in the back of the store to get it. Their psychology and my energy doesn't go together!

She simply did not have the strength and energy required to shop in a large supermarket. She further found that all the vegetables and fruit she liked to buy were heavy and hard to carry after they were bagged. There was only so much that could be bought at one time if the older woman did not have her own car or assistance with grocery shopping, such as someone to carry the purchased items.

Another issue for some of the women, particularly the oldest participants, was the distance of the Dining Room from a number of the apartments. Because of the physical layout of the building, residents living at the end of the longer wing had quite a walk to the Dining Room and other common areas of Colonial Square. For Mrs. Stokes, this walk could be physically demanding, and she often had to stop momentarily on her way to the Dining Room. Mrs. Monroe did not

---

[1] Pseudonyms are used for all participants and other persons named in this book.

live as far from the Dining Room as Mrs. Stokes, but used a self-propelled wheelchair, which made the journey to and from the Dining Room a tiring one, particularly because there was a downward slope away from her apartment that she had to maneuver up on her way back.

Mrs. Randall brought up another mobility-related issue, which was the appearance of assistive devices and "mobies" (the electric mobile chairs) in the Dining Room:

> Also, there was a problem about the mobies and walkers and walking aids and things like that. They [other residents] were saying that it doesn't look elegant. With those things sitting around the tables. So through the years, they have resolved: park it here in the living room and get inside. Now there's some people who can't quite do that. There have been comments through the years, "It's beginning to look like a nursing home." Well, those people, unfortunately, don't realize that some of those people when they came in here were walking around like everybody else. And this is the aging process in this facility. Well, a lot of that disappeared when Oak Ridge Manor opened. Because, there were about fifteen or twenty who moved there from here. So, there was a period when we didn't have as many of those mobiles and things.

Residents age in place at Colonial Square, and a number of them needed devices to help them get around or to help them as they rehabilitated after a surgery. Mrs. Randall had both her hips replaced and therefore was understanding about assistive devices for personal as well as intellectual reasons:

> But I have always thought - of course, I've been very sympathetic. Because you know, there was a time when I was on a walker. And I had been here a long time. And I would have hated for them to say you can't come in the dining room on that walker, when I, you know, when eventually I was going to be off the walker. These people should not be that critical, because who knows what they're going to be doing next week.

Another resident raised this issue in a conversation, but she was not as tolerant of assistive devices as Mrs. Randall. She seemed to assume that people who needed such devices perhaps should not be residing in an independent living community and implied that people did not want to see those sorts of things.

Thus, there was some social stigma for residents who exhibited frailty and required physical assistance with ambulation. Mrs. Richardson had recently fallen and utilized a metal shopping cart to support her when she walked around outside of her apartment; she said it helped her more than a walker and she felt more stable holding onto it. She realized that she was upsetting other residents by her actions and apparently was the recipient of looks and comments from other residents for using a shopping cart as a walker. The appearance of an older woman using a shopping cart was probably perceived by some residents as worse than if she used an actual walker. The reactions of other residents did not deter Mrs. Richardson, however, from continuing to use the shopping cart as an assistive device.

Other age-related health issues to some extent affected dietary practices. A few participants found that there were certain foods they had to avoid as they became older, because of digestive repercussions from consuming such foods (e.g., gas, diarrhea, indigestion). For example, Mrs. Donovan had discovered that it was better for her if she avoided foods that were spicy or acidic. Elevated cholesterol and blood pressure caused five participants to adjust their diets and/or go on medication. Over a third of the women reported bone health issues, which resulted in regularly taking calcium supplements. Supplementation practices are discussed further in Chapter Four. Some of the medications taken by participants required that they take them with a meal, take them with milk, or avoid certain foods. Mrs. Adams was on an anticoagulant medication, making it necessary for her to monitor her vitamin K intake, because she had to limit the amount of vitamin K she ingested while on this medicine.

Social Interaction and Relations

Interaction and relationships with family members, other residents, and the employees of Colonial Square played a role in the food- and eating-related practices of the participants, from what they liked to eat and who they ate with to how they expressed their views on the food served in the Dining Room. Family members, for the most part, had been an important influence in the past for the participants and were recognized as a continuing influence on current behavior. Specifically regarding food acquisition practices, a number of women depended on their interpersonal relationships, both with family members and with other residents, for assistance with food shopping. Social relationships and interaction with other residents of Colonial Square were very important in terms of food and eating; because the main meal was taken in the Dining Room, eating was a very social event for the residents and the participants made social arrangements for dining according to their inclinations for sociability. Social activities of Colonial Square often involved food and eating and this section briefly describes the participants' involvement in such activities. Finally, the section addresses relations with Colonial Square employees, particularly Dining Room management and staff, including how participants expressed their opinions to employees regarding the Dining Room.

Family Relationships

By far, the most commonly cited important influence in the participants' lifetimes on their dietary practices was upbringing. Participants felt that how they were raised, regarding food and eating, had a profound influence throughout their lives. The participants frequently identified parents, particularly a mother, as an important influence on how they ate. They referred to certain foods that were served by their mother in childhood or well-balanced meals that were served by parents and subsequently adopted by the participant herself. Mrs. Stokes remarked that she still loved macaroni and cheese, a dish often prepared by her mother. Three participants mentioned a grandmother as influential and as someone involved in how they were raised, at least in some aspects. Mrs. Provost, for example, stated that her grandmother, who lived with her family when she was young, was the biggest influence on her food and eating practices, because according to Mrs. Provost, "she started me off right, on good Southern food."

Upbringing was not always perceived so positively, nor did it always have positive effects. Mrs. Monroe, for example, purposely avoided repeating her childhood dietary experiences when she had her own family. Mrs. Monroe felt that she grew up in a crazy, unpredictable household, where there were always a lot of people visiting and things going on; she never knew who nor how many would be at her home. Because of this, her mother often prepared large meals that Mrs. Monroe felt were unappetizing, due mainly to their appearance and presentation. She also recalled her brothers coming in for dinner with greasy hands from working on cars and objected to the dirtiness of her brothers. She had always wanted nice things and resented not having them as she grew up. She developed an aesthetic taste for "pretty" dishes, as food presentation became important, and for neatness - her own children had to be clean and dressed for dinner. She desired structure and organization, and found ways to incorporate these characteristics into dietary practices throughout her life. Mrs. Monroe's preference for order and structure could be seen in her past participation and current admiration for the Weight Watchers program and in present practices such as consistently making grocery lists (even more useful since others began shopping for her) and having her breakfast dishes and breakfast foods set out the night before.

Families of origin were certainly influential, but families of procreation also exerted an influence, although that influence was generally felt much less now that the women were no longer cooking for their families. A number of women cited family members' preferences, particularly husbands' and children's likes and dislikes, as having an impact on their dietary practices. In a few cases, participants referred to a family member's health as affecting their behavior. Mrs. Wilson's husband's open heart surgery greatly changed their diet 25 years ago, as they both altered their food habits to follow what would be considered a heart healthy regimen. When she was in her early 20s, Mrs. Monroe's mother was diagnosed with diabetes. That diagnosis provided a great lesson, according to Mrs. Monroe, and it was a reason that she had always tried to eat fairly nutritiously. For example, she baked foods rather than fried them and enjoyed a wide variety of vegetables. Incidentally, Mrs. Monroe did not have diabetes.

Shopping for Food

The women in this study generally shopped once every week or two, to keep their basics stocked, such as milk, bread, juice, and fruit. At least four of the women had someone else shop for them, because it was too difficult physically for them to do so. For example, Mrs. Provost's fictive daughter did her shopping, while Mrs. Ford's sister, who lived with her, shopped for them both. For the women who were able to shop for themselves, where they went for groceries depended to some extent on their transportation and where their transportation could, or would, take them. Most of the women (12 of the 18 participants) no longer drove, and so they either had someone take them or used Colonial Square transportation. Mrs. Stokes' daughter took her grocery shopping (and did her shopping at the same time). Mrs. Richardson mainly just used the Loop, and Mrs. Jergens also rode the Loop, but if a friend or neighbor offered to take her, she went with them. The women who went on the Loop generally took rides from individuals to the store if offered. Some enjoyed the company. Mrs. Vossler could and did shop by herself, but she often accompanied her daughter, who shopped at a health food co-op, when she went shopping:

> Every Friday afternoon, I go with my daughter, just to be with her.
> She goes to the co-op, and maybe I'll pick up their oatmeal in bulk
> or mixed nuts or something to have in the house...I go to Kroger's.
> I just go to the co-op with her. I buy very little because it's very
> expensive. I don't see the need for that.

For Mrs. Vossler, spending time with her daughter was the point of the shopping trip at the co-op. The majority of the women went to, or used, Kroger as the preferred place for purchasing groceries; Kroger was also the closest supermarket. The store mentioned second most often was Meijer, a combination supermarket and discount store. Shopping could be a social and/or leisure activity, as suggested by the comments of Mrs. Vossler, who liked to shop with her daughter, and by the example of Mrs. Jergens, who just plain liked to shop. Mrs. Jergens loved grocery shopping, which she explained, was why her kitchen cabinets and refrigerator were so full of food.

Interactions with Other Residents: Dining Arrangements

Many participants stated how much they enjoyed the social aspect of eating in the Dining Room, particularly the widowed and single women. For Mrs. Brown, meal times provided good opportunities to catch up with others: "That's a good time - one of the visiting times." Mrs. Provost, who generally went to the Dining Room for dinner, remarked: "After the day is over, it's nice to be with other people." Similar to other widows, Mrs. Michaels found that after her husband died, eating alone was a big and difficult change. It meant a lot to her to have people to eat with now, and she asserted: "I enjoy the Dining Room. And I think it's a good way to keep from being lonesome, and it's a good place to meet different people."

The Dining Room was the main place where residents visited with one another, and as Mrs. Michaels pointed out, it was a place to make new friends. Mrs. Richardson occasionally attempted to make the acquaintance of new residents in the Dining Room:

> Sometimes, I tried to go in, with new people coming in, and ask them if they mind, you know, may I sit with them. But some people do not want, you know, they want to be so-called alone. But they're usually very receptive to you sitting with them. But this is how you really get to know people. And help them to feel at home.

Colonial Square had varied patterns of social arrangements of dining partners at meal times. Over half of the women had another resident or a group of residents with whom they regularly ate. At least two of the women met regular, but different residents or groups for meals, depending on the meal or day of the week. For example, Mrs. Faust and her husband had a regular group they ate with at breakfast, but they dined with different people each evening. Mrs. Donovan had a group she normally dined with during the week, but she ate with a different group on the weekends. Five of the women, like Mrs. Michaels, stated their preference for meeting different people, preferring to "mingle" or "circulate" among the residents rather than be a part of any particular group.

How much pre-planning went into social arrangements for dining varied.

Most of the women generally did not plan ahead to meet someone, either because they met their regular dining companions basically around the same times or because they just went down and sat with whomever they happened to find. Others often called or had someone call and extend an invitation to join them at a meal. Two participants had a certain table (or tables) where they preferred to sit when they had a meal in the Dining Room, but the rest sat wherever they found a place or someone with whom they wished to dine. Periodically, the furniture was rearranged in the Dining Room, forcing people to break their habits at least temporarily until they settled into new habits.

Interactions with Other Residents: Colonial Square Activities

Two-thirds of the women reported going on trips planned and organized by the Activities Department of Colonial Square; sometimes the destination was a place to eat or the trip included dining (according the Activities staff, trips further away than a 45-minute drive generally included a meal on the itinerary – often lunch). Trips that included a meal were popular with the resident population. Mrs. Nichols and her husband had taken advantage of such opportunities: "And we had gone out to dinner, oh, maybe 3 or 4, 5 times since we've been here, when they take a group to someplace we think we might like to try." There were also parties organized by the Activities Department that the women sometimes attended, such as ice cream socials or holiday parties.

For a few women, the weekly Social Hour (coordinated by the Activities Department) was a way of going out, without actually going out. At this happy hour, residents provided their own alcohol; according to Mrs. Monroe, there was an unwritten rule that residents should have no more than two drinks. Residents also enjoyed hors d'oeuvres and finger foods, as well as conversation and social interaction, before heading to dinner. Mrs. Monroe, who never missed a Social Hour if she could help it, asserted that she tried to mingle with different people at the Social Hour. Mrs. Monroe actually often observed the tradition of having a cocktail hour in her apartment before heading to the Dining Room for dinner.

Alcohol was also available in the Dining Room, as wine was served a couple of times a week, and several women would have a glass with dinner.

The Activities Department additionally oversaw the community's raised garden beds and garden plots that were for resident use. At least five of the women did some gardening, if not in a garden bed, then on their own porch or balcony. Two of the women's husbands' did some gardening in the raised beds. Gardening participants commonly grew tomatoes and green peppers, although two women also grew herbs. Those who gardened had past experience gardening before moving to Colonial Square; this was not a new hobby taken up in later years. The gardening participants (or those with gardening husbands) often shared the bounty of their agricultural efforts with family and other residents, which was a common practice among gardening residents in general. They sometimes discussed their gardens with others, sharing tips and experiences.

Communication with the Dining Room Employees

Residents, of course, could communicate with staff directly. About a third of the women reported speaking to Dining Room management and staff in the halls or in the Dining Room. A few participants had suggested specific items to be served or even not be served. For example, Ms. Carr found the serving of chili in the summertime to be an offense and let the Dining Room staff know this. Two of the women reported supplying recipes to the kitchen, such as Mrs. Donovan's pie recipes.

The residents could also communicate through the comment cards on the Dining Room tables, letting their thoughts and suggestions be known. Patterns of filling out the comment cards ranged from Mrs. Jergens, who said she had never filled one out (although her granddaughter does when she visits) to Mrs. Monroe, who said that she had filled out the cards quite often ("a hundred times"). The majority of the women reported filling them out either sometimes or occasionally. Although the written comments at times expressed a complaint, they were more often complimentary. Several women mentioned that they felt it was important to let the staff know when they were doing a good job; some would only fill out the card if they had something positive to write, presumably operating on the old maxim of "if you can't say something nice, don't say anything at all."

It was unclear whether the requirement that comment cards be signed by the residents affected if and how the participants filled out the cards. At least two women believed that the comment cards receive no consideration at all by the staff and management, even when signed. At least that is what they heard, for the rumor mill at Colonial Square did not spare food services. One participant heard that Colonial Square tried to save money through "pinching pennies" in the Dining Room. Another participant heard that being tight with the money in the Dining Room was one way for the corporation to make more money for the stockholders.

Social Roles and Statuses

More than a few participants referred to their roles and statuses as a parent and/or a spouse when discussing dietary practices and influences on their behavior. For some, being a parent meant teaching their children to eat healthy and modeling how to eat well. Mrs. Ford, with a college major in home economics, studied nutrition with great interest and tried to use principles of nutrition in selecting and preparing food for herself and her children. Mrs. Nichols also referred to raising children as influencing her: "I guess it just was the way I was raised. And then trying to carry that over to our children. I mean if you want your children to eat right, you have to eat right too. So you're forced into that." She felt at that point, however, the way she ate was largely habit.

For the women in the study who were still married, they continued in their role as the one mainly responsible for domestic food-related tasks. None of the husbands of the married women cooked, beyond simple food preparation, such as getting cereal. Their wives often helped them along, buying or preparing foods to have available in the apartment for their husbands. Mrs. Randall's husband got his own breakfast and lunch, but he would prepare something that could be heated up, dished out, or easily put together, like a sandwich. Mrs. Nichols and Mrs. Wilson both acknowledged that the fact that meals were provided at Colonial Square was a factor in their decision to move, because they felt some security knowing that if anything happened to them, their husbands would still be fed. Mrs. Nichols related this, as recorded in written fieldnotes:

> She feels that the dining room is a good thing for her husband. She says that he is helpless in the kitchen - he lets things boil over, and does not know what to do. She has to fix something for him if she is not going to be there during a mealtime. For example, if she will be gone during their regular lunchtime, she has to make him a sandwich ahead of time, so that it is ready for him when he wants lunch. Generally, he is not involved in food preparation. She told a story as an example. One time she and her daughter-in-law were out shopping, while her son and husband stayed at the apartment. They were out shopping later than they thought they would be and came home past normal lunchtime. Her son had gone into the kitchen and fixed himself something to eat. But her husband sat in his recliner and waited until she came home, so that she could fix something for him.

For many men of this generation, such as Mr. Nichols, traditional gender roles dictated that it was almost completely a woman's task to prepare food. However, the other husbands seemed able to manage better in the kitchen by themselves than Mr. Nichols. Mr. Wilson was the most able, having taken a cooking class with his wife, and assisted her often in the preparation of food for parties and entertaining. The rest were more along the lines of Mr. Randall's familiarity and ability in the kitchen, and perhaps did some limited cooking in the past.

The husbands of the married women were generally not involved in food shopping either, although there were exceptions. After Mrs. Florsheim's husband retired in the late 1970s, he began to take on more of the responsibility for shopping. She made the list and determined what should be bought. She thought that he needed to get out and do something after he retired, and particularly since moving to Colonial Square, perceived that he had not transitioned or settled in as well to their new environment as she had. Mrs. Faust reported that her husband would go shopping "once in a great moon," but it would be only to pick up some small item, not a regular shopping trip. Mrs. Faust stated that she had to tell and/or show him exactly what to get, which was no guarantee that he would buy what she wanted him to buy. Regarding shopping, therefore, Mrs. Faust willingly retained that role: "And if I ask him to get coffee or anything, I have to show him the bottle, show him what it is and how many ounces and...he'll do it once in a while. But no, he's not - that's my job. But at this point I want it - I want it to be my job." Mrs. Faust thought that she was better suited to perform shopping tasks and would not want her husband to have such duties anyway, even if he would be willing to take over shopping activities.

Larger Contexts

This section highlights contexts of the participants' dietary practices beyond personal factors and interpersonal relations. Before specifically discussing the spatial and environmental contexts of meals, this section presents an overview of basic meal patterns. This description itself provides a context for the following discussion of meals taken in the Dining Room and in their apartments. The food issue particularly focused on is meal taking, but food preparation and eating out are also considered. This section proceeds to consider community policy contexts (particularly dining hours, the dress code, and bringing food home), and ends addressing general political economic forces perceived as influencing dietary behavior.

Meals: Overall Patterns

The women generally structured the day's activities around meals and mealtimes, although a few participants structured their mealtimes around their activities during the day. All of the participants ate at least once a day in the Dining Room; for the most part, participants had just one main meal, either lunch or dinner, in the Dining Room. (Breakfast was no extra cost, and although a number of residents took breakfast, was not a main meal for any of them). All of the women consumed at least one meal, or some food, in their apartments.

The women decided on either lunch or dinner as their main meal, and then generally always went to that meal in the Dining Room. Mrs. Richardson, though, said she decided what meal she had in the Dining Room according to what was served, and might have both lunch and dinner in the Dining Room on the same day if she found the food at each meal especially appealing. In three cases, participants decided which meal to normally have each day based on their preferred personal schedule. Mrs. Donovan preferred to have her main meal at noontime, and so she had lunch in the Dining Room each day, and a light meal or snack at night. However, nearly all of the participants took their main meal at dinner. About half of the dinner-taking participants intermittently had lunch in the Dining Room on Fridays, because of the special brunch menu - a few specifically mentioned that they liked the Eggs Benedict.

Two of the women had just two meals a day, but the rest had three meals a day, even if two of the meals were light, such as coffee and toast for breakfast. A few participants remarked that they were not as hungry as they used to be, although that did not necessarily mean they ate less. A third of the women mentioned that they were attempting to control their weight and knew people, including themselves, who had gained weight since moving to Colonial Square. Meals served in the Dining Room could consist of four courses if a resident chose, often a temptation difficult to resist. The women conscious of weight gain mentioned cutting back on desserts, eating fruit for dessert, or not eating the bread, as there was always a basket of rolls with dinner. A number of women said other residents warned them when they first came to Colonial Square that they would gain weight, because everybody gained weight when they first came. Only Mrs. Wilson said she had lost weight, but attributed the weight loss to stress and affairs surrounding her husband's illness at the time that they moved.

Food and Eating in the Dining Room

The general view of the Dining Room, and the meals served there, was overall positive. Each woman had a particular critique of the Dining Room, but for the most part felt that any deficiencies were relatively minor, and could be overlooked. Quite a few were happy enough to not have to cook and felt unjustified in seriously complaining. Prior to her move to Colonial Square, Mrs. Vossler underwent an operation, and during her recovery at home, she was unable to cook food and had to no one to assist her; she essentially relied on canned items. She took simple pleasure in the knowledge that she could always get something to eat from the Dining Room. Three women recognized that when they first moved to Colonial Square, it was such a novelty to not have to cook or worry about fixing dinner and all the food seemed wonderful, but after being there a while, the novelty wore off and the food had become more institutional to them. Others mentioned that they recognized that it must be an impossible undertaking for the Dining Room staff to completely satisfy all the preferences of 200 plus residents and felt that considering their task (and staff turnover), the staff did a good job.

Many participants mentioned that they thought the Dining Room had a wide variety in their food offerings, although a few thought that lately the menus had been somewhat repetitious. A majority stated that the Dining Room served too much yellow squash and zucchini, and not enough potatoes. All but one of the participants were satisfied with the overall nutritional quality of the foods available. Comments regarding the desire for more fruits surfaced and a few women thought they could serve more green and leafy vegetables. Several appreciated attempts to offer more sugar-free, salt-free and fat-free options. Participants' nutritional assessments of Dining Room offerings are further discussed in Chapter Four.

It seemed the latest news about the Dining Room always got around; all but two of the women informed me that the Dining Room now served oatmeal at the continental breakfast and how well that had gone over with the residents, whether they personally went to breakfast or not. Almost all also reported that there was a new Chinese cook, although their reactions to the Chinese dishes have been mixed. They seemed to appreciate that the kitchen tried something new, whether they liked it or not. Other fairly recent additions to the menus included more contemporary entrees, such as pasta dishes and sandwich wraps (sliced meats and vegetables wrapped in a tortilla). These too have had a mixed reception by the women, as many of them preferred the standard "well-balanced" meal of a meat entree, with sides of potatoes and vegetables, which was the type of meal that most of them had always known. As Mrs. Adams clearly and simply stated: "As far as I'm concerned, my concept of eating is basically meat and potatoes." This concept of a meal also explained the dismay voiced by some women that more potato dishes were not on the menu. Other critiques included too many heavy and high calorie foods, too generous portions, seasoning issues (too many spices/salt or too bland), and women originally from outside of the South reported that "they cook different than I'm used to."

Most of the participants seemed to perceive the current head chef as performing well and trying very hard. They complimented her efforts, for example, her institution of a carving station once a week and omelet station once a month. Mrs. Provost appreciated the chef's introduction of frog legs and blackened catfish as menu items. The participants generally praised the service provided by the young men and women who waited on the residents. These young people did appear to make an effort to know the residents and pay attention to regular patterns of the residents. For example, Mrs. Randall remarked that she and her husband did not like to linger at dinner and noted that the servers knew to keep the food coming for her and her husband, bringing iced teas in hand when they came to take their order and serving their soup and salad at the same time.

The women also seemed to have found the food services director to be generally amiable enough, noting that he was fairly new, but approving of his performance overall thus far. He instituted the monthly Friday Night Out event, which was very popular and well received among the participants and other residents. Friday Night Out events made it very busy in the Dining Room, for it seemed that not only did many residents make an effort to go that night, but many also brought guests. However, residents also paid attention to actions of the management and staff that did not directly affect them. For example, Mrs. Monroe strongly disapproved of the director's promotion of one staff member, as she believed that another one deserved it more.

About two-thirds of the women commented that they have had guests eat with them in the Dining Room from time to time. They were pleased with the decor and had enough confidence in the service and food quality to invite non-residents to join them for meals. About a quarter of the participants claimed to think that it was nicer to bring guests to the Dining Room than to go out to eat. Entertaining at Colonial Square is addressed further in Chapter Four, and eating out will be attended to later on in this chapter.

One participant revealed a distinctive perceived difference between cooking main meals at home and eating them in the Dining Room. Referring to her previous residence as home, Mrs. Faust remarked:

> To me, the biggest change, I guess, is that your every meal is different. And when I cooked at home, often we had say, one dish one meal and maybe warm it up the next. You don't have warmed-over food here. And I think warmed-over food is good.

Warmed-over food, or leftovers, was something that some people just disliked, some people lived with, and some people, such as Mrs. Faust, enjoyed very much. Of course, there were no leftovers from meals in the Dining Room, and with the little cooking needed for other meals, leftovers were not common at home either.

Food and Eating at Home

Meals and food eaten in the private residential apartments (or "home") were generally simple, light, and prepared in small amounts, with an emphasis on quick and easy. Two of the women sometimes prepared big batches of food at a time, such as soups or vegetables, and stored or froze portions of it. Soup, sometimes homemade, but mostly canned, quite often was the base for a lunch or dinner. Cheese and crackers, a salad, or a sandwich might accompany the soup. Three women kept frozen dinners for quick meals. Mrs. Donovan always had quite a few of the Kids' Kitchen foods, which are little microwave-able plastic bowls of spaghetti and sauce or chicken and vegetables, for example. Meant for children, these bowls come in small portions, which are the right size for a light meal or snack.

The women all regularly kept bread, milk, and juice at home, and most of them stocked coffee and tea as well. Peanut butter typically made the list of foods on hand. The women who ate breakfast at home stocked foods such as eggs, oatmeal, cereal, and fruit for their breakfasts. A couple of the participants kept very little food in their apartments, such as Mrs. Richardson (although her freezer is full of ice cream), but all except one of the rest stored a moderate amount of food items. Mrs. Jergens was one who kept her cupboards and refrigerator full and readily admitted that she did not really need it all.

About half of the women also stashed snacks at home. Of the women who reported snacking, they commonly stated that it was a bedtime snack. Snacking was not necessarily a regular occurrence, as only a few described snacking as an everyday happening. Over a third of the women, however, insisted that they almost never snacked and that they never really had. Two of the women who snacked detailed more of a grazing pattern, where snacking was in place of a meal, instead of filler between meals. Mrs. Donovan, who generally ate light in the evenings, described her evening intake as more snacking than a meal. Mrs. Vossler stated that she became hungry every couple of hours and so she had to snack, sometimes on fruit, but she often had what she called "short" or "half" meals, four of them, throughout the day.

Health considerations to some extent influenced snacking and types of snack foods consumed. Mrs. Randall's gastrointestinal system dictated her snacking; she said she had a snack at night because she had a little acid reflux if she became "empty," and so would have a handful of dry Cheerios or something like that before bed. The type of snacks varied from healthful options such as fruit or Cheerios, to sweets such as cookies and candy, to the more unusual, albeit nutritious, choices of spinach or a piece of toast with cream cheese and green pepper. A few recounted how much they enjoyed nuts. Several consciously tried to limit their snacking. Mrs. Stokes, who was diabetic, monitored her carbohydrate intake to be sure she could afford to have a cookie and some milk before bed (she perhaps had water instead if she thought she needed to be careful). Ms. Carr was also diabetic and claimed to have exactly six Ritz crackers before bed. Ms. Carr and a couple of other women purposely did not keep candy around to avoid snacking on sweets. Mrs. Michaels said she knew she would snack for comfort or something to do, and so she tried to have fruit around instead of food such as candy or potato chips.

Where in the apartment the women consumed their food depended on several factors. One factor was where they felt comfortable eating. For example, at least two of the women preferred to eat in front of the television. Another factor was attitudes about where it was proper to eat. Mrs. Provost, for example, seemed to believe it was more civilized to eat at a table than in front of the television. A third factor was where they actually could eat, because of space issues and/or furniture use and placement. Two women had small tables in their kitchens, which took up significant amounts of space, but was where they generally ate. Others decided not to take up space in the kitchen with a table and ate at a dining room table or in the living room area. Three of the women, who had both tables in their kitchens and dining room areas, had one or both covered with clutter, and so were relegated to eating at only one of the tables or in the living room area. Finally, two women did not have dining room tables at all; Mrs. Florsheim did not have a table in her dining area, eating mainly in the kitchen, and Mrs. Nichols gave away her dining room set to family.

The kitchens at Colonial Square, as previously described, had the basic modern conveniences most people now depend upon, such as a full-size refrigerator, a full-size oven with stovetop, and a dishwasher. The women generally brought additional appliances with them. As a result of the desire for quick and easy meals, the microwave was an appliance that all of the women had. Mrs. Stokes cooked just about everything in the microwave. Coffeemakers and toasters were also common appliances found in the women's kitchens. Over half of the women rarely used their ovens, if they turned them on at all. Mrs. Brown, for example, had only used the stovetop in her kitchen to heat soups. Only three of the participants, those women who continued to do a fair amount of cooking and/or baking, regularly used their ovens.

At least three of the participants used their ovens to store things, mainly pots and pans. For Mrs. Adams, who used oven space for storage, this caused her to be less likely to use the oven, because she did not want to bother with emptying and reloading it. The kitchens lacked storage space if a resident had a number of kitchen-related items to store. One participant related that she knew of people who used their dishwasher to store things. Mrs. Randall and Mrs. Wilson both had large cupboards that they had put in, because both still did some cooking and needed extra space to hold cookware and bakeware. Mrs. Wilson stated that the kitchen facilities in the apartments of Colonial Square were a major reason she and her husband chose Colonial Square over other retirement communities in town. Mrs. Wilson's cabinet also had a pullout shelf, for additional counter space. Mrs. Adams noted:

> And there's not that much counter space for cooking. It's a funny kitchen. It's got this wonderful equipment, and this big oven - you could roast two turkeys. And it's got a full-size refrigerator and a full-size dishwasher. And twin sinks. But there's just not that much counter space to - the way I was used to working.

However, Mrs. Adams added: "But I don't need to do that much cooking, so it doesn't matter much." Ultimately for Mrs. Adams and most of the other women, counter space was not much of an issue.

Although Mrs. Randall and Mrs. Wilson still had cookware and bakeware, they gave away larger items, such as stockpots. A number of the women gave away most of their cookware and bakeware, retaining only what they needed, such as a couple of pots and pans and a skillet or two. This divesture of cooking items sometimes occurred just before the move to Colonial Square, in anticipation of the limited time that would be spent in the kitchen, but for several, it came after they moved. At least a third of the women expressed that they felt they had brought more than they needed to their home at Colonial Square, despite their efforts (and children's efforts) to pare down their belongings. Mrs. Florsheim recalled preparations for her and her husband's move to Colonial Square:

> I remember when we were packing up and the two daughters were there with us, and I had this old pot that I depended upon. And I remember Kate or Veronica, one saying to me, "Mother, you're not going use that." And I thought, well, why aren't I going to use it? I've used it all my life. I sure am going to use it. I think I brought it, but I don't think I've used it.

Mrs. Florsheim later donated an electric skillet to a sale; she liked the skillet, but she just did not use it. Mrs. Jergens had practically all the cooking items she had before her move, but she planned to begin "weeding out" items as soon as she was physically able (at the time her left arm was in a sling).

If the participants had finer dishes and utensils, such as china and silver, they gave most of it to children. Mrs. Wilson, who gave away most of her silver, was planning to pare down even more as well:

> Gave away silver. Kept very little of it. I kept the tea service, not to use, but just because I'm used to seeing it sitting on the table over there. But we really got rid of a lot of things. As a matter of fact, when I get around to it, I'm going to get rid of more stuff, because, you know, we're not going to use it.

She kept the tea service for the sake of its familiar and sentimental qualities, not for utilitarian reasons. But most other things, unless they were used, would likely be given away. Mrs. Richardson had also given china and silver to her daughter, and would be passing on her Spode china pieces. It seemed to comfort the women who were able to pass on items, such as cookbooks, china, silver, family cookware (e.g., a mother's pot) or even dining room furniture, to adult children, as these were family heirlooms in a sense and symbolized the passing on of family history. Mrs. Nichols had her mother-in-law's cookbooks, and it pleased her that one of her daughters wanted to have them. It was important to be able to keep these objects in the family.

Almost half of the women mentioned that when asked to supply their favorite recipes, they had to "dig" them up. If they had cookbooks, they were not usually handy, as they might have been when they were cooking regularly. Mrs. Brown gave away all of her cookbooks and several other women gave most of their cookbooks to family, particularly daughters. A few women still had recipe boxes, although Mrs. Ford kept hers in her bedroom, as it was no longer used for recipes, but as a source of memories and nostalgia. Four of the women recited recipes from memory. Cookbooks and recipes were no longer consulted, at least not on a regular basis. If they brought a dish to a function, family dinner, or holiday celebration, it was often a dish that they knew how to prepare without looking it up, such as salads (vegetable, fruit or Jell-o) or baked goods.

Eating Out

Eating out was, of course, an option for residents; in independent living facilities, residents come and go as they please and are not restricted to eating only in their apartments or the Dining Room. However, participants in this study generally did not eat out very much. Quite a few of the women never really ate out much at restaurants before moving to Colonial Square, but others did not go as much as they previously had. Mrs. Richardson, for example, ate out most of the time before moving to Colonial Square, but after moving, she only went out occasionally.

This pattern of infrequent dining out largely had to do with the fact that they paid for one meal a day at Colonial Square and felt they might as well eat there. Mrs. Vossler affirmed that because meals were provided and paid for at Colonial Square, she did not go out to eat. As Mrs. Ford bluntly articulated: "As long as it's going to be there and we're paying for it, we might as well use it. That's the way I look at it." Mrs. Florsheim and her husband very seldom went out to eat, but finances were first in mind when they did: "And when we do, we are actually horrified at the size of the servings and the size of the bill. To me, it's just unconscionable to eat a $50 meal. It's absolutely out of my line." The women reported eating out with friends occasionally, but more often mentioned eating out with family. A few regularly went out to eat after church on Sundays.

If they chose where to eat, stated preferences for restaurants tended to be places where American, regional (Kentuckian/Southern), country-style, or "home-cooked" food was served. The women mentioned chain restaurants (such as Bob Evans, O'Charley's, Steak-N-Shake, and Cracker Barrel), steakhouses, cafeteria-style restaurants (such as Morrison's and Picadilly's), and places where they could eat ribs or catfish. Those who liked cafeteria-style restaurants said that they liked to see the food they chose and know just what it was that they were getting to eat. They also found such restaurants to be more economical. Some also mentioned country clubs or more upscale independent restaurants, generally of a regional reputation. These restaurants were for special occasions. Only three women mentioned ethnic restaurants; Mrs. Randall and Mrs. Nichols reported enjoying Chinese, and Mrs. Ford, a Northeasterner, reported that she liked to have Italian sometimes. Take-out or delivery from restaurants was rare. Occasionally, Mrs. Ford and her sister craved something they had not had in a long time, such as pizza (the Dining Room's version was not to their liking), and ordered the delivery of a pizza from Papa John's.

Almost all expressed little to no interest in fast food, with two women blaming fast food for ruining American diets and health and contributing to the decline of the family dinner. If the participants had fast food, often it was because a family member had taken them. Family members' choices of places to dine were not always the preference of the participant. Mrs. Adams, for example, related that sometimes she took her daughter's family out to eat. Two granddaughters in their mid-twenties still lived at home and would chose someplace they liked, such as the Applebee's chain, which serves "American" food. Mrs. Adams' problem with those types of restaurants was not the food served, however: "Where do college kids like to go? Oh noise, noise, noise. I guess that's one reason I don't enjoy going out more. It's the places the kids like tend to be noisy." Mrs. Adams wore a hearing aid and found conversation in noisy restaurants to be rather difficult.

Mrs. Adams took her family out to eat when her daughter had to work on

Sunday afternoons; generally, she was invited to have Sunday dinner at her daughter's house. Women who had adult children or other family in the area reported sometimes eating at family homes, particularly for holidays. However, several had family members eat with them at Colonial Square. They more often reported bringing them to the Dining Room to eat, as opposed to in their apartments, although meals were sometimes prepared for, or by, family members in the apartment. Mrs. Nichols related that that her daughter-in-law would frequently prepare a special meal for her and her husband when her son and daughter-in-law visited; in fact, she had a shelf of spices and sauces in her kitchen that she said only her daughter-in-law ever used.

Colonial Square Policies: Food and Dining

Colonial Square had a number of community policies, some handed down from the corporate office and others devised at the community level. Particular policies that affected the residents' dietary practices were the Dining Room hours for mealtimes, the dress code for the Dining Room, and the policy regarding taking food from the Dining Room.

Meal hours could be problematic. At least three of the participants were not on any type of schedule, as far as when they ate meals, before moving to Colonial Square and found it trying to adjust to regular meal times. Mrs. Wilson, who generally went to the Dining Room for dinner, related that she and her husband ate whenever they felt like it before living at Colonial Square:

> Mrs. Wilson: And we have to struggle to be hungry here. You know, with our meals, we've never really been on a schedule. We'd be having dinner, depending on how the day went, at nine o'clock at night.
>
> LC: But here you have to plan ahead.
>
> Mrs. Wilson: Oh, you absolutely have to. And you have to be hungry enough to eat. Which means, you can't have a very late lunch. Or if you do, you better not eat much. And we're still struggling a little bit to manage that. Because we'd been so not on

a schedule. You know, we'd just get to working outside and all the sudden, it's late. And so, we just went haphazard, just eating when it was convenient. So now, we really have to struggle to be hungry enough to enjoy our dinner. And I know you're supposed to eat regularly, but it's still a problem for us. I find that we're - I'll say, "Oh my soul William! Here it is 1:30, 2:00 we can't have but just a bite."

In another example, Mrs. Monroe did not go down for the continental breakfast because she found getting up early enough to be difficult, and since she ate a late breakfast, she almost never went down for lunch.

The perceived needs of the staff, particularly the servers, to some extent influenced when a few participants went to dinner:

And here, you have to have dinner early. Uh, 6:15 is as late as you should go. You really should go earlier, because the servers are college students and the sooner they can serve everybody, the sooner they can go home. So we don't like to go late. (Mrs. Wilson)

I go about 5:30 now. And that's too early. I don't like it. But I go. The little school girls - our waiters and waitresses, the schoolchildren, and they want to get through and get away, you know, so we go earlier and earlier so that they can get through and get away these short days. (Mrs. Provost)

There was the feeling among those who preferred to eat later that they should not go to the Dining Room too late, because of the young people who worked there. Although no one said that any of the servers had explicitly expressed wanting to go home as early as they could, it seemed that residents felt a bit rushed through their meals when they went later, even though they should have been able to receive service until 7:00 p.m.

The dress code for the Dining Room was a community policy devised and established by the residents many years ago. Nearly all of the participants stated that they were satisfied with the dress code in its current form. Almost a third of the women remarked that lately many residents had not been following the dress code, especially for dinner, as closely as it could or should be followed, and they observed people becoming more "lax" in how they dressed. However, they were inconsistent in whether they thought it was the men or women who were not as nicely attired for the evening meal. A small number of women thought that it was quite important to have a dress code and that it was good for people to make an effort to look nice for meals, especially dinner. Mrs. Michaels, however, did not attach as much importance to the dress code:

> Well, I think it's more lenient than it used to be. They used to dress up quite a bit, and a lot of people do now, because that to them is the highlight of the day, and of course it's the social time. I don't feel that it's that necessary. I sometimes put on some earrings and beads and wear what I got on. You know. Maybe a fancy sweater or something.

She explained why she thought that she and others had become more lenient about dressing up for meals:

> I think it's harder for older people to get dressed. You get dressed once for the daytime, that's about as much as you're going to - you know, it's hard to get dressed. When you have arthritis and all these ailments that we all get. I know by the time I get dressed, I'm tired.

Another factor that may have affected how closely the dress code was followed was the activities of the residents themselves. Mrs. Randall recounted the evolution of the dress code, from its institution to the current policy, which was apparently more casual on the weekends in its present incarnation than in the past. She asserted that this was due to people going to or coming from sporting events on weekends. She sometimes left right after dinner for bridge club; others had evening activities also that did not require dressing quite so nicely.

A community policy issue brought up by several women regarded taking food from the Dining Room. The policy was that no food could be taken from the Dining Room, with the exception of desserts in a container provided by the resident. A few residents, such as Mrs. Faust, found fault with this system:

> If they bring you too much food and you can't eat it, you can't bring it up to your room. People fussed about that enough, and now you can bring dessert up. And if you order grapes for dessert, they bring you grapes for dessert and you can bring that up, but if they bring you a pile of grapes on a fruit plate, you can't bring that up...That makes no sense to me. There are a few people who abuse

that. You know, I understand that...But you have to take your own container, but you don't know what dessert's going to be until you go down to supper. And so you never quite know whether you want to bring something down or not. But most of the time, I order a half of meal. Particularly the entrée, because generally the servings are really generous. More than people need. And if you have ham or something that's very - such that could be used for lunch, I don't see any reason why you couldn't bring that back. It's going to be thrown out. It doesn't make any sense to me.

Mrs. Faust's thrifty side found the policy to be rather nonsensical, for reasons of both logic and waste. She later revealed how she occasionally used this policy to her advantage, finding something of a technical loophole:

Sometimes I ask for a banana - if they have bananas available, they'll bring me a banana for dessert. That's when I'm too full to eat a dessert, and I bring it up and save it for breakfast. Because that's a dessert I don't have to bring a container to put it in.

Some residents found other ways to get around the policy, but without using loopholes like Mrs. Faust; they deliberately violated the policy by smuggling food out of the Dining Room. Mrs. Adams, for example, reported that she knew of people, mainly women, who sometimes sneaked food from the Dining Room. Mrs. Monroe admitted once to "squirreling away" a half of a baked potato in a little plastic bag, because she loved to fry it up for breakfast.

Politics and the Economy

Two women mentioned larger political and economic forces as a perceived influence on dietary practices. Mrs. Faust was one participant who took a rather political economic approach, as she explained that availability and cost of food had influenced her as much as her family's preferences. Recently, current political events played a role in dietary practices as reported by another participant. Mrs. Stokes' concern about the global issues of terrorism and biological warfare became personal matters for her:

Mrs. Stokes: Are you concerned about this anthrax thing?

LC: Not really. [Gives more explanation why she is not.]

Mrs. Stokes: Well, I'm worried about it getting in the food. Because a lot of our food comes from out of country. A lot of the countries in South America. So I wash everything real good, grapes and all that. That is a terrible disease.

Although Mrs. Stokes was the only participant to bring up such events and relate it to food, several of the women did bring up the similar issues and the events of September 11, 2001. They shared their anger, sadness and patriotism, and compared the fall of the Twin Towers to another event that they remembered all too well: the bombing of Pearl Harbor.

The Interaction of the Various Influences

This chapter demonstrated multiple factors that influenced dietary practices of these older women and that the women themselves perceived multiple factors at work, recognizing various levels of influence from the personal to the international. Personal factors surfaced, in terms of psychological processes and physical aging changes. Social processes emerged as important factors, as the social relational components of food and eating were key aspects of, and almost inseparable from, dietary practices, from food shopping to interacting with Dining Room staff. Social aspects of dietary practices as related to family statuses and roles illustrated the continuing influence of various social roles, whether past experience became over time a natural part of a current repertoire of behavior or current experience reproduced what had always been the case (e.g., wives who prepared food for their husbands, as they always had).

The larger contexts of behaviors were quite important for understanding certain food- and eating-related practices. Contexts included physical spaces and environments at Colonial Square, but also policy controls on behavior. The ethnographic approach of this research no doubt greatly stimulated the identification and detailing of the contexts of practices, but it did not appear to be at all difficult for the women to discuss and recognize contextual factors.

Taken together, these various factors represent a life course perspective on dietary behavior, where earlier life course experiences affected later experiences and behaviors, personal factors interacted with social factors, and location in time and place influenced behavior both directly and indirectly (through affecting the factors of influence themselves, such as the content of certain social roles and statuses). Life course experiences and events, such as the health problems of a loved one or a national crisis, played an important role in how the participants related to food and eating. The next chapter focuses on dietary themes and meanings of food and eating practices throughout the lives of these women, as they were developed and modified by life course experiences and events.

Chapter Four

Dietary Themes in the Lives of Older Women Residing in a Retirement Community

Numerous dietary themes emerged from analysis of the women's narratives. However, four overarching themes distinguished themselves as approaches that the women took toward their food and eating experiences: dietary morality, dietary wellness, dietary sociability, and dietary duty. Though found in varying degrees throughout the lives of each of the women, for most, one theme was more prominent in their lives. Each of the four themes is presented through a close examination of a particular participant who serves as an exemplar of the theme, with summarization of and support from other participants' comments.

Dietary Morality: The Rules of Food Consumption

Next there should never be any wasted or thrown away that can be turned into account, either for your own family or some family in poor circumstances. (Gillette & Zeimann, 1887, p. 540)

Figure 4.1: Mrs. Stokes' Recipe for Diabetic Pumpkin Pie

Diabetic Pumpkin Pie
1 (no. 2) can of pumpkin
2 eggs
1 can condensed milk
4 packets Sweet-n-Low (more if you like it sweeter)
1 teaspoon pumpkin pie spice (a little more if you like it spicier)
1 teaspoon vanilla
Mix all the ingredients together. Pour into a pie shell. Put it in the microwave on high for 45 minutes. Test it with a knife to see if it comes out clean.

Mrs. Stokes was born in an urban area of the Midwest, the oldest child of a German immigrant and his first generation German-American wife. Her parents eventually had three sons and one other daughter (one son died from diphtheria at age three). She helped look after her younger siblings, as well as assisted with other household duties, such as setting the table, drying dishes, and sewing. At the time of the study, Mrs. Stokes was an 88-year-old widow with a pleasant smile and a ready laugh. Her spectacles could not hide the twinkle in her eye, and her easygoing demeanor invited others to engage her.

Perhaps her positive personality had helped her to cope with her physical conditions. For over 25 years, Mrs. Stokes had lived with diabetes. Her mother was diabetic, her husband was diabetic, and her 64-year-old daughter was diabetic (diagnosed 10 years ago). When asked for a favorite recipe, it seemed only natural that she readily responded with directions from memory for a pumpkin pie suitable for diabetics. Diabetes created a whole set of "rules" for how Mrs. Stokes needed to manage her diet and lifestyle. Dietary regulation was a large component of her overall management of the disease; for several years she managed diabetes through diet alone. But she eventually needed insulin, which she took twice a day, just before breakfast and just before dinner.

However, these are not the only factors influencing food consumption in the life of Mrs. Stokes. She began following one particular dietary rule long before she was ever diagnosed with, and probably before she ever even heard of, diabetes. The rule is not related to health, but rather is related to a moral (and economic) standard summarized in a well-known proverb: "Waste not, want not."

Rule #1: Thou Shall Not Waste Food

Mrs. Stokes recalled that, as a young child, her parents expected her and her younger siblings to eat everything on their plates at meals:

> My mother was always telling us about the starving Armenians. No, we were supposed to belong to the clean plate club. In fact, I believe it is a sin to waste food. When you think of all the hungry people in the world. You see these poor kids in Africa.

Her parents, particularly her mother, emphasized the importance of eating what they were given and eating it all. There were obviously good economic reasons for not wasting food, especially in a family of seven supported only by their father, a carpenter. Although her childhood occurred prior to the Great Depression, it is very likely that it was still important for her parents to use money and resources frugally. Whether the moral overtones (eat your food because other children in this world are not so fortunate as to have food) were meant simply to motivate children who lacked an understanding of economic issues or whether Mrs. Stokes' parents actually believed in the moral aspects of wasting food, Mrs. Stokes took from her childhood a moral imperative that wasting food was wrong, even using religious language, that it was a "sin," to stress the depth of her moral conviction.

As Mrs. Stokes grew up, her parents' admonitions about wasting food went with her as she ate in school cafeterias. She recalled how the cafeteria workers would monitor the students' food selections, sometimes not even giving the students a choice:

> Mrs. Stokes: And if you didn't pick the right thing, they told you about it too. [Chuckles, then pretends to be a cafeteria worker] "Don't you want some of these green beans?"

> LC: So they were watching to make sure you were eating okay.

> Mrs. Stokes: Yeah, they were watching. I know there was one lady...She says, "Now you're gonna take some of these." She just put them on your plate. And of course I was taught not to throw food away. That was good for me though, that was really good for me. The other kids wouldn't eat it if they didn't want to, but I wouldn't do that. I would eat it.

Mrs. Stokes graduated from high school and began working at a laundry. A few years later she married and the newlyweds lived with his father for a couple of years before moving out on their own. Over the next ten years, a daughter and two sons were born. Mrs. Stokes also told her children about the starving Armenians, laughing about how she had to pass that along, though believing in its moral and authoritative power: "But it was a good thing to tell. I thought it was very effective." Mrs. Stokes was supposed to belong to the "clean plate club" as a child, but she noted that if there was something that she or her siblings did not like, they were only expected to eat a little bit of whatever it was they did not like. Mrs. Stokes derived her rule of "at least taste a food" from her mother's rule of "eat a little bit of the food":

> They had to taste it. They didn't have to eat the whole thing, but they had to taste it. And they'd act like they were gagging and…they put on quite a show. And my husband would sit there, and he says, "Now, you're going to eat that." And they would take the littlest portion.

Mrs. Stokes relaxed her childhood rule somewhat from eating a little to just tasting the food. She laughed as she talked about how her children responded to this rule. She also talked about one child who would feed peas to the dog under the table and of another who would sneak cookies and cans of Pepsi cola.

Such was Mrs. Stokes' indoctrination in the "do not waste food" rule, that if she broke the rule, even at the age of 88 years, she felt guilty. For example, due to a long-time practice of cutting salt out of her diet, Mrs. Stokes was taste-sensitive to salt and she could not eat food that tasted too salty to her. Occasionally, she came across an item in the Dining Room of Colonial Square that tasted too salty: "The dressing is always kind of salty. And I don't like the French Onion Soup either. That's always very salty…If it's just too salty, I don't eat it. Always feel bad about that too. Because that's wasting food."

Other participants spoke of their belief in "not wasting food," and this belief had various expressions in their practices and views of others who were perceived as wasting food. Mrs. Florsheim and Mrs. Adams both made use of turkey carcasses from Thanksgiving celebrations, carcasses that, in their view, their children were not going to put to good use. Mrs. Florsheim recounted what usually happened at Thanksgiving at one of her daughter's homes:

> We ate at our daughter's and they cut all the turkey off the carcass that they wanted, but, oh, they left a lot on. A lot. And as we often say, they did not grow up in the Depression. So each Thanksgiving

evening, and when we leave, why they'll say, do you want to take home the carcass? We'll say yes. They wrap the thing up and we brought it home. So the next day, we unwrapped it and took the big pot that we had brought with us and put all of the carcass bones into that. First we cut off a lot of meat - I have four packages in here of frozen turkey. And then we make the turkey broth from the bones.

Mrs. Adams told a similar tale, observing the difference between her sister (who used to always cook the Thanksgiving turkey) and her daughter (who now cooked the Thanksgiving turkey):

And I get the carcass. Ed cuts off for their dinners and sandwiches and things, and then I get the carcass. For my sandwiches and then I make soup. Michelle doesn't like - doesn't have time and I guess she never did care much about cooking up the carcass. My sister always - she had got more use out of a turkey. And she wanted a big enough turkey so there were plenty of leftovers. There'd be cold sliced turkey to eat, sliced turkey for this recipe, and turkey for that recipe, and soup. And, oh boy, did she get all the meat off the bones. Of course she cooked the bones, but...none of that turkey was wasted with my sister.

Both women noted possible reasons for why their children did not cut off more meat and cook the carcass. Mrs. Adams in part attributed this to her daughter's personal preferences, but also to a lack of time to cook. Mrs. Florsheim attributed it to the fact that their children did not grow up during the Depression and therefore presumably did not develop an appreciation for thriftiness and ensuring that nothing went to waste. Technically, Mrs. Florsheim herself did not grow up during the Depression, as she graduated from high school in 1930. But because she graduated from high school in 1930, she might have had an even better appreciation for the Depression, as it would have been a difficult time to become a young adult. When asked further about it, Mrs. Florsheim actually credited her upbringing more for her heightened awareness of wastefulness, because while growing up, her family did not have much money. This economic and moral philosophy had become second nature to her: "Not because I have to, but because it's just a part of me, not to waste things. There's a saying, 'Waste not, want not.'"

As Mrs. Florsheim alluded, societal forces and historical events may be powerful shapers of behavior. The Depression left a lasting impression on those who experienced it. Many of the participants' adult children grew up in a time of post-World War II affluence in this country, which could have also left an impression. As parents of young children during this time, the women made rules similar to those of their parents regarding food, but several perceived themselves to have been more lenient than their own parents. In addition, although they also generally portrayed themselves as obedient when it came to cleaning their plates or as unaware that there could have been any other way ("We just ate what was put before us"), they did not always portray their own children as such. They told anecdotes about how their children broke the rules, although often with amusement. They likely were not so amused when such incidents occurred, but are able to laugh and joke about it now that time has distanced them from those instances of "rebellion" and dimmed any seriousness of the incidents.

Mrs. Adams related how she had thought her daughter loved rutabaga, as she always cleared her plate of it. So she fed her daughter a lot of rutabaga - until she found out that it was really the dog that liked rutabaga so much. Mrs. Richardson spoke of how her youngest son put broccoli in a radiator by the breakfast nook, due to the clean plate rule. However, she and her husband did not always enforce the rule in its strictest sense:

> Mrs. Richardson: But we never dreamed that he would put it in there. Because at that time, you finished your plate. And thank heavens that went out.
>
> LC: Now what happened if they didn't finish their plate?
>
> Mrs. Richardson: Well, their father was pretty strict. And he would make them sit there a while. Now they're all, all big eaters. And eat everything.
>
> LC: So they had to sit there until they finished?
>
> Mrs. Richardson: Uh, approximately. Until their father got tired of waiting.

When it came to a battle of wills between parent and child, it was not unusual for the victor of the power struggle to have been the child. Mrs. Burkholt recalled one of her children getting around the rules, not through any deception or waiting game, but through simple logic. When told that she would have to clean her plate before getting dessert, her daughter responded that she did not want dessert and therefore would not have to finish what was on her plate. Mrs. Burkholt referred to "laying down the law" in the way that she did as a "mistake," because of the loophole that her daughter found.

Mrs. Michaels, like Mrs. Stokes, spoke of being expected to be a member of the clean plate club as a girl, but she and her husband consciously decided not to be as strict about that rule with their own children. When asked whether she fixed different foods for different family members when she was cooking for her family, she responded:

> No, I usually just fixed one meal and if they didn't want - didn't eat it, they didn't have to. I mean...of course you know, a long time ago we were supposed to clean up our plate - you had the clean plate club. And we found out that that wasn't the best thing to do and we were more lenient about it...I remember one time we were over in Berea...and they had all these little extra things at first, and our Bill, when we got to the real food, he couldn't eat it, and his dad said, "Well, this time, it wasn't your fault," because they brought all these little things and he had filled up on those. But we always tried to make - if they took it out, they were supposed to eat it. When they were serving themselves. Now if somebody else served them, then that was a different story.

Both Mrs. Michaels and Mrs. Richardson suggested that the "clean your plate" rule was not really a good rule for children anyway. Also, the rule, or the enforcement of the rule, changed according to this shift in attitude, as the women became the ruler-makers. However, they do not seem to have always been the rule enforcers. Mrs. Stokes, Mrs. Michaels, and Mrs. Richardson all indicated that their husbands were the enforcers of food rules as they raised their children, whether that was to make the children follow the rule or to allow the rule to be broken.

Wasteful practices were not limited to an association with younger generations or with raising children. Mrs. Brown explained that in the Dining Room of Colonial Square, she tried to only order as much as she knew she could eat, but observed, with a bit of incredulity, that other residents did not follow this practice:

> I have found that a number of the people are, particularly the women, are ordering everything that's on the menu and then maybe take five or six bites and that's it. It's been really amazing to me the amount of food that is ordered that goes untouched. Whether - and I'm not going to ask anybody - whether it appeals to them at the time and they think that it's going be good or whether they do it because, to get their money's worth. That always has bothered [me] - on cruises, when you know you have more food than you can shake a stick at - people go to everything and take everything they can, so they get their money's worth. Of course, if it makes them sick, then - they get off and gained 5 or 15 pounds. And that to me is so silly. I guess I'm a moderate at heart, so…

Mrs. Brown continued, stating that she thought it was ridiculous for people to order so much food and not eat it, but believed that it was their privilege to do so. In this case, she attributed the wasting of food to people trying to get the most out of their money, although she attempted to give some residents the benefit of the doubt. It seemed that some people, who did not want to waste their money, ended up wasting food in the process.

Rule #2: Thou Shall Not Consume Bad Foods

As these women aged, rules regarding food shifted in emphasis from rules about wasting food and trying foods to rules about what one should and should not eat for health reasons, particularly because of specific health conditions. Mrs. Stokes, as mentioned, had diabetes and was insulin dependent, but also managed the disease through diet. However, she had other physical conditions for which she made, or was supposed to have made, dietary adjustments, such as diverticulosis, high blood pressure, and congestive heart failure. With regard to diverticulosis, she was to avoid foods with seeds, such as corn or berries. For high blood pressure, she had to cut salt. Because of congestive heart failure, she needed to watch her fluid retention.

As a result, she developed another type of dietary morality, resulting in a number of rules about the right foods and wrong foods to eat. Mrs. Stokes distinguished between good foods and bad foods, or "no-no's":

> My husband just loved fried eggs and bacon for breakfast and potatoes. Real crisp potatoes. And of course that's a no-no now.

> I don't have her [Mrs. Stokes' mother's] butterscotch pie recipe though! Of course, that's a no-no anyway for me now.

> And that's a good [diet] book too, by the way, but he was heavy on cream. You could have cream unlimited. And now, you know, that's no good.

> But most of the time it was oats. And they're so good for you now.

> Of course, we learned how to eat papayas and all that good stuff. But that's all good stuff for you.

She additionally categorized foods as something one may or may not have, based on whether they were good or at least not bad. Foods or ways of eating that are okay, according to the rules, are "allowed": "I always have to have a glass of milk and something to eat with it before I go to bed. And I'm allowed to do that, too." When discussing what she was allowed to eat, her language sometimes became more legalistic: "Of course, I do have the regular orange juice, and I make lemonade with the lemon that you buy in the jar and then I add sweetener to it. And that's a legal drink." Referring to something as legal was evidence of the degree to which her rules for dietary management of diabetes had become dietary laws, such as those that might be found in certain religions.

Who made these rules and decided what was and was not allowed? Mrs. Stokes remarked that "I have to do what they tell me," following the orders of her doctors and sometimes her daughter, who lived in town and took her grocery shopping. Yet, Mrs. Stokes admitted to sometimes breaking these dietary rules. Occasionally, when her husband was alive, as a fellow diabetic, he would be a co-

conspirator in purposefully deviating from the rules: "Once in a while we would go out and we would sin a little bit. It's nice having company when you do that too. I would sin with ice cream, 'cause I just love ice cream." Again, the use of religious language regarding the breaking of a dietary rule suggested a fundamental moral orientation that she had taken toward foods.

Mrs. Stokes often accounted for breaking the rules, offering rationalizations for what she did. Occasionally she bought doughnuts, but she took precautions: "And every once in a while, I do get some without any sugar on them. Of course, I ration myself with those." She acknowledged that even though she was not supposed to eat seeds because of her diverticulosis, that did not mean that she did not ever eat foods with seeds, such as strawberries or corn: "Well, I know the doctor told me at the time, 'Don't eat corn.' But now I do a little bit. Of creamed corn. Not very much though." Presumably, Mrs. Stokes rationalized that doughnuts without extra sugar on them were not as bad as glazed, iced, or powdered doughnuts, and in both the case of doughnuts and corn, she limited her intake, careful to consume only a little at a time.

Mrs. Stokes also felt it necessary to account for "wrong" dietary practices in the past. For this accounting, however, she did not use personal justifications, but pleaded ignorance, appealing to a lack of scientific and public knowledge about nutrition: "I always thought I was pretty good, but I guess I wasn't careful enough. See, we didn't know years ago about eating." She continued, referring to her husband's favorite breakfast trio of fried eggs, fried bacon, and fried potatoes, and how that was not a "good" breakfast, but noted "nobody told us that was wrong."

However, it seemed a main reason now that Mrs. Stokes did not mind sometimes breaking dietary rules was because of her age. When asked if she thought she would change the way she ate in the future, she replied:

> No, not really. I'm gonna die happy. I figure I don't have that much time ahead of me anymore. I might as well enjoy what I've got. Of course, the doctor doesn't agree with that. But I tell him anyway. I think he thinks I'm a cranky old lady. A feisty old lady.

She later reiterated this idea, when asked whether she drank regular or decaffeinated coffee: "Regular. I only drink one cup a day. So I figure I can have that much caffeine. As I said, I'm gonna die happy. And of course I drink milk too." In subsequent comments, Mrs. Stokes revealed that she drank whole milk instead of low-fat or skim milk, because she liked whole milk better: "Skim milk is practically nothing, you know. And on cereal, forget it. I think I would just as soon put water on it." Determining that her remaining days were limited, she let her personal preferences and enjoyment of foods take some precedence, using her age as a license to break the rules - albeit in moderation.

All of the women expressed differentiation of foods that were good or bad for health. Some participants classified certain practices as good or bad; for example, cooking techniques (frying versus baking) or meal patterns ("I really just have two meals a day now, and I think that's very bad."). More than a few believed that moderation was the key when it came to good and bad foods, letting themselves have a little of the foods that were considered bad. "I think anything you do in moderation is not bad" was a common sentiment among the moderates. Mrs. Nichols felt that it was easier for her to avoid eating too many sweets if she let herself have just a little. Occasionally, religious language was used again to denote when something was bad. Mrs. Monroe, for example, considered her love of dark meat to be wrong: "And most of the time they have baked chicken, you can get the dark meat. And that is a sin. Because I like the dark meat better than the light meat and the light meat is better for you."

Others also accounted for past behavior that was contrary to current dietary recommendations because of a lack of knowledge at the time. For example, when Mrs. Michaels recalled the breakfasts she used to prepare for her husband, she prefaced her comments: "And back earlier, before we knew about fats and cholesterol, we had a lot of bacon." Mrs. Michaels was a home economics major in college and had previously noted that they did not discuss such things: "And cholesterol wasn't mentioned. We didn't know that word really."

In addition, Mrs. Stokes was not the only woman who used her age as a reason to enjoy foods that might otherwise be considered bad. Mrs. Richardson tried to eat more vegetables than she used to, because she liked them and thought they were healthy, but she also clearly articulated that she did not necessarily restrict herself from bad foods. "They'll have something and if it's something that sort of strikes my fancy and I'll say, mmm. So eat what you want. I don't try to deprive myself because it's something I shouldn't have. I feel like at this age, eat it and enjoy it." She wished other residents had her same philosophy:

> And I was sitting there with six or seven people, and this one gentleman, I'll never forget him, Mr. Taft. And I said, "I'm going to get up and get dessert. May I get anyone dessert?" And he said, "Oh no, it isn't good for you." Mr. Taft is 93. It was not good for you. When I came back at the table with my really fattening dessert, I felt a little guilty, but not guilty enough not to eat it. Do you know three days later Mr. Taft had died, and I thought, oh, I wish he had eaten some dessert. Because I knew he wanted it, you know.

Although she expressed feelings of guilt for breaking a rule, it seemed her philosophy of "at this age, eat it and enjoy it," tempered her guilt.

Other women who had health conditions that required dietary adjustments also used moralistic terms to discuss what they should and should not eat. Ms. Carr was diabetic; at the age of 72, she was younger than Mrs. Stokes, and with nine years since diagnosis, had not lived with diabetes as long as Mrs. Stokes. For Ms. Carr, "it is a constant battle with the diabetes." She sometimes felt overwhelmed because there was so much she had to be mindful of about her diet. Mrs. Stokes, however, felt that much of what she did regarding food had become almost automatic (for example, counting carbohydrates) and it seemed to be less of a "battle" for her now. Unlike Mrs. Nichols, the moderate, Ms. Carr thought it was better for her to stay completely off sweets, because when she tried to have a little, it ended up turning into a lot.

Ms. Carr in particular talked about what she was allowed and not allowed:

> Now one of the things they allow me to have is one slice, twice a week, of angel food cake plain. No icing. And that was fine.

I do have permission to drink diet drinks. It [her diet] says I can have as much as I want. Or I'm even allowed to have coffee.

And I figure, I can have eggs - well, in fact, this diet I have says I can have eggs two or three times a week.

I am allowed a bedtime snack.

And it's very interesting, but seems like people get all upset about the amount of fluid I drink. And I say, well, it's on the diet, it's there.

She referred to the diet that had been prescribed for her as an authority to be deferred to, but also as a defense to others who observed her practices. She was bothered by residents who took it upon themselves to monitor her dietary behavior: "And one resident will come up and say, 'Well, I'm just checking on what you're eating. I want to be sure you're eating right.' And I thought, well, I don't say one word to you about what you're eating."

Sometimes when Ms. Carr broke her dietary rules, she felt guilty, but at other times, she laughed it off:

And they're beginning to know us and they know that I'll accept the chocolate sugar-free pudding. Unless there's something they have that I just simply can't turn down. And see, I'll check my blood sugar before I go down. And if it's not completely out of whack, why…I know it. I am terrible, I know it. I know it. But I'm rotten. I think I get by with it too. [Laughs]

It almost seemed as if she regarded herself at these times as something of a mischievous child who did naughty things but meant no harm. Her swings between guilty and a devil-may-care attitudes were reflective of her battle with diabetes. In some way, her struggle was not just a health issue; it was also a moral issue for her, about rules that she should not break but did anyway.

Food rules regarding health and nutrition, reflecting moral ideas about food and eating, came later in life for these women. Their regard for the rules also depended to some extent on their views of nutrition - what it meant to eat nutritiously and where they got their information about health and nutrition. The

138

next section goes beyond moral aspects and rules to the broader role of nutrition in their past and present dietary practices.

<u>Dietary Wellness: Nutrition Advocacy</u>

> *That the flavor of cod-liver oil may be changed to the delightful one of fresh oyster, if the patient will drink a large glass of water poured from a vessel in which nails have been allowed to rust.* (Gillette & Zeimann, 1887, p. 494)

Figure 4.2: Mrs. Wilson's Recipe for Granola

<u>Granola</u>

1 cup raw wheat germ
2 cups rolled oats
1 cup oat bran
¼ cup sesame seed
½ cup sunflower seed
1 cup chopped nuts (not fine)

Mix together. In a separate bowl, mix:
¼ cup oil (safflower)
¾ cup honey

Work throughout the dry ingredients. Bake in 300° oven in roaster sprayed with Pam - for 1 ½ hours - need to stir every 15 minutes. After cooled, put in plastic bag. Should be a light tan color - don't overdo it, but it needs enough. Towards the end of baking, may want to taste a teaspoon to make sure it is crunchy.

Mrs. Wilson went over old recipes that she liked. Some of them were party appetizers and some were family recipes. She also had some recipes that were particularly healthy:

> And granola. Now this dates from when William had his open-heart surgery. Because that's when I started doing research. That's when I got the Jane Brody book, and started eliminating, well, egg yolks and fats. You know, downgrading sugar a great deal and started incorporating the whole oats and grains and things like that.

It was over 25 years ago that Mrs. Wilson's husband underwent quadruple bypass heart surgery, an event that lead to a complete and radical change in their diet and the way the Wilsons ate. Since that time they never looked back, allowing themselves the rare treat (e.g. bacon or waffles), but typically consistent in maintaining their low-fat, low-salt, high-in-fruits-vegetables-and-grains diet.

At the time of this research, Mrs. Wilson was 79 years old, a tall thin woman with a soft voice and sensitive soul. Mr. Wilson was her second husband, although they had been married for 33 years. She had two children from her first marriage and three stepchildren. She also had 5 grandchildren, 5 step-grandchildren, 5 great-grandchildren, and 7 step-great-grandchildren. Even the young ones were well aware of the dietary practices of their grandparents, as Mrs. Wilson related:

> Well, I think I told you about my little granddaughter, who had to write a three or four page essay. And she wrote, I like to go and visit my grandparents, but there's just one thing. When you go to their house, you have to eat health food.

Family was very important to Mrs. Wilson, who kept in close contact with all her siblings and the children. Over her lifetime, she often cooked and prepared food for them, at family gatherings and as gifts; she also tried to have a positive influence on their eating habits, sharing her knowledge of nutrition and impressing upon them the importance of good nutrition.

It was Mr. Wilson's surgery that spurred Mrs. Wilson's study of nutrition, which resulted in the transition of their eating habits. Before then, Mrs. Wilson's knowledge and practices were based on how she grew up and what she learned in school. Mrs. Wilson was born and raised in the rural South with four siblings. For her family, cornbread crumbled into milk was a standard meal. The family owned livestock, which supplied them with fresh meat, eggs, milk, butter, and clabber. They also cultivated a garden, producing an abundance of fresh vegetables. She described how her mother made fresh biscuits and ground fresh coffee every morning. She also described a favorite dish called pot likker: "You crumble corn bread in a bowl and pour the juice that you cooked the turnips in over it. And eat it with a spoon. And that's what pot likker is. And that was just a favorite. And you can imagine how nutritious, you know, the juice, the broth from cooking turnips, plus the corn bread." She credited her parents with providing wholesome meals and a variety of foods for the family.

Mrs. Wilson received her first training in nutrition in high school, where she had a health class in which food was discussed. After high school, she went to business school and then moved to Washington D.C. to take a job in the civil service. It was in Washington that she met and married her first husband, a Northerner, and learned how to cook, because as she put it, she "didn't know how to boil water." She prepared dinners of meat, potatoes, and one or two vegetables, which was all her husband wanted anyway, just meat and potatoes. At that time, such dinners were the concept of a well-balanced meal. She made sure her two boys ate fruits and vegetables, and always kept carrot sticks around, which became a snack staple for them.

They were living in the Northeast when she and her first husband divorced. After the divorce, Mrs. Wilson attended college, and her younger son.

> But with college, we had nutritious food. For instance, we had a lot of tuna fish salad, with a lot of vegetables in it, you know, and we both liked it. We had - on the weekends I would cook full meals, and maybe make a roast and we would have some sandwiches then. But cooking really got to be - we used some frozen foods. Because I worked really hard to get through college...But we did have a healthful diet. I made sure that we got protein and vegetables and fruits.

She married Mr. Wilson a week after graduating from college. At that time, his main meal had been steak and potatoes, a meal that continued to be in their diets, except that Mrs. Wilson added vegetables, salads, and desserts in order to provide what she considered a well-balanced meal. When Mr. Wilson retired, they moved from the Northeast to Louisville, Kentucky, where Mr. Wilson had a brother and sister-in-law.

Shortly after they moved to Louisville, Mr. Wilson went to the doctor, sensing that something was wrong with him physically. Subsequently, he was admitted to the hospital for quadruple coronary bypass surgery. Mr. Wilson's doctor informed them that if he had had a heart attack, he would have died. Mr.

Wilson's father actually died at the same age from a heart attack. Mr. Wilson recovered well from the surgery, and Mrs. Wilson described his last post-operative appointment with the cardiologist:

> I went in after his surgery, after 6 weeks, he'd be going in for his dismissal thing. Well, I went in with my little notebook and pencil ready. And after he [the cardiologist] finished talking with William, I said, "Well, I'd like for you now, if you would please, to tell me what he should - his foods." He said, "He can eat anything he wants to. I've fixed his heart." And I looked at him. And just got upset. Now, he's a wonderful fixer. But I had already read that 80 percent of open-heart patients are back in five years for more surgery because they had not changed their life. So I thought, well maybe he needs more business later on. But that didn't keep me from believing what I had read.

Her research on nutrition became a very important project for her, and she put her love of reading and study to use in improving her husband's health:

> I subscribed to Prevention magazine, that was one thing and of course, you know, books from the library on nutrition and all kinds of things. And you know, it was just a matter of reading. Just a matter of reading. And then finally, recipes - and I also found a book to give me suggestions on how to modify recipes. If you have a favorite recipe, how to modify it. So, and, of course, I love to study. I just soak it up. Still do.

Studying up on a health-related topic was not new for her; during her pregnancies, she recalled reading books and following recommendations. Mr. Wilson's surgery, however, required a much larger, permanent change in their lifestyles and resulted in a serious plan of action.

Mrs. Wilson cut fats from their diet, reduced their salt and sugar intake, frequented health food stores, added nutrients to already healthy foods (such as adding oat bran and sunflower seeds to plain oatmeal), and learned not only how to modify recipes, but also new ways to prepare healthy and tasty meals, such as stir-frying in a wok. In addition, they began taking supplements, including a multivitamin, vitamins C, D, and E, and folic acid. Mr. Wilson took an iron supplement, but she did not. She took a calcium supplement. They had not cut out desserts, but instead of pie or cake, they chose frozen yogurt or sherbet.

142

Mrs. Wilson was quite happy with the foods that they were able to choose from the Dining Room:

> They use very little salt. There are always choices that are good for William's diet, which I follow also. They have plenty of vegetables, plenty of fruit. A wide choice of fish. They serve different kinds of fish and good fish. You know, the kind that has the omega-3. Except catfish, but we eat that anyhow. They have blackened catfish that's just wonderful. And it does not have omega-3, but we eat it anyhow. But it's not fried. We don't eat fried foods at all. But they have good vegetables and salads. Now, they don't have whole wheat breads. But they have to please the majority of the people and I understand that the majority of the people don't want whole wheat bread. So, you know we don't make a fuss about that. And we have cranberry juice as sort of an appetizer at dinner every night. And they always have some, a fruit plate available, with lovely fresh fruit. And you can have that with cottage cheese or chicken salad or tuna salad.

She was willing to make small concessions (e.g., the whole wheat bread) due to the overall perceived nutritional quality of the food choices available in the Dining Room and her recognition that not all residents were following her dietary lifestyle. The servers in the Dining Room always filled any of their special requests, such as "going light" on a cream sauce or getting a salad of greens not listed on the menu.

The adjustment in diet and dietary practices was not a very difficult one for them to make, even when Mrs. Wilson was preparing their main meals, because of the seriousness of the situation and the threat to Mr. Wilson's health, even life. As she said, "William knew and I knew what was at stake." She remarked that Mr. Wilson never complained, but also that she had been able to prepare food for him that tasted good. Her support, both emotional and instrumental, meant a lot to Mr. Wilson, who credited his wife with his survival: "I'm still here because of her. I wouldn't have made it without her." Mrs. Wilson had no complaints about changing her lifestyle either, but for somewhat different reasons:

> I'm a very docile person. You know, what suits anybody else, suits me. Well, and of course, that's reflected in William's situation.

When he - it never has crossed my mind to make something for me. I love pecan pie. But he shouldn't have it, and so I - I wouldn't think of making anything just for myself. I just - I'm a people pleaser. That's what I am.

Additionally, this change has not been without its rewards for Mrs. Wilson. In conveying that her husband's illness made the biggest impact in her lifetime on her eating behavior, she explained why: "I really studied food...I've studied it. And have actually made a plan. And I'm very proud of it." She continued:

> I told you that Dr. Harper, his cardiologist, when we first went in to her, and said, well he had four bypasses, 24 years ago, and he hasn't had any trouble since, and she was just astounded. She said she had never heard of such a thing. And of course, his food I eat - we eat the same diet. So, it's been good for me too.

She took pride in the fact that she organized and engineered their dietary transformation. She also had seen success from all her efforts. His cardiologist's response and the fact that he only recently had any recurring heart troubles proved to her that their diet had been "wonderfully successful." She evidently believed that she also benefited from the health effects of such a diet, noting that it had been good for her too. Mrs. Wilson even used nutrition to improve her mental health, talking of the time she made an orange juice and yeast concoction, to which she gave some credit for helping to pull her out of an "air of depression."

She also felt that she had been a good influence on her children and step-children, nutritionally speaking. Although sometimes she saw them eat in ways that she wished they would not, she was secure in her knowledge that they did know good nutritional practices. Mrs. Wilson did not plan to make any future changes in their dietary behavior, satisfied with their current eating practices.

Not all of the participants were as staunch believers in the power of nutritious food as Mrs. Wilson was. Some even expressed skepticism about various dietary recommendations that they had come across in different media sources:

> And you know, you read articles that supposed to be people in the know and one six months you're supposed to eat this and that [sic].

Now, margarine for instance. How long you weren't supposed to eat butter - it wasn't good for you and you're supposed to eat margarine. Now butter's better for you than margarine. And all those changes, you know. I try to keep up with them. But I never did do without my butter. I love butter, sure enough, butter. But that's just one instance. I mean, often they change - what was good for you one time is not so good for you the next six months. (Mrs. Provost)

I find myself, when I look at the menu here, thinking, oh that's fried and it's not going to be as good for me. Now I've begun to think about my weight too. But there have been a lot of food fads through my lifetime, latter lifetime. And we never paid much attention to those. You know, for instance, eggs for a while were so bad for you. We continue to have eggs every once in a while. (Mrs. Nichols)

[I read] some articles about nutrition. But they change their mind so often; I don't pay any attention to those anymore. Really. That's true. I think the one thing that I've tried to change is not to eat so much pork. I think that was not good for my body particularly. But mother, when she ate her meat, she wanted half lean and half fat. And she lived just about longer than anyone else. Now figure that one out. I guess she worked it off - I don't know. (Mrs. Faust)

There was a perception among the skeptics that dietary recommendations changed frequently, sometimes contradicting or negating previous recommendations, making them difficult to follow and trust. Other women, such as Mrs. Faust, additionally noted that someone they knew, be it a parent, an aunt, or a sister, lived a very long life on a diet that by today's standards might be considered almost deadly. In fact, Mrs. Burkholt, at 86 years old, found some recommendations did not apply to her at all: "Don't tell me that pork isn't good for you. I grew up on it." Ever the meat lover, Mrs. Burkholt found that among her peers, she was something of a nutritional outcast:

Nobody likes to eat like I do. I say anything about grease or pork...They say, "How on earth can you eat that stuff?" And I say, "Boy, it's good. Got to have a little grease go through your bones."

In the face of the contradictions of experts and proof that said otherwise, some women did not take much stock in the latest nutrition information.

Almost all of the women trusted in the well-balanced meal concept and in moderation, feeling that it worked for their parents and served them well over the years. In their early years, participants cited parents as a main source of knowledge about nutrition and healthy food. Except for the few from urban areas, many of the women's parents did some type of gardening, resulting in fresh vegetables served at meals. Those who lived on farms also had fresh meat, eggs, and/or dairy products. Additionally, they identified school and clubs, such as 4-H, as places of learning about food and nutrition, again mostly in terms of food groups and the well-balanced meal. Just over half of the participants mentioned they first learned about nutrition in a health or home economics class.

As the years went on, all but one of the women married, and all but one of the married women had children. None of them remembered doing anything particularly different as far as their dietary behaviors during their pregnancies (except Mrs. Wilson, although she could not recall specifics). Three of the participants mentioned being unable to drink coffee during their pregnancies, not for health reasons, but because it was unappealing to them. Mrs. Faust had inquired about her diet when she was pregnant, asking her doctor's advice:

> Some people think they have to eat special things when they're pregnant. I asked my doctor about that and he was a man of few words. He says, "You eat don't you?" And I thought everybody when they got pregnant had to take vitamins, special vitamins. He said, "You eat, don't you?"

Nearly all of the women fed their families based on their upbringing and any health classes they had in school. A few recalled perusing women's magazines, such as Ladies Home Journal, in which they read articles addressing nutrition or procuring nutritional information from a cookbook.

Regardless of the source of information, the concept was still the same: a well-balanced main meal of meat, potatoes, and one or two vegetables. They often served more salads (e.g. vegetable salad, fruit salad, or the always-popular Jell-O salad) with the meal, however, than their mothers had served. Dessert after the meal continued to be the custom. The participants did not particularly mention beverages, although three mentioned soda and reported that they either did not buy much soda when they were raising their children (especially as compared to what they perceived as a high rate of soda consumption by today's families) or they limited their children to one soda a week.

In later years, the media became a regular source of nutrition information, as nutrition became a frequent topic in magazines, newspapers, and books, and on television. Friends and peers also began to more often discuss nutrition issues and share information and tips. Mrs. Adams explained that she learned about nutrition from reading and from talking to others: "I guess a friend talked about taking vitamin C. She had a lot of colds or something, and she found vitamin C helped her. So I tried that..."

As seen in Table 4.1, the top three vitamin and mineral supplements used by participants were vitamin E, calcium, and multivitamins. Ten women took calcium for bone health, and about two-thirds took at least a multivitamin. Three women took Ocuvite, a supplement with minerals specifically for eye health (e.g., lutein and zinc) which was recommended by their ophthalmologists.

The majority did not begin to take supplements until their later years (with the exception of one who began taking vitamin supplements in high school for extra energy to play basketball). Of those able to estimate how long they had been taking vitamins, three women had been taking supplements for 1-3 years, four for 5-10 years, two for 15-20 years, three for 24-25 years, and the one who began in high school, for 70 years. Often they began on the recommendation of a doctor (10 participants), some took self-prescribed vitamins (5 participants), and two women began based on the counsel of adult children (one step-daughter and one daughter-in-law). Mrs. Adams began to take vitamin E based on a lecture she heard given by a researcher from a local university: "I take vitamin E to avoid the plaques from Alzheimer's." She emphasized that she had her doctor approve her use and dosage of vitamin E.

Table 4.1: Vitamin and Mineral Supplement Use of Participants

Supplement	# of Women Using
Beta carotene	1
Calcium	10
Folic Acid	2
Glucosamine	2
Multi-antioxidant	2
Multivitamin	11
Ocuvite	3
Shark cartilage	1
Tums	2
Vitamin A	1
Vitamin B's	2
Vitamin C	5
Vitamin D	3
Vitamin E	7

Participants reported receiving minimal nutritional advice from health professionals, beyond physician recommendations for vitamin and mineral supplements. Mrs. Provost's doctor instructed her to drink Ensure, and nurses recommended that she drink green tea; health professionals advised Mrs. Randall and Ms. Carr to drink cranberry juice. For those with high blood pressure or cholesterol problems, nutritional counseling essentially consisted of advice to reduce salt or consisted of a sheet of paper with foods to avoid for reducing cholesterol.

Four women reported receiving nutritional advice from their children. Mrs. Burkholt talked about her daughters and their eating, and then noted: "And they know a lot about nutrition. In fact, they've gotten so they tell us." Mrs. Vossler claimed that she learned much from her daughter, who is a vegetarian, about nutrition. For her, nutrition seemed to be a family issue. She affirmed she learned from her daughter, when she said: "Because who else was going to teach me? My mother cooked the way I did, you know." Mrs. Vossler did not become a vegetarian herself, but since her residential transition to Lexington and now close proximity to her daughter, she has incorporated more vegetables into her diet, had come to appreciate meatless meals, and was generally more aware of nutritional issues than she had been earlier in life.

All but one of the women generally concurred with Mrs. Wilson's assessment that the Dining Room of Colonial Square had nutritional options. Two issues that were consistently brought up by the women were one, a lack of potato selections on the menu, and two, some lack of variety in vegetable selections. Yellow squash and zucchini were perceived as making too frequent appearances on the menu; according to Mrs. Brown: "As everybody says, they're [food services] addicted to yellow squash." A related issue was balancing medications and food; for example, Mrs. Adams was on a blood thinner and consequently had to limit her intake of foods high in vitamin K, found in leafy and green vegetables such as spinach, kale, and broccoli, to no more than three cups a week. She expressed concern about this situation. First, it was difficult for her to determine how much 3 cups exactly was, particularly because she was eating mainly in the Dining Room: "And so that would be easier to manage at home, on my own. Like how much is a half a cup of broccoli?" A second difficulty occurred when all the vegetable choices at dinner were high in vitamin K:

> All the sudden [they] get peaks of it. And it seems as though, sometimes the alternatives - you have to choose between which vitamin K you will eat that day. And sometimes, you know, they'll have stuff two, three days in a row. Broccoli, spinach, Brussel sprouts, three days in a row.

Almost none of the women mentioned fruit as an issue, only Mrs. Ford, who would have preferred more fruit be available in the Dining Room at meals.

On the whole, the women varied in their interests in and knowledge of nutrition. They ranged from Mrs. Wilson, a self-taught student of nutrition who practically revolutionized her diet, to Mrs. Burkholt, who gave it little thought, relying on her common sense and daughters' advice, but really having changed very little about her diet since she was a child. Almost all had some heightened nutritional awareness as compared to their awareness at younger ages, although two women qualified their awareness, such as Mrs. Faust who asserted, "I'm not a real nutritionist," or Mrs. Brown who stated she "never made any special study of it." A number of participants were either skeptics or had no reason to change, feeling that their well-balanced meals and vitamin supplements provided adequate nutrition. If nutritional changes occurred, it was often a conscious attempt to consume more fruits and vegetables or as part of a plan for weight management (e.g. altering dessert patterns).

Mrs. Wilson also enjoyed cooking, and she had entertained socially quite a bit over the years, welcoming friends and family into her home. The concept of feeding others in social situations was another theme to emerge from the stories of these women.

Dietary Sociability: The Art and Activity of Feeding Others

I enjoy preparing any kind of meal, but I prefer meals that have a special meaning - meals for guests...No matter how tired or how busy I may be, I always rise to the occasion when a party is in the offing. (Vanderbilt, 1961, p. viii)

Figure 4.3: Mrs. Randall's Recipe for Brunch Casserole

Brunch Casserole
12 slices white bread - crusts trimmed, buttered on both sides, cubed 1 pound cooked sausage, crumbled ½ pound shredded cheddar cheese 4 to 6 eggs, lightly beaten 3 cups milk ½ teaspoon salt - pepper
Butter 9x13 baking pan or dish. Sprinkle sausage and cheese over bread cubes. Combine remaining ingredients. Pour over bread cubes. Cover and refrigerate overnight. Bake covered for 45 minutes to 1 hour at 350°. Serve immediately.

For Mrs. Randall, one of the great aspects of the Brunch Casserole was its ease of preparation. Another great feature was that you could make it in huge quantities: "You can see, you can imagine, you can line six pans up and do 125 people, which is what I had to do." As Mrs. Randall noted when discussing her recipes, the ones she chose to discuss were representative of her and her life.

The reason why she had to make so much Brunch Casserole reflected a major dimension of Mrs. Randall's approach to food and food preparation. The recipe was 30 years old and from a friend. Mrs. Randall used it for Holy Week breakfasts at the Methodist church she attended, when many years ago she was the cook. For about 10 to 15 years, she and another woman cooked for church breakfasts, church suppers, wedding rehearsal dinners, wedding receptions, and other special occasions, feeding the congregation. She enjoyed cooking for the church a great deal and felt she was skilled at it. Mrs. Randall also had 20 years of entertaining experience as a military wife. She was a master at preparing food for social situations, be it entertaining, church functions, social clubs, family gatherings, gift giving, or charitable work.

Mrs. Randall at 73 years old was one of the younger women of the participant group, but she had lived at Colonial Square the longest, having moved in when the building opened. Born in the rural Midwest, she had little interest in domestic activities or experience with social events when she was a girl. She was rather tomboyish, hunting and fishing with her father, and even received a shotgun at age 16: "My dad thought I was a boy. For years." Her first real cooking experience occurred at a restaurant where she worked part-time, after school and on Saturdays. As a teenager, she prepared spaghetti for the bus drivers who frequented the establishment. When she married, she could make spaghetti, fried chicken, and chocolate cake. She knew a little more than she thought at the time, as she also was familiar with gardening and cleaning and preparing game.

She met Mr. Randall while at a Midwestern college and they married after he graduated from dental school. They went on a short honeymoon to Niagara Falls and then reported for duty at Walter Reed Hospital in Washington, D.C. The next twenty years took them to one foreign country, four state, and back to D.C., before settling in Kentucky. The almost simultaneous marital and occupational transitions completely changed their lives. Her new role was not just that of wife, but that of an army officer's wife. Socially speaking, much was expected of an army officer's wife during the 1950s and 1960s. Her only previous experience with the military was writing letters and sending cookies to soldiers. As an army officer's wife, she had to know the social rules of the military, which other experienced military wives helped her to learn. She was obligated not only to do private entertaining for other officers and their wives, but also to be involved in social activities involving only wives.

Once she got the hang of it, however, her wifely duties almost became a matter of routine. Mrs. Randall always entertained at home, never at the officer's club. She organized her entertaining to make it as easy and yet as successful as possible:

> When Johnny was in the military, I had about five menus that I knew to the nth [inside and out]. How long it took, what it took ahead of time and so forth. And those were the ones that I pretty much - and it was food I could get - those were the ones I pretty much used the entire 20 plus years of cooking for or entertaining for the military. And we laughed about it - I said, "You know," I kept saying, "You know, we can't stay too long here because I've gone through all five!" The only thing was, most everybody had left and new people had come in, but we never left, that was the problem, see. So I said, "Well I've gone through all five of them, now I'm going to have to figure something different. But, oh well, most everybody's gone, you know." So anyway, it was pretty much the same ones all the time. Typical. The ham dinner, the beef dinner, you know.

In addition to the use of set menus, she also found that she could use essentially the same social rules, as entertaining was basically the same wherever they were.

She characterized some of the places she and her family lived during her husband's military career. During the Texas and Hawaii assignments, they struck her as very military and very proper, where tradition was highly regarded and given much emphasis. In D.C., she found the atmosphere to be more executive and rank was considered to be very important. They also really only associated with other medical officers and their families in Washington. In Europe, there was no officer's club yet where they were stationed, and she found them to be a very social group that enjoyed getting together at social events. During one of their tours in Texas, she was in charge of organizing all the activities for the dental wives (a dental training school was there and thus many dental wives).

When Mr. Randall retired from the military, he accepted a faculty position at the University of Kentucky. Although not their last residential move, the relocation to Lexington would be the last time they moved to a new town. Mrs. Randall discovered that as a professor's wife, it was much more relaxed socially. They became involved in coordinating departmental get-togethers about once a semester, and she taught bridge to other faculty wives. She took on the duty of church cook; also through her church, she became involved with Meals on Wheels. Mrs. Randall contributed food to the local food bank and had contributed food to those in need in the past. She referred to an example when they were living in Texas:

> Johnny went hunting down there several times and we got deer, he got venison. And a couple of times, well most of the time, we would keep the tenderloin. Pretty much that was it of the venison. And then we'd give the rest of it to a church or one of the agencies or so on. And they always gave it - they all had families that really loved the venison. And they'd grind it up and put it in a tamale and things. So they were always glad to get it and we were glad to get rid of it. And it fed someone. You know. And that was a good way to use venison.

Mrs. Randall, of course, was familiar with game and how to clean and prepare it from her days of hunting and fishing with her father.

When Mrs. Randall and her friend stopped working as the church cooks, the church had to hire someone to come in and cook: "Well, we retired and there wasn't - nobody else was going to do that for nothing! Just us nuts!" She also discontinued her involvement with Meals on Wheels, and her husband eventually retired from the university. Even at Colonial Square though, Mrs. Randall still actively cooked for others. Family especially continued to benefit from her skills. She and her husband had three children. Their daughter lived in Lexington, one son was a few hours drive away, and the other son lived in Washington, D.C. (he was in the military). Birthdays were usually a family affair, and the whole family got together when they could for the holidays. Mrs. Randall was in charge of Thanksgiving this past year (due to a daughter-in-law's health problems), which involved not only planning and cooking on Thanksgiving day, but planning the meals for the entire weekend, as family members came into town and stayed through the holiday weekend. She often made food to give as gifts to family and friends (such as tins of roasted pecan clusters or wrapped-up English shortbread). She always brought food when her bridge club had potluck, from fruit salad to barbeque meatballs.

Mrs. Randall used her extensive culinary experience at Colonial Square, offering advice and suggestions to those in food services. She was able to add insight to the menus, based on her experience as a cook and a long-time resident:

> I've got a few ideas I'm going to turn over to them shortly. Again. I feel free to offer some suggestions. I think it's easier for somebody who's been here also, who knows the problems. You can say, oh well, do my favorite recipe. Well, "my favorite recipe" won't hold and it won't multiply. But mine do…And yet I know some short cuts and some things like that.

Mrs. Randall was on the residents' food services committee in the past, and though she was not on that committee at the time of the study, she communicated with the staff on her own, suggesting menu items (for example, tuna melts and gingerbread) and changes to the menu cycle. For example, she recalled, "I suggested several years ago that maybe they needed to add an extra week. Because we discovered in Meals on Wheels, that we needed really five weeks. 'Cause you don't want the fourth Monday to be the same."

Mrs. Randall and her husband usually had their dinners in the Dining Room and stocked food for breakfasts and lunches. She prepared items to have on hand, generally soups and salads. She usually had something to start the soup with, such as a can of condensed tomato soup, but always added things to it, such as seasonings, pasta, and vegetables. She did the same with cake; she would start with a box mix, but "doctored" it up. Her creative food tips occurred throughout the interview, such as suggesting that the Brunch Casserole be served with hot salsa on the side, how to make bacon-wrapped green bean bundles tied with red pepper strips, and how to make a tortellini soup.

There were no frozen dinners or other pre-made meals in her kitchen, with the exception of some frozen pizzas that Mr. Randall sometimes had for lunch. She shopped at Meijer because she found they had fresher and more exotic produce in stock, but she occasionally went to Sam's Club (a chain warehouse club which specializes in bulk quantities), if she was "going to have a mob." She still had quite a bit of cookware and a very large cupboard (really a small hutch) full of cooking and baking equipment. She gave away the big items, such as huge stockpots. They had the cupboard custom installed in their apartment when they moved in to Colonial Square, knowing that she needed the space for storage of her cookware. She had, for example, six 9"x13" metal baking pans.

Mrs. Randall voiced concerns about contemporary cooking practices, or rather the lack thereof:

> Mrs. Randall: But oh - it's so much easier now, because - oh, everything is so - you know, you can get spiral sliced ham, and it's a breeze now. And it's a darn shame, because people have quit cooking, haven't they?

> LC: Yeah. I would say a lot of them have.

> Mrs. Randall: I think so, because these foods that are packaged and already put together - good grief, you've got TV dinners and everything - that are really quite nice.

Although she was a fan of dishes that were easy to prepare and made use of items such as canned soup and box cake mixes, her definition of cooking was more than warming up food. She perceived that while there are good pre-made options for meals, it also meant people who bought those foods were cooking less. She perceived homemade meals to be healthier as well:

> Mrs. Randall: We took health classes in high school. And I knew the food groups. And what I was supposed to be eating. I don't know whether they're giving those anymore, but they ought to. Maybe we'd have few less fat kids. Seriously. Of course, I don't

think so, because people don't cook anymore. And you know, we were talking about people who need food, and I know this, and I contribute to God's Pantry [a food bank] and all these other things. But you know, when they used to give coupons, I don't whether they still give them - are they giving food coupons to people and they're using them to buy food?

LC: [Confirms that the program still exists]

Mrs. Randall: But anyway, I would follow someone through the line who gave those and I didn't begrudge them that a bit. But their selection of the food they got indicated to me - because they could have gotten - do much more and better food if they had shopped differently. But they weren't cooking. They were warming up. And I think that's one of the problems with the microwave.

Her discussion here had tones of "class-ism," as she specifically targeted low income, food stamp recipients as doing a poor job of food selection in their shopping. However, she in a sense blamed the food industry and technology also, for making it so easy to simply warm up food.

Other participants did not lament the lost art of cooking quite as strongly as did Mrs. Randall. About half of the other women simply heated up food for their meals eaten at home, whether it was a frozen meal or a can of soup. However, Mrs. Brown mentioned that she thought people raising families today were not well-practiced in the "art" of preparing a meal for a family: "Then with the children you definitely tried to make balanced meals and learned to cook in quantity and learned to time things so that everything came out at the same time and that's an art. It's an art - a lost art I'd venture."

Two women mentioned that their children and young people today also did not seem to entertain or throw parties like they used to do. Over three-fourths of the women did not remember their parents doing much entertaining, outside of family get-togethers. Three of the women recalled that their church pastor coming for Sunday dinner about once a month. As children, sometimes whether the participants had friends over was a matter of family economics. Mrs. Adams noted that if her mother served pork chops for dinner, there were only so many to go around and therefore friends would not be invited to dinner. But if it was leftover roast, then maybe she could have a friend over for dinner.

After they were on their own and had families of their own, for the most part, the women became more involved in preparing food for family gatherings, often hosting holiday celebrations themselves. Friends and neighbors would sometimes get together for dinner or wives together for lunch. The women became involved in group and organization activities (e.g. PTA, church groups and functions, women's groups and events), which provided opportunities to host luncheons, bring potluck to suppers, and participate in bake sales. Two of the women mentioned cooking for a group to which their husband belonged, such as the Masons. Four women talked about entertaining because of their husband's career, a more obligatory type of entertaining for their husbands' bosses, co-workers, and business associates.

The participants' later years had seen much less private entertaining, particularly after moving to Colonial Square. Mrs. Wilson no longer entertained, other than for family, and one reason was limited space. If Mrs. Florsheim and her husband had visitors, they ate in the Dining Room or dined out. Mrs. Faust also liked to bring any guests to the Dining Room, as she thought it was nicer than eating out. However, she did have one problem with the current meal accounting system:

> They used to let us - we're invited out quite a bit to friends' houses, so we don't use our ticket for that meal. But we invite them to our house and have them use our unused tickets. But you can't do that anymore. We have to pay for a months' worth of tickets, and it has to be us that uses it.

Mrs. Monroe reported a similar difficulty:

> And we got tickets in the back [of the ticket book] each month, five extra ones for lunch only. And I used those for my bridge club once a month. I took them to lunch. They loved it and I loved it. It let me pay back for all the things they do for me, you know. And that [the system change] was a big blow to me. Now they bring out a sandwich, and I make up some tuna fish and something to eat.

Guests to the Dining Room were scanned as a guest meal to be charged to the resident; guests could not pay for themselves at the Dining Room. Also, any unused meals by residents resulted in a small refund, but they could not be used by anyone else, and there were no more bonus meals. These changes affected patterns of guest invitations and personal systems of reciprocity.

Family gatherings, of course, were still important. All but one of the women mentioned celebrating holidays and other special occasions with children and other family members, but had long relinquished the coordination of such gatherings to their daughters or daughter-in-laws. A couple of the women mentioned that they were not able to get to a family gathering due to physical difficulties. At Thanksgiving, Mrs. Stokes did not join her daughter, because she could not make it up the steps to her daughter's house. Mrs. Provost's back and legs kept her from making the two-hour drive to her family's place. Both had their Thanksgiving dinner at Colonial Square.

Over the life course, women referred to social expressions of affection and compassion through food, such as gift giving and charitable work, mostly in donations to a food bank, though three women mentioned involvement with Meals on Wheels. All but one of the women talked about bringing food to someone in times of sickness or a death in the family, usually either a casserole or baked goods. Some participants mentioned such rituals had changed since moving to Colonial Square, in that they did so less often, partially because it was a fairly common occurrence at Colonial Square for someone to be ill or have a death in the family. Mrs. Richardson stated that she did not bring food to a grieving person at Colonial Square, because the provision of food and meals at Colonial Square negated the helpful aspect of bringing food to a grieving person. Mrs. Richardson therefore expressed her sympathies by offering her companionship and prayers.

Not all the women threw themselves into and enjoyed feeding others to the creative extent of Mrs. Randall. For many, cooking was more a matter of obligation and doing what was expected of them. They saw it as part of their job description as a wife and then as a mother, the theme of this next section.

Dietary Duty: Fulfilling the Role of Wife and Mother

I believe that the ability to prepare and serve good and attractive meals is a delightful feminine virtue. (Vanderbilt, 1961, p. vii)

Figure 4.4: Mrs. Brown's Recipe for Chili

<u>Chili</u>

1 pound ground beef
1 medium onion chopped
1 can condensed tomato soup
Chili pepper
1/2 can water
1 large or 2 medium cans red kidney beans
Catsup

Brown beef and chopped onions. Season with chili pepper. Add tomato soup and water. When well mixed, add kidney beans - including liquid - add 2 or 3 dashes catsup (add another 1/2 can water if needed).

Microwave's the best thing. And the coffeemaker. And I haven't even had the stove on except to heat the soup. I don't think I've ever had the oven on. I would say about maybe a third of the people prefer to fix their own breakfast or a meal, and there are a few who love to do baking. Just bake every day. But I don't - that's one reason I came around here, so I wouldn't have to cook. I've done my duty. (Mrs. Brown)

Mrs. Brown's last sentence in this quote succinctly expressed her current philosophy regarding involvement in food preparation: "I've done my duty." This philosophy did not develop overnight, but rather came about over time and was a fitting conclusion regarding all her years of putting in her time in the kitchen. It reflected a view of cooking in which she did what had to be done, because it was expected of her in her role as a wife and a mother. She did not resent meeting the expectations of her role nor did she consider that there could be any other way. That was life, and as a wife and mother, she shopped, cooked, and fed her family. She could do no less. She did not have to do more, however, and if the opportunity arose to do less, and it still allowed her to meet the demands of her role, then she gladly took it. For Mrs. Brown, preparing and serving meals was neither delightful nor a virtue, as suggested by Vanderbilt (1961). It was, however, definitely feminine.

Mrs. Brown was 90 years old and widowed for three years. She moved to Colonial Square a year ago, which she felt was "a logical thing to do," as her sons were beginning to worry and she not only did not want to cook, she also did not want to do as much housekeeping. Cooking did not really become a part of Mrs. Brown's life until she was married. She grew up in the South, the oldest of four children. Her experience in the kitchen was limited, as her mother "didn't particularly let us help very often." She remembered that around the age of 11 or 12, she started making an angel food cake every Saturday for the family to eat on Sunday. As far as learning to cook, she conjectured: "But my mother was an excellent cook and I guess I just picked up a lot of things just from watching her - never did a lot of it at home." She recalled that her mother served well-balanced meals, always having a meat, potatoes, a green vegetable, salad, and, of course, a dessert.

After graduating from high school, Mrs. Brown enrolled in a nearby university. This was during the Depression, however, and after her third year, she could no longer afford to attend college. She left school and worked for a few years before getting married and becoming a full-time homemaker. She really learned to cook when she married, now that it was her responsibility as a wife and soon as a mother. She thought there was some difference in cooking when a couple is first married and when they began to add children to the family: "I think you take a little more care with what you did and maybe had slightly more elaborate recipes. Then with the children you definitely tried to make balanced meals and learned to cook in quantity..."

As Mrs. Brown's family grew, eventually four sons rounded out the household. By then, cooking for her family had "just become such a matter of habit." Chili was a meal that was quick and easy to prepare, a mainstay for her family, and something her children all liked. It made a regular appearance at the dinner table, showing up, in Mrs. Brown's estimation, about twice a month. She generally tended toward the quick and easy when it came to food preparation: "When I was working and the kids were growing up...after that I did anything that was easy. It's amazing how many things developed in the food field that you could do real quickly too." Appreciative of box mixes and canned foods, she took advantage of changes in the food industry that kept her from having to prepare foods from scratch. She wished that technology had developed a little sooner though: "The crock pot and the microwave came along just as everybody left, and I said, if we'd only had those when the kids were all here, it'd been much easier."

Mrs. Brown continued to prepare the same type of meals that her mother had prepared, serving well-balanced dinners of meat, potatoes, vegetables, salads, and desserts (according to Mrs. Brown, "A meal's not a meal without dessert."). Peanut butter was a staple for the boys and for one in particular. She recalled that one son lived for two years on raisin bread, peanut butter, and milk, with the occasional hamburger. This did not bother Mrs. Brown though: "I was glad that he'd eat that...I figured he was getting plenty to eat. By that time I was on the theory that they'll get by." She performed other food-related duties, obligingly participating in PTA bake sales and contributing to church cookbooks. Mrs. Brown returned to work after her youngest son started school, which also fueled her desire for quick and easy meal preparation. Being creative was not a priority. During these years, the Browns only occasionally entertained, because Mrs. Brown was too busy to do much entertaining. They occasionally ate out; they also belonged to a country club, where they ate about once a week.

As her children began to leave home one by one, she further altered her attitude towards her cooking responsibilities:

> And then, of course as they gradually went away, well, and then I went to work too, why, I started doing the easiest things, sort of quick things. I think that really the time that I began to loose my grip, or whatever you want to call it - became more disinterested - was when the two younger boys were both in college and I'd fixed dinner as usual and one of them said, "I've got a meeting and I can't stay," and the other said, "Well, I promised somebody I was

going to do such and such." So I said, "No more cooking for you all." If they were going to be there, we'd work something out. But be sure they ate a good substantial lunch at school. Not from the vending machine, but an actual lunch. I'd have things on hand if they wanted to have something, but they were active in so many things and they were gone a lot.

Although her younger sons were still living at home, their schedules and activities were such that there was no need for her to put the effort into preparing something for them, and it was easier and more efficient for her to keep foods on hand rather than prepare full meals for them.

Eventually all her sons left home, and she and Mr. Brown were living alone. She felt that things fell into more of a normal routine with regard to meals. A period of additional change occurred, when they ate out more often: "For a while there, just shortly after they were gone and while we were both still were working and then when I first retired, because I retired before Al, we ate out some. As my husband said, I could make three meals out of what I brought home in a doggie bag. Really we did use those a lot." They also began to eat a lot of soups. But there was a reason it was only for a while that they ate out: "After Mr. Brown's health started to decline, we stayed home more. It was good, just more a matter of a routine type meal. Can't even remember what all we had. I still fixed the chili though - he liked the chili." After Mr. Brown died, she consciously thought about her eating practices:

Well, the one thing I did try to do - because I had told so many other people that you must do it - was to eat three even fairly light meals a day. See, now I've changed it since I now only eat two. But I always felt that was an important thing to do. I mean light ones, I would say. And not stand over the sink and eat a cracker with peanut butter on it, but to sit down...

Although she only ate two meals a day at Colonial Square, she made sure she was ready in time each morning to have a substantial meal at the continental breakfast served in the Dining Room and then had either lunch or dinner in the Dining Room. She stocked little food in her apartment, and her typical supply consisted mainly of soups, crackers, cheeses, bread, butter, and carrots, with milk, juice, coffee, tea, and hot chocolate for beverages. Regarding her typical food reserve, she said:

> Well, I just keep some so in case I - if I think I'm going to eat a scant dinner, then I have some to fix for lunch, and if I eat the lunch, then I'll simply have maybe just a soup and crackers or something. I really find that just breakfast and either lunch or dinner is sufficient.

As remarked earlier, she greatly appreciated her microwave and coffeemaker, but used her stove only to heat pre-made soup. She had little cookware and gave away all of her cookbooks, because she had no need, and no desire, to cook anymore. She seemed satisfied with her food options in the Dining Room; her only critique was that the selection of vegetables was sometimes not to her liking.

Mrs. Brown observed that her responsibilities as a wife and mother were common, at least in her family: "I think we all of us assumed about the same responsibilities. Those were years when you did. Even if you worked outside the home, you were the one responsible for the home." As far as her food-related responsibilities, she did not particular enjoy them, but they never posed much of a problem for her. She did not mind cooking, "it was just one of those things you do." Since she did her tour of duty in the kitchen, however, she was content to let someone else take charge.

It was no revelation that the women of this study were expected to do the cooking and other food work of their household because of their female gender. Ms. Carr was young when her mother died, and after, as the only other female in the family, she assumed her mother's domestic responsibilities:

> It was really - I mean, I don't mean that it was cruel, but the woman of the family was expected to do the cooking and house-like duties and it didn't matter how old or young the girl was. I was only 13, not quite 14, when Mother died. And I assumed the responsibility, almost seemed to believe it was an honor.

Ms. Carr's case was unusual among the group, as the only one who experienced the death of a mother at a young age and subsequent assuming of the family's domestic duties, but she illustrated the role of the head female of a household. The women accepted their responsibilities and in turn did not expect that men would assist them or be involved in food chores. Regarding her first husband's involvement in food preparation, Mrs. Provost remarked, "He had such long hours and I never expected him to [help with meals]. I thought that was my range."

For half of the women, their cooking careers could be characterized like Mrs. Brown's: one in which they merely did their duty as the woman of the house. They had no particular interest in cooking, as communicated so clearly by Mrs. Adams: "I'm not a - someone who just really loves to cook. To me, cooking's [a] means to an end." Overall, a number of the women had few responsibilities in the kitchen as girls, despite future expectations that they would be running their own kitchens one day, among other domestic chores. Several explained simply that their mothers did not have them help much in the kitchen. Many of them recalled providing minimal assistance, such as setting the table, washing dishes, and sometimes chopping food or stirring pots. Some women, similar to Mrs. Brown, would bake cakes, pies, or biscuits.

Birth order was used in various ways to explain why they did not help much in the kitchen. Some explained that as the oldest, they were too busy helping to take care of the younger ones to help in the kitchen. Others explained that as the youngest, their older sister got the benefit of helping their mother in the kitchen. More than a few admitted that as young girls, they were not that interested in cooking anyway. Some never really became that interested as they matured and left their parents' home, beyond what they felt they had to do for their families and the obligatory social functions that involved food.

As a result of their inexperience in food preparation during childhood, two-thirds of them really learned how to cook when they married, just as Mrs. Brown did. Mrs. Jergens only knew how to make salads; as a girl, that was her contribution to family meals. As it was for others, cooking on her own was somewhat trial and error: "And I ruined one meal...I didn't have anything that was worth eating. We just sat there and laughed. Nothing, *nothing* was any good." Roughly a third of the women mentioned getting a cookbook, such as the *Joy of Cooking* or *Better Homes and Gardens*, from which they learned. Mrs. Randall learned to cook meat from the butcher at the market she went to after she first got married. Three women avoided cooking for six months to several years, because they were living with in-laws or parents. Only Mrs. Stokes seemed to mind this, as she did not like her father-in-law's cooking. All in all, the ones who learned to cook as they began to set up house were fairly resourceful in how they learned. They essentially did what needed to be done to feed their families, and what was expected of them when there was obligatory cooking as for a potluck or bake sale.

As children grew up and left home, cooking often became less of a priority. A couple women spoke of eating out more, as Mrs. Brown and her husband did. Mrs. Richardson and her husband ate out most of the time after they retired. Regarding the move to Colonial Square, Mrs. Brown was not alone in her current view of cooking; quite a few of the women appreciated that they no longer had to cook much:

> I still fix breakfast and we eat a good breakfast usually. And then I fix lunch. And if I feel like cooking, I make something that, you know, requires a little doing...Now, I do enough cooking just, you know, being in the kitchen that I don't miss [it] and every afternoon at about four-thirty or five o'clock, I think, oh, isn't wonderful not to have to think about dinner. (Mrs. Nichols)

> You'll be sitting at a table and everybody's just fussing about the food, and I'll think, I didn't have to cook it and I don't have to wash the dishes. Enjoy it. (Mrs. Richardson)

> I would have to work all day and then come home at night and fix three or four dinners. And the joy of cooking sort of left, and it got to be kind of a chore. So I'm very happy here that we can go downstairs and eat. (Ms. Carr)

One participant found an additional reason to exult in her freedom from cooking for her family:

> Mrs. Faust: Phil loves fish. In fact, that's one of my joys out here. He used to want fish all the time, and I didn't - wasn't - well, I don't care a whole lot for fishy fish.
> LC: So an advantage for you of living here then is that he can eat what he wants and...

Mrs. Faust: He can eat whatever he wants, and I can eat whatever I want. And that really is a joy.

As a married woman, Mrs. Faust was now able to eat only the foods she liked, avoiding the foods she did not but that her husband preferred. Some of the single women also appreciated being relieved of some of their cooking duties, because they did not like cooking for one. Ms. Carr, for example, upon retirement began to pull away from cooking: "It became more and more, easier let's say, more and more often to go out and get something to eat than for me to go out and buy the groceries and come home and cook for one." It seemed that changing family and work roles played a large part in the women's dietary experiences.

Summary

The important overall point of this chapter is that the dietary approaches of the women and their resulting dietary behavior are better understood in terms of their life course experiences. For example, food moralities may be developed at young ages and carried throughout life. They may also be developed later in life, in response to aging and health changes. The extent to which nutrition is an integral aspect of dietary behavior might be influenced by the extent to which it matters to family members, because of a health crisis or a lifestyle choice, for instance.

Of the four themes, dietary duty was the predominant theme, characterizing about half of the women. They had performed according to their role requirements, but it was a responsibility that they easily relinquished. All of the women had a sense at a basic level that shopping for and preparing food for their husbands, children, and/or other family members was their duty, but there were some for whom food and eating was more socially oriented, some for whom food and eating were important regarding health and wellness, and a couple for whom food preparation (and consumption) was regulated by moral imperatives.

The women who exemplified each of the four approaches represented somewhat of an extreme of the particular theme. Yet these themes were found running in and out of each of the women's stories of their lives in various manifestations, degrees of strength, and at various times. Mrs. Vossler's experience could be described as dietary duty until she moved to Colonial Square; this residential transition resulted in a change, where her experience was more a combination of dietary wellness (now that she was close to her vegetarian daughter) and a variation on the theme of dietary sociability (cooking and eating with others). Mrs. Burkholt's experience was much more stable, with little variation in her preferences and practices over her lifetime, and she truly seemed to fall into a dietary version of the saying, "The more things change, the more they stay the same."

Early life experiences, relationships, work and family roles and transitions in roles, residence, and health seemed to have influenced the dietary experiences and behavior of the women in this study. It also influenced the meaning associated with food and eating practices, which was reflected in their various approaches to food and eating. These findings, along with the findings of Chapter Three regarding the various levels of social influence, are discussed in the next chapter.

Chapter Five
Discussion: Interpretations & Theory Development

Levy (1981) advocated using personal narratives as a key to understanding consumer behavior and contended that marketing research needed to uncover the meaning and significance of foods, rather than simply survey people about product attributes. Levy (1981) suggested:

> One way to interpret consumer behavior is to consider consumer protocol (remarks made by people about their attitudes and behavior and those of others) as a kind of story to be interpreted, not so much for the facts of consumption, but for an understanding of why a consumer tells a particular tale and what it reveals beyond its literal meaning. (p. 97)

> Through the narrative, we see the organization of the behavior, its justifications, and something of the processes by which sheer sensation is made so strangely human. (p. 106)

Similarly, through the narratives of the older women who participated in this study, one can see the organization of dietary behavior, its justifications, its processes and its significance beyond actions themselves.

The narratives in particular illustrated the influence of life course factors in developing and modifying the participants' dietary behaviors and the importance of social situations as past and present influences on dietary practices. Intrapersonal processes, such as beliefs and attitudes, were relevant, but social experiences interacted with and affected personal processes over the lifetime to form current dietary practices. This chapter discusses interpretations of the findings of Chapters Three and Four, situates the findings in previous literature, and presents a theoretical model based on the findings, using a life course perspective and integrating elements of symbolic interactionism.

Social Influences on Dietary Behavior: Development and Maintenance

One of the goals of this research was to explore how social milieu affected the development and maintenance of dietary behaviors of older women over their life course. Most of the women perceived social experiences, especially family life, as highly influential on dietary behavior and this influence spanned from early in the life course through later years. References to upbringing, parents, other significant family members (e.g., grandparents), and the types of foods and meals served in their childhood were common and regarded as the basis of current preferences and practices (even if such behaviors represented a rejection of childhood experiences). Participants recalled eating as children the same food that their parents or grandparents ate, with little choice in what they consumed. They were socialized regarding food in various ways; for example, Mrs. Provost's affinity for good Southern cooking was a result of her upbringing and developed as an aspect of her regional and cultural identity.

The women were most strongly socialized in the well-balanced meal concept and the serving of meat, potatoes, and vegetables for a main meal. This lifelong preference for a meat-potatoes-vegetables main meal is a prime example of the influence of early life experiences. This was usually the type of main meal that was served to them as children, that they served to their families (often with the addition of salads), and that they now expected to have in old age. Notions of what constitutes a proper meal expanded for the participants, but the meat, potatoes, and vegetables meal was still the preferred "proper" meal, with contemporary versions of main meals gaining in acceptance, but not fully incorporated into the diet. More contemporary types of meals and foods, such as sandwich wraps, were just not in their repertoire of preferred foods. This meal type preference illustrates a distinct period effect, as the meat-potatoes-vegetables meal option pervaded American society as the ideal of a balanced diet during their younger years.

Because the meat-potatoes-vegetables main meal was considered to be a well-balanced meal, it was therefore nutritionally sound. Nutritional concepts learned earlier in life frequently provided the foundation for ideas about nutrition for most of their life, with a few exceptions. Mrs. Ford believed that her training in nutrition in college, particularly using the food groups, to prepare well-balanced meals had been the biggest influence on the way she ate. Others cited the well-balanced meal concept as the basis of their nutrition concepts, learned from parents and health classes in high school and college. A number of women reported trying to keep up, at least somewhat, with changing dietary recommendations.

The addition of salads to the main meal perhaps reflected the increasing emphasis of dietary recommendations on food groups (and number of fruit and vegetable servings) that began when they were young wives (Davis & Saltos, 1999). However, the nutritional skepticism exhibited by the elders in McKie et al.'s (2000) research was also found among the participants of this study, as several of these women questioned the reliability of nutrition information and contrasted nutrition advice with personal experiences. That recommendations did change, combined with evidence to the contrary (e.g., someone they knew who had regularly consumed fatty meat and had a long life), caused several of the women to mainly trust the one premise that they had always known, that seemed to remain constant among the various versions of dietary recommendations, and that had essentially become habit to them: the well-balanced meal of meat, potatoes, and vegetables. Additionally, these women were already in middle age when the media and public really made nutritional science a topic of everyday conversation. Several women noted that no one discussed issues of cholesterol, fats, and sodium when they were younger. This demonstrates a cohort development added onto period effects.

The influence of early life can also be seen in their approaches to food and eating. For example, a few of the women had developed a dietary morality regarding wasting resources, particularly food, at a young age, socialized into this orientation by their parents and influenced by the events of the Depression. This moral imperative was an underlying principle regarding their food consumption throughout life, affecting both their actions and feelings toward food and waste even now. However, this moral principle was not considered to have been always passed on to children, and in some cases, the women purposely did not emphasize the food waste rule to their children, believing that it was better for children to not be forced to eat food, but only try food. This could partially be the result of post-World War II affluence, when many of the women were raising children, and when abundance in resources did not necessitate the conservation efforts required of families during and before the war. Therefore, ultimately economic forces could have altered the transmission and socialization of this particular food morality to the next generation. Moral meanings of food and eating are further discussed later in this chapter.

Findings such as these are consistent with the findings of Devine et al.'s (1998) study of fruit and vegetable trajectories. The lasting "food roots" from early life experiences and food upbringing as a key influence were two of their findings that accurately describe social influences uncovered in this research. Additionally, Lupton (1996) had contended that childhood patterns of dietary preferences and practices never completely disappear, based on her research and her assessment of others' research. The findings of this research also appear to support the contentions that childhood is a critical period for the development of health behaviors. Although parents were predominant influences, other family members such as grandparents were recalled as influences also, indicating that a focus in research on parents alone might be misleading or at least incomplete. Socialization processes regarding food began in childhood for the participants, as parents and family modeled dietary behavior, although a lack of choices regarding food indicates a social control mechanism. Clearly, the social relations that are connected with food early in life were influential.

Social Relationships and Interaction

Family relationships in childhood were apparently quite important as influences on the development and maintenance of dietary behavior.

Relationships with spouses and children also played a role in the women's evolving dietary behavior. Food preferences of husbands and children to some degree influenced what the women ate when they were raising their families. In the women's later years, adult children became a source of nutritional information for some, whether offering advice on how to eat or introducing them to vitamin and mineral supplement use. Adult children could also be an influence on food consumption; Mrs. Vossler, for example, had come to appreciate meatless meals because of her vegetarian daughter. However, she continued to consume her well-balanced meals when eating in the Dining Room with other residents. This suggests that dietary practices might be adapted depending on the relationship with the mealtime companion and/or on the social situation, consistent with Connors et al.'s (2001) research. Mrs. Vossler had additionally mentioned that her husband never would have tolerated a meatless meal. Social support of husbands regarding dietary practices might have also played a role. This is further illustrated in the mutually supportive relationship of Mrs. and Mr. Wilson and how they have continued with the dietary changes made after his heart surgery.

Interactions with health professionals have influenced practices for some, most notably in terms of vitamin and mineral supplementation. Health professionals had recommended a few alternative dietary treatments for illness, such as green tea or cranberry juice. This possibly suggests that social support from doctors and other health professionals could have positive effects on the practices of older adults, although this could alternatively represent a cohort effect, whereby the perceived authority of doctors and health professionals is deferred to by this generation of women. The finding is consistent with Holmes and Gates' (2003) research, in which health professionals emerged as an influence on older men's eating habits, and Weng et al.'s (2004) research, in which a majority of respondents reported that their doctor advised supplementation.

Relationships with other older women and residents were another source of nutritional information, but social interaction with friends and other residents were also an important part of dietary experiences for the participants. The Dining

Room afforded opportunities for mealtime companionship at least once a day. Social arrangements related to dining at Colonial Square reflected a loose social organization of these relationships, as some women joined certain companions or groups in the Dining Room, and others avoided attaching themselves to groups. A few women mentioned that there were residents who they particularly avoided sitting with at mealtimes, generally because the resident was perceived as being a negative person. Although the details of the social organizational aspects of retirement community life that Keith Ross (1977) had observed in France were different from what was reported and observed at Colonial Square, the Dining Room at Colonial Square was the main arena for public contact among residents, and a central place for meeting other residents, as it was at Les Floralies. However, residents at Colonial Square did not all dine at the same exact time as they did at the noon meal at Les Floralies and so social integration (or lack of integration) was not quite the public display that it was a Les Floralies.

Connors et al. (2001) emphasized the part that social relationships play in how adults managed their food choices and dietary behavior, indicating that consideration of others' food preferences, even if they represent conflicting food values, takes priority, especially for women, who tend to be more accommodating. This consideration helps ensure that social interaction at meal times is pleasant. Mrs. Faust had pointed out that in this past she had accommodated her husband's food preferences, but now no longer needed to because of the ability to select different foods in the Dining Room. This suggests that the Dining Room has an additional role in facilitating management of food values while maintaining harmony in social relationships.

Mrs. Randall exemplified how social relationships were an important motivation behind the development and use of her culinary talents, shaping her social orientation toward cooking and food preparation. But her cooking also was an aspect of her social roles, whether as an army officer's wife or a church cook. Social relationships entailed associated social roles, which also emerged as significant influence on dietary practices.

Social Roles and Statuses

In their role as parent, some women acknowledged attempting to positively influence their children's eating and to teach them to eat good (healthy) foods, through modeling healthy eating and socializing children in principles of nutrition and balance. For the participants of this study, this often meant relying on the well-balanced meal, but for Mrs. Ford, for example, it meant actively teaching principles of nutrition and use of the food groups. This supports Lupton's (2000) findings, in which parents saw themselves as responsible for their children having a healthy diet. Mrs. Wilson still tried to emphasize healthy eating to her grown children and even grandchildren, but for a few, roles in this sense have reversed, as the adult children, particularly daughters, are conveying nutritional advice to their parents and watching after the health of their parents, sometimes by monitoring how they are eating.

Gender effects on practices were detected among the participants, particularly in terms of social and family roles. The women of this study generally had traditional roles as wives and mothers, and even Ms. Carr, who never married, took over homemaking duties after her mother passed away. Food preparation was a central obligation in the role of wife and/or mother (or female head of household). Husbands' occupations sometimes added the responsibility of hostess to their job description as wife, as occasionally their spouses' careers required at-home entertaining of colleagues and business associates. Husbands' social activities, such as membership in a men's lodge, might have involved their wives in food work and hostessing for their groups. Similarly, children's activities, at school and/or extracurricular, might have involved them with PTAs, scouting, or fundraisers and associated food work.

A number of the women learned to cook when they married, in order to fulfill role expectations as a wife. The women who began their cooking careers in the theme of dietary duty generally carried that view of food preparation with them across their life course and disclosed the salience of their family role as it related to food activities of their household, as well as the obligatory nature of the performance of such activities. In this view, cooking was necessary because it was a role expectation of the mother, wife, or female head of the home, and while it was not to be resented, it also was not an activity that they reveled in; it was considered a fact of life. When duty demands lessened, however, the women acted accordingly, lessening their efforts. The relief of that duty for many of these women brought about a new freedom, not only from the chores, but also from having to put their preferences and wants on the "backburner." The duty to cook at Colonial Square was minimal and the duty-oriented women easily adjusted, happily turning that duty over to someone else. This is in contrast to the women in Gustafsson et al.'s (2003) study, for whom maintaining a traditional female role through cooking and homemaking functions was important and protected.

Marital status continued to play a part in dietary practices during the participants' residence at Colonial Square. The married women, though demands lessened due to the use of the Dining Room, continued to fill remaining food roles of the family. They attended to the other meals, and even when their husbands helped themselves in the kitchen, the married women made sure that their husbands had foods that could be heated up, dished out, or easily assembled. The men did not completely take over even non-main meal preparation. Food shopping was still generally in the women's domain, although Mrs. Florshiem's husband was the one exception, for whom shopping became an activity, something for him to do after he retired. He illustrated a possible reason why older retired men might become more involved in food purchasing, a finding by Schafer and Schafer (1989), who had thought it was perhaps because the men had more time. In this case, Mr. Florsheim had more time, but his wife turned over the responsibility so that he would have something productive to do with his time. It was not just having time; it was the meaning of what they did with their time. Additionally, Mrs. Faust articulated the idea that it was better if she did such things as shopping anyway, because she was better at it, a justification that has been found in the literature (Brown & Miller, 2001).

The widowed and single women were most minimally involved in food-related activities, with the exception of Mrs. Donovan, for whom baking was a hobby and leisure activity initiated in an attempt to fill the time that used to be consumed with caring for her husband before his death. Generally, the widows mirrored much of what was found in the literature about widowhood and dietary practices regarding the use of convenience foods and the lost meaning of cooking (Callen & Wells, 2003; Shahar et al., 2001; Sidenvall et al., 2000; Valentine, 1999).

The women did have the appearance of having a gatekeeper role in their families regarding food and eating as described by Lewin (1943), although it seemed to be somewhat of a false appearance, as put forth by McIntosh and Zey (1998). About a third of the women were homemakers and therefore were mainly economically dependent on their husbands; a few even spoke of having a food allowance or budget when they were in their early years of marriage. Additionally, many women did want to please and accommodate their families and showed some deference to their husbands' tastes, but also much deference to their children's expressed preferences. However, for some this accommodation needed to have its rewards, and when cost outweighed benefit for women such as Mrs. Brown, the effort put into food activities decreased. The gatekeeper role is not an accurate description for the married women in their residence at Colonial Square, as the food services department becomes the gatekeeper for main meals.

Learning to cook for such women came about because of a life course transition, becoming married, and demands generally lessened in response to life course transitions, such as child launching. Transitions from married to widowed also affected dietary practices. Life course transitions and such consequent effects on dietary patterns were additionally identified in this research.

Life Course Transitions: Modification of Dietary Behavior

A second aim of this research was to examine if and how life course transitions potentially modified dietary behavior. Several transitions appeared to alter dietary practices. Family life course transitions were important initiators of change. Marriage, for example, was the catalyst for some to learn how to cook. Although somewhat surprising to this researcher that they were not socialized more in actual cooking practices before then, this transition clearly had implications for their dietary behavior, thrusting them into a role that required them to be responsible for food duties that they had not previously had. Learning to cook and sometimes to shop were two changes that accompanied marriage. Because their husbands also enjoyed meals of meat, potatoes, and vegetables, cooking was not perceived generally as problematic, and few dietary differences were recalled.

The addition of children to a family introduced a resolve to teach proper eating behavior, as discussed above, and shifts in how and how much they cooked. The launching of children meant reduced quantities of food to prepare and an overall reduction in food preparation demands. The loss of a spouse or co-resident family members (as in the case of Ms. Carr) resulted in a number of changes and was a significant transition. Eating alone was a difficult adjustment, but one that was eased by eating in the Dining Room of Colonial Square.

For many of the participants, health-related transitions influenced their dietary practices. For some women, health-related changes might be rather subtle, and therefore not recognized necessarily as having much of an impact on dietary behavior, such as taking calcium supplements to treat (or prevent) osteoporosis. At least four women reported that changes in health that shaped dietary behavior, though the health transition could be a family member's; it did not have to be the woman herself who experienced a change in health. The change in the health of Mrs. Wilson's husband obviously had a large impact on both his and her dietary trajectories, changing the theme of her dietary life course into one of dietary wellness, in which healthy eating became a lifestyle and nutrition became a hobby. Mrs. Stokes and Ms. Carr's diagnosis of diabetes created a new dietary morality theme in their lives, where rules about good and bad foods became prominent.

The transformation of Mrs. Wilson's and her husband's diets demonstrated how life course transitions in the lives of significant others, most particularly family members, have the potential to result in alterations in behavior and approaches to food and eating. The occupational transition early in Mrs. Randall's husband's career began the evolution of Mrs. Randall from a country tomboy into the ultimate social hostess, who turned serving food to others into an art form. Subsequent career and residential transitions influenced the incorporation of regional foods and ways of cooking into Mrs. Randall's and her families' foodways. Changes in a husband's occupational trajectory variously affected the women who had been or were currently married. A husband's retirement resulted in a residential transition for a few of the women, either seasonal or permanent; for example, Mrs. Stokes and Mrs. Ford relocated to Florida, where they incorporated citrus and other Florida produce into their diets, and Mrs. Richardson moved to a southern Atlantic coastal town, which resulted in the incorporation of seafood into her diet.

The experiences of the women in this research are similar to those of the older adults of Quandt et al.'s (1997) study, in that they also perceived various processes that affected their current eating patterns, such as changes in work patterns, family life, health, and health awareness. Food had social meanings that related to gender and family roles for the respondents of Quandt et al.'s study, and life course changes in these roles brought about changes in meal patterns (e.g. the loss of a spouse, followed by fewer cooked meals), and in the social meanings of food and meals. This was confirmed in this research as well, with the women acknowledging changes in behavior and in social meaning associated with life changes.

Devine et al.'s (1998) results suggested that life course transitions are times when food choice systems may undergo change and illustrated the importance of role transitions and social status, especially familial. Role and family transitions, such as childbearing, marriage, divorce, employment, empty nest, and return nesters, affected fruit and vegetable trajectories in their study.

Similarly, the findings of this study indicated that family and occupational life course transitions affected dietary behavior, but residential transitions as an influence emerged from this research as well.

The dietary experiences of the participants during their residence at Colonial Square demonstrated that a residential transition to a retirement community, particularly one where dining services were available, had an effect, albeit in different ways, on the food- and eating-related experiences of the women and their current dietary behavior. The findings suggest that the ways in which the transition and the new social and environmental context affected the women depended on the previous life experiences of the women and then their particular experiences in that environment.

The Retirement Community: Shaping Current Dietary Behavior

The third aim of this research was to explore the influence of the retirement community environment in shaping dietary behavior. This study demonstrated that relocation to Colonial Square certainly and variously impacted the participants' dietary practices and experiences. The residential transition modified approaches to food; for example, Mrs. Vossler became much more socially engaged after her move to Colonial Square and this was reflected in her dietary experiences, as she emphasized dietary duty much less and dietary wellness and sociability much more. Meals and food-related responsibilities, such as grocery shopping, became social occasions for Mrs. Vossler, and her daughter's vegetarianism influenced her new nutritional awareness. Additionally, as mentioned, social opportunities and social relationships at Colonial Square influenced the social aspects of meal times.

A focus on living alone versus not living alone, which some studies have used, e.g., McIntosh and Shifflett (1984), would be too narrow to apply to the women of this study. Although some of them live alone, they still dine with others at least once a day and have interactions and relations with others (e.g. family members, health professionals) that have influenced them. Living alone might have fostered more reliance on convenience and frozen foods than if they lived with someone, but the community environment and their social network constitute a broader context that is important to take into account when examining the effects of living arrangements on dietary behavior of these older women. It also could be that gender made a difference, as Horwath (1989) contended, who also found that living alone did not adversely affect the diets of women. The findings regarding older women who live alone in this study additionally support the conclusions of research such as Schlettwein and Barclay's (1995).

In Asato's (1992) survey of residents of a retirement community, the residents averaged about four appliances per household, and the most frequently owned appliances were microwave ovens, coffeemakers, toasters, and blenders. The findings of this research are therefore consistent with Asato's findings regarding frequently owned appliances. The findings of this research are also consistent with some of Percival's (2002) findings regarding the use of domestic space for eating meals. A couple of factors influencing where the women ate in their apartments were comfort and suitable space, just as Percival had found. An additional factor, alluded to in Percival's research but not explicitly explored, is the notion of where it is "proper" to eat meals; a few of the women in this research believed that it was more proper to eat at a table than in front of the television, for example. Also similar to Percival's results, between one-third and one-fourth of the women regularly ate meals in their living room areas.

Percival's (2002) interviewees did have a concept of where it was proper to eat meals when having friends and family over, as seen in the preference for the more formal arrangement of dining at a table in the kitchen or dining room when guests visited. Those who lacked space or physical ability to entertain felt they had lost a meaningful role of host for family and friends. An advantage that the women of Colonial Square had, that Percival's respondents did not have, is the Dining Room of Colonial Square. The availability of dining services meant that those who no longer entertained due to their own or their apartment's limitations did not have to lose the role of host, as Percival's interviewees did, but could (and did) take guests to the Dining Room for meals. Although the change in the accounting procedures for using the Dining Room affected entertaining for some, most participants felt that the Dining Room was a very nice place to take guests.

How Colonial Square affected the participants' dietary practices could be considered in terms of how the community both liberated and constrained their dietary actions. In some ways, the structural characteristics of the community created new freedoms or liberations for the women, but in other ways created constraints that they had not previously known.

Structural Characteristics: Liberations

Several structural factors of the Colonial Square environment produced new liberations (or opportunities) for many of the women. These freedoms and enhancements included: freedom from food-related responsibilities and catering to family members' preferences, food security, social interaction opportunities, and easier entertaining.

All of the women cooked much less than they had before moving to Colonial Square, if they cooked at all. For some of the women, the Dining Room and meal service provided a new freedom from the chores of planning meals, cooking meals, and cleaning up from meals. Those women whose lives were characterized by dietary duty found this especially liberating, because, just as Mrs. Brown stated, they had done their duty. They were no longer in a role that prescribed they coordinate meal preparation and seemed to rather easily put as little effort as possible into the preparation of non-main meals. This also gave them more time to enjoy activities they really liked, more than cooking and baking, and/or released them from duties that became more physically difficult to perform.

The women who were still married discovered another new freedom related the freedom from cooking: the freedom from having to cater to the food preferences of family members. Mrs. Faust expressed this sentiment when she related her joy in not having to prepare fish for her husband any more. They could both eat whatever they wanted to eat at Colonial Square. As discussed previously, this allows Mrs. Faust to follow her own food values without concern that her relationship with her husband will be disrupted at mealtimes. This also indicates that a transition to such a community can instigate a re-construction of a couple's shared gastronomy, extending Paisley et al.'s (2001) findings. Because rules, norms, practices, and perhaps even meaning concerning food change after moving to Colonial Square, then the couple gastronomy necessarily changes as well. In this case, it becomes a more divergent or inclusive gastronomy, because although commensality continues, choice alters and the exact same foods no longer need to be eaten by the couple, at least in the Dining Room.

The liberation related to food security is more in the sense of a freedom from worry and fear. Food security in terms of having enough food is not the issue per se, but rather in terms of the ability to prepare food for oneself and others. Mrs. Vossler, for example, enjoyed the fact that a prepared meal was available whenever she needed it and all she had to do was walk downstairs. A couple of the married women took comfort in food security for their husbands, for whom a lack of skills, inclination, or physical strength would render them less able to prepare meals if their wives were not able to do so for them. For these women, the Dining Room was an insurance policy, guaranteeing that their husbands' dietary needs would be taken care of, should anything happen to them and their ability to perform their wifely duties. The dining services, combined with other services such as housekeeping, gave them some peace of mind about the care of their husbands, in terms of some instrumental activities of daily living.

For many of the women, the enhanced opportunities for social interaction were a very positive aspect of living at Colonial Square. Social activities involving food (a large portion of activities) provided social interaction. However, eating in the Dining Room was an important and main mechanism for social interaction for the women, and particularly for the widowed and single participants. The Dining Room was a place to not just have a meal, but to share a meal. They enjoyed the companionship of others at mealtimes. Residents visited with one another and caught up on daily happenings in other residents' lives and in the community. Current events might be discussed, but past history was just as likely to be discussed, thus reaffirming stories from the past and keeping memories alive. Cohort experiences might have also provided a sense of connection with others who could appreciate what it was like, for example, during World War II. The simple act of being with others (whose company they enjoyed) at meals was important and illustrated an important social function of mealtimes for many women. This is consistent with Russell and Porter's (2003) findings; although their research was of older men, it illustrated that eating was a social activity for them, and such an everyday activity held much social meaning, as it did for the women of this study.

Another social function of meals was being able to continue to practice the civilities associated with a meal. For some residents, this meant, for example, sitting down at a table and having a "proper" meal, instead of standing over the sink or in front of the television, eating cheese and crackers. In the Dining Room, residents dressed nicely, sat down with their companions, and ate a proper meal, even if this was not done for the other meals.

As previously mentioned, having an easily accessible place to eat such as the Dining Room additionally made entertaining easier for the women, even if it was only family that visited. Food and meals were an important aspect of entertaining guests. Residents of Colonial Square could bring their guests to the Dining Room to fulfill this entertaining obligation, instead of preparing meals and food at their home. Additionally, a couple of women had taken advantage of the private dining room for family functions. In this way, even for those for whom food preparation was difficult, they felt that they were able to continue to be hospitable to guests. It also met the needs of some for reciprocity purposes. By taking visitors to the Dining Room, some women were able to reciprocate for what others did for them. Mrs. Provost's fictive daughter shopped and ran errands for her. She took her to lunch often when she came to visit; Mrs. Provost considered it a nice treat to take her to the Dining Room and buy her lunch.

Structural Characteristics: Constraints

In some ways, structural characteristics put constraints on entertaining and reciprocity. Structural factors of life at Colonial Square also constrained the participants in terms of: a lack control over when and what they would eat, getting to meals, and social pressure/control (e.g., peer pressure to follow group norms or expression of paternalistic concern).

As for entertaining, there really was not enough physical space inside the apartments to have many people over at one time, although this seemed to be a more minor issue, as many of the women appeared to prefer not to put the effort into entertaining that they perhaps once had. Social reciprocity was not as easy to fulfill with dining services as it had been in the past, because of changes in the accounting system. The change to an electronic system and stricter enforcement of meal allocations meant that a few women were less likely to bring guests because they could no longer give away unused meals or extra lunch tickets.

A lack of a certain amount of control regarding dietary practices was another constraint resulting from features of the system at Colonial Square, and could be manifested in different ways for different women. To some extent the Dining Room hours and consideration of the perceived needs of the young men and women who worked in the Dining Room determined when the women dined. A continuous seating system as described by Nickels (2000) would alleviate the schedule constraints felt by some of the participants. What they ate was limited to what was offered and served in the Dining Room. For some women, this could create difficulties in terms of nutritional and medication management, personal preference, and personal control. A lack of control over items served could be problematic for someone like Mrs. Adams, who had to monitor her vitamin K intake, due to an anticoagulant medication she took. She was unable to control how many items high in vitamin K were served, and had difficulty determining how much of an item was served to her. Mrs. Wilson and Mrs. Richardson both preferred more green and leafy vegetables as menu items, for nutritional reasons.

Personal preferences played a role for Mrs. Ford, who finds the food preparation and options at Colonial Square to be different from what she is used to. This is likely due at least in part to regional differences in food preparation, and her taste for Northeastern styles of foods and food preparation. Actual item choices were limited, but more food than was normally consumed at home for a main meal was available. Having four courses, breads, and tempting desserts tested the willpower of several women, and a few gained weight. Because they could not control the amount and types of foods available to them, they tried to learn to better control their impulses, with varying degrees of success. Changes in quantities of food consumed for some and types of foods for others contradict findings such as Cluskey (2001b), whose survey of retirement community residents resulted in the finding that food intake had not changed as a result of living in the community. The types of questions asked and the survey method itself perhaps was inadequate to uncover changes in food consumption in Cluskey's study.

For older women such as Mrs. Stokes, the physical design of the building was a constraint in the sense that her long walk to the Dining Room required she left her apartment with enough time to make her journey, because of all the rest breaks she took along the way. This also meant that she did not venture to main public areas of the building often, as it was too tiring to go back several times a day. Physical design could be an issue even for those not as far from the Dining Room, as physical capacity and disability could make even short trips tiring. It seemed that in some ways living in such a retirement community offered less flexibility in accommodation of physical changes and lowering activities of daily living (ADLS) and instrumental activities of daily living (IADLS) with age as they influence dietary behaviors. This is one element for which living in an independent home in the larger community may be somewhat advantageous for an older person.

Social pressures put some level of constraint on the women. Pressure to conform to the dress code, although viewed by many of the women as appropriate, caused the need to account for a lack of close adherence to the code.

Mrs. Michaels offered her age and the physical difficulty of dressing as a justification for her leniency when it came to the dress code. Pressure from other residents regarding dietary behavior can also be perceived as intrusive. Ms. Carr expressed her perturbation with residents who found it their business to keep a watchful eye on her dietary practices, noting that she did not tell others what to eat or not eat. Her health conditions apparently prompted some residents to paternalistically monitor Ms. Carr's eating patterns. Although it did not necessarily mean Ms. Carr felt pressured to eat in a certain way, it could have added stress to an already stressful circumstance for her.

Further Considerations

As far as personal factors affecting dietary-related actions of the women, psychological processes appeared in the narratives, with references to moods, feelings, and personal preferences, but the women more frequently and strongly mentioned physical aging effects on their dietary practices. Physical mobility-related issues came out, such as shopping for food and getting to the Dining Room. So did issues related to the use of assistive devices, particularly the social stigma of dependence on such devices, presumably because the use of walkers, mobile electric carts, etc. represented morbidity, mortality, and perhaps less than successful aging in the eyes of other residents.

The effect of health concerns and medical conditions on food choices and behaviors observed in some studies appeared to also affect the participants' dietary behavior, but to varying degrees (International Food Information Council, 2001; Rainey et al., 2000). Health concerns played a major role for Mrs. Wilson and her husband, because of his heart condition, whereas health concerns played a much lesser role for Mrs. Brown, who simply took a multivitamin for her health, because her doctor recommended it and she thought it was a good idea since she was getting older. All the women in the study took vitamins regularly, and past studies have shown that being female and Caucasian is associated with supplementation (Daniel et al., 1995; Weng et al., 2004).

Aging had a non-physical effect in the sense that at least two women acknowledged their age as a license to break food rules, according to an internalized food morality of what one should and should not eat. Food and moral meaning did emerge in the narratives of the participants, in terms of a food morality developed earlier in life regarding wasting food and then later in life regarding foods that are good and bad for one's physical health, which in essence reflected one's moral health. These findings confirm Manton's (1999) assertion that guilt is usually first linked with food in childhood, due to parents' tales of starving children and emphasis on the importance of not wasting food. They also provide further proof for the existence of the "should syndrome" identified by Paisley et al. (2001). Lupton (1996) discussed a moral discourse in which the consumption of "bad" foods was a sign of moral weakness. This too is indicated in the narratives of some of the women, particularly in the use of religious language to convey the consumption of "bad" food and the concomitant breaking of a rule, e.g., "sinning" by eating dessert.

Social rules are culturally defined ways of ordering life, and the rules identified in this research are perhaps strongly associated with not only the individual's own cultural identity in life (e.g., Southern, Anglo-American, Protestant), but with the local culture of the retirement community (e.g., dress code), and even the regional culture of Lexington or Kentucky. Such rules are intimately related to a person's cultural identity and mediated by a host of other cultural factors that are part of the person's lived environment. Additionally, food and eating identities of the women came out in the research, also related to "rules" and particularly found in the dietary themes that characterized the women and their approaches to food and eating; these approaches spoke to who they perceived themselves to be in relation to food and eating - dietary self-concepts – and the research demonstrated that the development of these self-concepts had various influences. This is in line with Bisogni, Connors, Devine, & Sobal (2002, p. 135) study of identities in food choice, in which they found "that a person constructs her/his own identities related to eating and that the sources of these identities may be eating practices, personal characteristics, and reference groups and social categories."

It should be noted that I have discussed only a few of many possible dietary rules. Additional rules regarding dietary behavior might include the importance of certain meals (e.g., the noon meal is the main meal), the timing of meals (e.g., some cultures would not think of eating dinner/supper until just before bed), or the content of meals (e.g., all dinners must have soup and bread).

The themes of dietary morality, dietary wellness, dietary sociability and dietary duty reflect meanings assigned to food and eating practices by the women, which impacted their approaches to dietary behavior performance. Meaning therefore can be a very important influence, which in turn is influenced by varied social factors. This is consistent with Connors et al.'s (2001) findings:

> Meanings of foods and food categories can and did change with new information, new situations, new relationships, and new environments...When change or new information was introduced into people's lives, they struggled and redefined what was acceptable behavior and when or what values became most important, what foods fit into various categories, and even what constituted a meal. People brought skills that they had acquired throughout their lives to the re-defining process. They acquired information from professionals, the media, and through dialogue with friends and family. These resources enhanced their possibilities in redesigning a workable personal food system. (p. 198)

One can see the experiences of the women in this research mirrored in the experiences of Connors et al.'s participants.

There are a number of additional significant linkages that can be made between the findings of this research and of previous research. Regarding dietary behaviors of older adults, several points made in the literature showed up in the data from the participant sample. In terms of food acquisition, shopping among the women who were physically capable was sometimes more of a leisure activity, whether shopping was enjoyed for the sake of the activity itself, seen by Bonnel (1999), or because of the company enjoyed on such trips, illustrating that shopping trips can be an avenue for social contact, as noted by Read and Schlenker (1993). For those who were more physically disadvantaged, shopping was problematic, because of lessened strength and stamina, also noted in the literature (Read & Schlenker, 1993; Sidenvall et al., 2001). The participants demonstrated a variety of strategies in acquiring and purchasing food, including the use of their own cars, use of the retirement community's transportation, going with family, friends, and neighbors, and having family, friends, neighbors, and/or a hired aide pick up items at the store. The use of employed workers was not a strategy commonly found in the literature.

Similar to the older women in Sidenvall et al.'s (2001) study, some of the participants purchased convenience foods, such as frozen dinners, to reduce food preparation work. Another way that participants made food preparation easier was by the use of the microwave oven, a strategy that appeared in Bonnel's (1999) research. Although meals structured the day for the participants as it did for the women in Brombach's (2001a) study of older German women, the structure was in some sense imposed because of the set hours during which they could eat in the Dining Room, as it was for Gubrium's (1975/1997) participants. The women therefore accordingly structured the timing of their meals based on when they planned to have their main meal and when they could have their main meal, incorporating personal preference for timing of meals to the extent that they could.

With a few exceptions, the participants ate three meals a day, and all had breakfast, which are reported common patterns for older adults (Read & Schlenker, 1993). The exceptions were two participants who generally ate two meals a day and one who sometimes had four small meals a day. However, of those who reported three meals a day, a number had at least one meal that was considered a light meal. The heaviness or lightness of meals of older adults has not been widely investigated.

Occasionally, the participants consumed meals away from home. For Mrs. Adams, it was a weekly ritual with her family, eating either at her daughter's home or going out to eat. Mrs. Randall and her husband generally ate out each week after church. For most of the participants, eating out at a restaurant was not a common occurrence; some preferred to eat with family and friends in the Dining Room than to go out to eat. The participants of this study were not compared to younger age groups, but their patterns on the whole support findings that older adults do not eat out very much (Paulin, 2000; Wakimoto & Block, 2001). Fast food was infrequently mentioned and even looked down upon by at least three of the participants, one of whom said she had fast food only because her sons took her to get fast food, but it would never be her choice. Note that this illustrates a compromise in food values due to social relationships, as in Connors et al.'s (2001) research; thus, the Colonial Square Dining Room does not solve all food value issues for the women.

Development of a Theoretical Model

The findings and previous discussion indicate that social influences throughout life, including earlier life experiences, affect the development of behavior, that life course transitions have the potential to modify behavior, and that the context of a living environment, such as a retirement community, can prompt the renegotiation of certain aspects of behavior for female residents. Taken together, these points suggest the usefulness of a life course perspective for understanding dietary behavior. Additionally, as the meaning associated with behavior is important to the performance (or non-performance) of behavior and an emphasis on roles and interaction emerged as important influences, a framework such as symbolic interactionism provides valuable elements to incorporate into a life course perspective. Therefore, in an effort to advance theorizing in health behavior and aging, focusing on dietary behavior, a theoretical model of influences on older women's dietary behavior, utilizing primarily a life course perspective and integrating symbolic interactionist elements, is developed out of the data from this research.

This model of processes of influence on dietary behavior is socially focused, derived from the findings of the study, and guided by the theoretical foundations of this research. The model has five components: Precursor Influences, Filters, Actions, Outcomes, and Feedback Influences. The precursor influences consist of four elements: the person, social roles, social relations, and contexts. Filters include temporal processes and meaning systems. Actions involve the dietary practices as performed by the individual, and outcomes are physical and psychosocial well-being, which ultimately contribute the individual's quality of life. The feedback influences indicate how processes of influence are not linear, but loop back on each other, such that the outcomes of behavior can affect behavior performance and/or the precursor influences. The behaviors themselves in turn can affect the precursor influences.

Figure 5.1: A Model of Influences on Dietary Behavior of Older Women

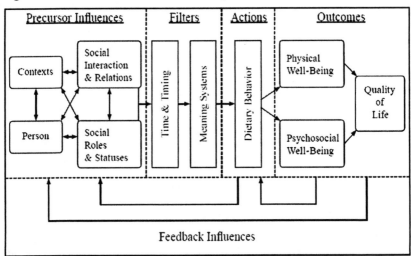

Precursor Influences

The precursor influences more fully encompass and feature various mechanisms of social influence than previous theories. The four elements of Person, Social Roles and Statuses, Social Interaction and Relations, and Contexts interact and reciprocally influence one another. Though social in focus, the model retains the potential for psychological and physiological influence, encapsulated under Person factors. The Person element groups together characteristics of the individual. Psychological processes encompass internal phenomena, such as cognitions, beliefs, feelings, and values, and includes personal preferences and tastes. Physiological processes are further included under this element. Physical aging, health and illness, and food sensitivities are clearly involved in behavior performance. However, these sets of processes interact with social factors and contexts. For example, a "taste" or preference for Southern food should also be interpreted as a socially constructed preference, because of regional context and socialization by significant others into that particular food culture.

Social Roles and Statuses refer to the positions within social systems that the individual occupies and the roles that may be attached to those statuses. For example, a participant may have been a wife and mother and therefore acted according to the role expectations of those family statuses. This element also includes the broader social categories of gender, seen as an influence in this study particularly as related to social roles, and presumably would include class and race as they affect roles and statuses.

Social Interaction and Relations embrace interpersonal processes that influence dietary behaviors. Social relationships and interactions reinforce patterns of stability or stimulate change in dietary behavior. This might occur through various mechanisms, such as socialization, social support, and social control. The others in these relations are frequently significant in some way, whether in power and authority and/or emotional attachment. The influence can result in a negative response on the part of the individual. For example, someone could model behaviors that the individual consciously rejects and decides not to imitate. Relationships are important influences on roles too, in that they to a large extent determine roles. For instance, one has the status and role of a wife only if one is in a social relationship with a husband. There may, however, be exceptions to this in lagged behaviors following life course transitions. A woman may publicly lose the role of wife, for example, with the death of a husband, but she may retain her personal identity as wife, with some associated behaviors, for some period of time as she adjusts to widowhood.

Contexts are the background influences such as place (the physical environment and geographic areas), culture, policy (from the level of national dietary recommendations down to Colonial Square regulations), and economics (market forces such as cost, availability, but also personal resources). The Colonial Square spatial and political environment is a context that exerts a strong influence currently on the participants, both constraining and liberating residents in the performance of dietary practices and modification of dietary patterns.

Filters

The two elements under Filters, time and timing and meaning systems, represent two particular processes by which the experiences of the precursor influences are "filtered" and ultimately affect behavior. The time and timing element represents, at one level, an intersection of age, period, and cohort effects, at another level, aspects of stability and change, and at a third level, the timing of transitions and events and duration within a particular state. The time and timing of the previous four elements affect how an individual responds to those influences. Continuing with the example of the role of a wife, the role may change with age (e.g., the wife role at 25 may be different from the wife role at 75) and it may change over historical time (e.g., the role of wife in 1950 is different from the role of wife in 2005). The timing of taking on the role of a wife has different effects, as becoming a wife at age 18 has different implications than becoming one at age 30, but the timing of losing the role and duration of time in the role may also be relevant.

Such influences of time, i.e., timing of a lost role in conjunction with duration in a role, may potentially be very important regarding the previously mentioned notion of lagged change in behaviors and adjustment processes. The widowed woman might have lost the role of a wife socially, but psychologically is still in the role and acts accordingly. As she mentally accepts her new social circumstances, her behaviors may then begin to alter at that time. Alternatively, there could be the potential for psychological disengagement from a role prior to the actual loss of the role and, in anticipation of the transition, the individual makes preparations for the change. Thus the individual could possibly modify behaviors before an actual event and/or transition occurs. An additional consideration regarding this particular filter is the time and the timing of events and transitions in the lives of others significant to the individual. As illustrated in this research, changes associated with husband's occupations and health affected the married woman and her behaviors.

The second filter consists of meaning systems. The meaning attached to influences and transitions, in other words, how they are interpreted and defined by the individual, will affect the meaning and performance (or non-performance) of the behaviors. As previously stated, the themes of dietary morality, dietary wellness, dietary sociability, and dietary duty reflect meanings assigned to food and eating practices, which impact approaches to dietary behavior performance. For example, moral meanings attached to food and eating, developed through social interactions with others (e.g., parents and health professionals) and according to the era (e.g., reinforced by the Depression), affected behavior performance (following or not following rules) and consequent feelings associated with behavior performance (e.g. guilt for breaking a rule). These feelings are an aspect of psychosocial well-being and ultimately quality of life.

Actions

Dietary behavior encompasses the food- and eating-related practices performed by individuals. This includes a wide range of behavior, from meal planning, food purchase, and food preparation, to actual eating and drinking (including the use of supplements), to aspects such as the storage of cookware and dressing for dinner. Meal schedules and social arrangements for dining are examples of temporal and social aspects of dietary behaviors.

Outcomes

Physical well-being encompasses the general condition and functioning of the body and its physiological processes. Good physical health indicates physical well-being and an overall lack of physical problems, whereas poor physical health, including illness and disease, indicates bodily problems. The meaning and definition of health, in terms of physical well-being, are also relevant to dietary behavior, as what constitutes "good" health is dependent to some degree on subjective interpretation.

Psychosocial well-being refers to the general condition and functioning of the individual's mind (internal state) and social relations and circumstances. Psychosocial well-being indicates psychological and social well-being and a general lack of problems and difficulties, whereas poor psychosocial well-being indicates psychological problems and/or difficulties in social relationships or situations. Again, people define psychological and social well-being in unique ways, and what may be a satisfactory social situation for one person maybe unsatisfactory for another.

Both of these concepts contribute to overall quality of life. Certainly dietary behavior as it contributes to good physical health and/or manages health conditions can lead to reduced morbidity, delayed mortality, and increased physical functioning - all aspects that can be factors in quality of life. However, for many people, there is more to life than living longer and in good physical health. It is as important (and for some people more important) to have psychosocial well-being, for which a concept such as life satisfaction is one indicator of this aspect of quality of life. Due to the profound social meanings and relevant social aspects related to food and eating and the psychosocial implications of food-related experiences, to be able to enjoy one's dietary practices and experiences can greatly contribute to psychosocial well-being and thus quality of life.

For example, for Mrs. Stokes, who sometimes broke her dietary rules regarding the management of her diabetic condition, it appeared that her psychosocial well-being, in terms of her enjoyment of food, was a more important contributor to her quality of life than physical well-being. It was sometimes more important in her view to enjoy food than to be concerned about possible physical consequences of not strictly adhering to her dietary regimen. She in part determined this through the lens of time; her age and the amount of time that she thought she likely had left in her life weighted psychosocial factors in quality of life issues as related to food.

Feedback Influences

As mentioned, the feedback loops indicate how processes of influence are not simply linear, but can be circular, such that the outcomes of behavior can affect behavior performance and/or the precursor influences, and behavior performance can affect the precursor influences. These loops add necessary complexity to the model, because of the non-linearity of interactions among the various components. The feedback mechanism also allows for greater ability to address temporal dynamics, for example, adjustment to life course transitions and events.

Summary

This theoretical model highlights social influences on dietary behavior, an aspect generally treated rather superficially in previous models applied to health behavior. It also incorporates temporal considerations, to account for change or stability over time, and meaning-making, reflective of the processes of interpretation applied to influences and behavior; these are again neglected facets in theorizing about health behavior. These aspects represent strengths of using a life course perspective, supplemented by symbolic interactionist elements, to better understand dietary practices of older women. To view behaviors in terms of quality of life issues further informs understanding at the concrete and theoretical levels.

A final point to bear in mind is that these influences can be in both positive and negative directions with regard to dietary practices. In other words, dietary actions or changes in dietary actions may be such that they worsen physical or psychosocial health, resulting in lessened life quality life, or they may improve physical and psychosocial health, resulting in overall improved quality of life. The model is at this time gender-specific and older adult-oriented. These are two possible limitations of the current form of the model, although there is not presently reason to think that it would not apply to men or other age groups. The limitations of the model are limitations of the research overall, which have implications for future investigations. These and other implications for research and practice are considered next.

Chapter Six
Conclusions

Dietary behavior occupies a very socially situated place in the lives of older women. This research showed that psychological and physiological processes are indeed relevant in understanding behavior over time, but cannot be divorced from social processes at both micro and macro levels of concern. Moreover, application of social theoretical perspectives proved useful in thinking about the development and progression of dietary practices. With these points in mind, I conclude, considering implications of this study for future research and practice. Additionally, as this research was about biographical stories of women and this book began with an autobiographical note, it seems appropriate to end autobiographically as well.

Implications for Research

A number of key elements emerging from this research would benefit from more focused study. Particular life course transitions or various sequences of transitions appear in this research as potentially strong factors influencing dietary behavior. For example, widowhood is a significant life course change that has repercussions for all facets of life, including food and eating. Such a transition causes immediate alteration in the social setting of meals, and there is evidence that loneliness impacts food preparation (e.g., less effort) and eating habits (e.g., perhaps increased food consumption if feeling bored or decreased food consumption if suffering from depression). The ramifications of widowhood for dietary practices, and potential alleviation of negative impact on practices, are only just beginning to be understood. In another example, residential transitions are inadequately addressed by research in terms of the effects on dietary patterns. These effects might stem from adjustments to new and different food choices, costs, areas of food preparation, or sociocultural milieus. This research showed some effects of a residential transition to a retirement community, but a specific focus on seasonal migration or transitioning to co-residency with an adult child could provide valuable additional insight to how residential change and adjustment potentially acts to modify dietary choices and behaviors.

Furthermore, such research could be expanded to explore the influence of other types of residential settings, as an increasing number of elders relocate to age-segregated communities. These communities evolve quite differently; there are numerous and varied models of retirement communities, based on an array of management styles with various food and dining service arrangements. Understanding how different features of these residential contexts affect the dietary practices and quality of life for residents can reveal which features may be more liberating, or at least less constraining, for residents.

Although this research included only women as participants, there was strong indirect evidence suggesting important gender differences. The roles and statuses of men, their social relationships, and the contexts in which men live might differentially influence their dietary behavior. Future studies should consider men and explicitly probe gendered life course elements. Such studies might shed valuable light on the notions of power in the family, and how power and control might shift through life, thus informing dietary choice, food preferences, and eating behavior. Likewise, studies that examine other social classes and races/ethnicities would be instructive for understanding variation in social experiences and the effects of life course factors and transitions. Differences in dietary behavior might be based on differences in factors such as upbringing, education, economic resources, and cultural identity.

An interesting idea which research might follow-up on regards how people deal with conflicting dietary rules (i.e., expressed normative perceptions and behaviors that are considered right or wrong, beneficial or deleterious). For example, a rule to clean one's plate might be based on long-term familial influence, but a local cultural rule is to eat only enough to satisfy the appetite. Which rule takes precedence? Individuals living in a retirement community that offers communal dining are immediately placed in conflict between rules of personal cultural identity and rules of the institution, and additionally with cultural norms of community and region if a distant residential relocation has occurred. How do they react to the conflicting rules? Given the duration of which elders have lived with their own rules, it might be conjectured that adjustment to different norms of behavior might be more difficult for them than for younger adults. Independently living elders (i.e., those living in their own homes as they have throughout life) do not have such conflicts to deal with. Their meals are basically private affairs and are governed by rules established almost solely within the family unit and/or maintained as individuals living alone. Such a line of research might be meritorious, not only theoretically in our understanding of cultural diversity and conflict, but in our abilities to better accommodate and provide for the dietary needs of institutionalized elders and elders residing in retirement communities.

All of these suggested directions in research would add to the theoretical model presented in this study, illuminating aspects that need improvement and refinement and strengthening existing factors that continually emerge from data. This research has demonstrated the value in applying socially-oriented theoretical frameworks to conceptualize processes that develop and support or transform dietary practices. Further elaboration of particular components or interactions among components would be informative.

I have suggested several lines of research thus far. I now provide a few examples of potential findings of such research endeavors. The examples I use are hypothetical and based on how I extend my findings, and the findings found in the literature, to future eventualities. For example, expanding on the notion of identity and food rules, personal cultural identity is dramatically variable, as are other imposed institutional, local, and regional cultures. If an older woman lived in her own long-time home in a community at large, she does not encounter conflicting rules, issues related to physical distance from a dining facility, and she does not have to abide by the temporal schedules of meals as she would living in a retirement community such as Colonial Square or various other age-segregated residential settings. In these ways, she is more "free" at home than if she lived in a retirement community. However, with advanced age, she might experience malnutrition, due to decreased physical abilities for shopping and cooking or a lack of social meaning of meals, and especially if she is widowed, divorced, otherwise living alone, or of limited economic means. Thus there are also constraints for community-dwelling elders that retirement facility residence might help them avoid.

In another example, an older woman might live at a community such as Colonial Square, but is East Asian and accustomed to light meals, high in certain complex carbohydrates (e.g., rice), diverse vegetables, and fish. She also has a low educational level. Her personal rules might immediately be at conflict with institutional/local/regional rules, but her exposure to others at Colonial Square might enhance (albeit late in life) her knowledge of nutritional needs and result in possibly valuable changes in her dietary behavior. However, she might suffer psychosocially if she is unable to obtain her preferred ethnic foods and meals or to enact social customs tied to food in her culture.

The participants of this research had profound experiences from both the pre-WWII depression and post-war economic largess. Interestingly, they seemed more influenced by the Depression (controlling for their family's relative economic situation), given the clean plate club principle. So the age at which they experienced the period event (the cohort-period interaction) appears to be quite important, but so too is the parental cohort-period interactions. Thinking about the future of Baby Boomers, it is possible to speculate along the same lines using anecdotal observations of contemporary middle-aged adults. Consider first the example of a male born in the mid-1950s, who could be considered a member of the clean plate club, but only because of his parents, who were both young children of the Depression, but post-war lived in relative poverty because both their fathers had died. Most of this boomer's friends, childhood and currently, were not really of the clean plate ilk because their parents had gained full benefit of post-war economic recovery. Although the clean plate notion stayed with him, he has changed because of a period (post-Vietnam) emphasis on college education. He still holds a meat-and-potatoes meal as a preference (due to his upper Midwest upbringing), though such meals are now few and far between; they have not been eliminated, but their frequency decreased because he is more familiar with the meaning and value of balanced nutrition. He now believes that people cannot live on meat and potatoes alone.

As far as this baby boomer's dietary behavior in the future is concerned, it seems likely that cohort and family effects will maintain the clean plate motif. Period effects will moderate that motif in that he is willing to spend more money on better foods (but will logically take smaller servings because of his education). Some of his friends (and maybe the more typical Boomer and Boomer child) will be equally concerned about nutrition value, but not so concerned with waste, and so they might be less likely to overeat. However, the pace and style of recent economic development has more deeply commodified time, leading to the rise of fast foods and rapid meal preparation, often with the sacrifice of nutritional value. Structural response to commodified time has been increased advertising for fast foods and increased competition among fast food chains to seemingly offer the most food for the lowest price. So, people look for the bargain (the notion of economic rationality, seen also in the popularity of restaurant buffets), and tend to eat and drink more than is nutritionally necessary. This seems to have become habit for many in our society and, as individuals grow older, either they suffer from more heart disease or diabetes, are faced with greater problems of adjustment in later life to a better dietary lifestyle, or simply die from chronic inattention to dietary needs. Furthermore, there are the individual experiences that serve as a persistent influence in addition to period and cohort effects. The boomer in this example participated in professional sports in high school and college, and the constant exercise and weight loss habits remain with him. The exercise is beneficial, but the weight loss might be deleterious in that even now he easily suppresses hunger sensations and can go for days without eating.

In a brief second example, a peak boomer woman became vegetarian in her thirties. Her decision to become vegetarian had less to do with health and more to do with her respect for animal life. Her vegetarian diet excludes meats, but she does eat dairy products. Although her life has been characterized by risk-taking ventures, the societal dietary climate renders such a choice less of a social risk, as society now seems more accepting of such alternative diets and vegetarian options are increasingly available in grocery stores and restaurants. Such diversity will need to be reflected in the options available to future generations of elders. Diversity in terms of foods of other cultures might also need to be reflected in menus, as a variety of ethnic foods have become, and continue to become, more mainstream in typical American gastronomies. Fast food restaurants now offer quick Chinese, Mexican, and Italian meals. Mall food courts offer Japanese, Greek, and Middle Eastern cuisines in addition to burgers, subs and pizza.

Similarly, retirement communities and senior meal programs of the future might need to serve foods such as tofu burgers, sushi, gyros, sesame chicken, and enchiladas to satisfy the tastes of their clients - even if the clients are middle class, white elders. However, dishes such as meatloaf and macaroni and cheese or pot roast and mashed potatoes have recently been termed "comfort" foods, because for many Baby Boomers these meals are reminiscent of what their mothers used to prepare and carry with them some sentimentality and nostalgic sense as foods eaten in the "good old days" and simpler times. Therefore, these meals might still make occasional appearances at dinner times in Baby Boomers' futures, in addition to the dietary diversity embraced by many.

These are specific examples among a population of almost infinite heterogeneity. My conclusions from these examples are that the life course influences associated with age, period, cohort, and unique personal experiences all shape the dietary behaviors of individuals. This has implications for both theory and practice, in terms of accounting for behavior and satisfactorily meeting the dietary needs of older adults, both physically and psychosocially.

Methodologically, investigations might employ similar methods when studying older adult populations, as the narratives and probing for participant perceptions, in addition to observational techniques, revealed a full and rich picture of the phenomena under study. Additionally, the gathering of recipes from participants seemed to be an effective method to use for informational and recall purposes. Incorporation of other methods, such as food diaries, might also be insightful. Prospective types of studies, which, for example, interview an older adult before and after a later life transition, could be valuable for revealing what aspects of the transitions cause change, and if they do not cause change, why they do not. Health transitions would difficult to anticipate, but a residential move often can be anticipated.

Some practical applications of research would need to be based on some assumed generalizability. The establishment of generalizability is not generally a strength of qualitative research, but more the forte of quantitative methods, such as surveys. Some concepts uncovered in this research that might be suitable for exploration by survey methods include quality aspects of meals rather than quantity (e.g., heavy versus light meals), aspects of eating out, strategies used for food acquisition and food preparation in age-segregated independent residential settings, and the notion of constraints and opportunities related to food and eating in retirement communities.

Implications for Practice

As indicated above, the research additionally has implications for practice, as this and future research might assist professionals in better meeting and accommodating the dietary needs of older adults. More specifically, just as Levy (1981) suggested that collecting interview narratives from consumers would benefit market research and ultimately enable companies to better serve consumers, I suggest that conducting dietary histories and collecting food narratives from incoming residents might help retirement communities, assisted living facilities, and nursing homes better serve residents. Food and eating has been recognized as an area of much import when considering overall quality of life at residences, and improving satisfaction with food and eating experiences would improve overall quality of life. The identification of features of community contexts that are perceived as constraining or facilitating would allow communities to work on rendering the residential context as facilitative as possible with respect to food and dining services.

Additionally, residential communities need to consider cultural diversity in the provision of dining and food services, whether that diversity is regional, ethnic, or otherwise. Bermudez and Tucker's (2004, p. 25) "characteristics of a culturally competent nutrition professional" can be applied to dietary services directors:

> Is aware of own food values and possible biases.
> Respects the unique, culturally defined eating patterns of different groups.
> Has appropriate knowledge and understanding of the values and eating patterns of clientele.
> Acknowledges the profound effect of culture on eating practices.
> Is flexible and understanding of possible resistance to change.
> Understands that diversity within is as important as diversity between cultures.
> Integrates cultural knowledge and sensitivity into strategy and everyday operation of food and nutrition programs. (p. 25)

Dietary narratives and improvements to services can boost public relations and marketing efforts and need not be costly to implement. Nickels (2000) asserted that a continuous seating system, for example, does not cost any more than using traditional set seating times.

When it comes to health care and dietary interventions for older adults, Wellman and Johnson (2004) stated that food and nutrition has been viewed quite differently by two systems that provide services to older:

> The social service system, including the aging network, tends to view food as nurturing, emphasizing the emotional, social, and quality-of-life aspects of eating. The healthcare system has

traditionally focused on food and nutrition primarily as therapeutic treatment for chronic diseases and more recently has come to value the heath-promoting and disease-preventing attributes of a healthy diet. (p. 6)

Although there is room (and a need) for both views, a sentiment echoed by Wellman and Johnson, this research suggests that dietary interventions do need to focus less on physical indicators of well-being or, rather, increase attention to psychosocial indicators. Dieticians and other health professionals would better serve their clients by increasing efforts to consider and include psychosocial well-being as an outcome in health education and promotion. Reducing morbidity and improving function might mean very little to an elder who is miserable because of dietary restrictions.

Furthermore, understanding that dietary practices are more than just personal choice and understanding other aspects, such as moral meaning associated with practices, might enhance the effectiveness of educational efforts to improve the food choices and dietary quality of older adults. Barr and Schumacher (2003) asserted that using a quality of life survey as an adjunct to nutritional interventions can both improve the effectiveness of the intervention and determine how well the client is adapting (and if the dietary recommendations are even realistic for the client at that point in time). Furst et al. (1996) had similarly emphasized the usefulness of considering social factors:

Greater understanding of the interplay of their clients' life course influences, values, and personal systems during food choice can improve practitioners' diagnoses of problems in implementing dietary recommendations and suggest ways to resolve these difficulties. (p. 263)

Practitioners who are informed about the contexts of behavior and how an individual is socially situated also can prevent prescribing dietary recommendations for older adults that could potentially cause elders to feel frustration, disappointment, and self-reproof if they do not fully follow the experts' advice, and take into consideration what will work best for the elder.

Practitioners additionally should consider the skepticism in which older adults might hold them and their recommendations. It might not always be possible to earn the trust of those who do not "believe," but it would be important to know why they are skeptical and how far reaching their skepticism is. The practitioner can then work with the older adult within those limits.

Wellman and Johnson (2004, p. 6) observed: "In our aging society, the connections between nutrition and health and independence and the relationship between food and quality of life are merging into a more holistic view of food and nutrition." Indeed, increasing efforts have been, and continue to be, made in a promising direction among dieticians and nutritionists. Barr and Schumacher (2003) noted that the American Dietetic Association (ADA) has issued at least four commentaries and position papers in which the organization emphasizes that dieticians have a role in improving quality of life for their clients. They cited the ADA's 2000 statement on nutrition and aging, which recognized that "the enjoyment of food, along with its social and nurturing aspects, contributes to quality of life for older adults" (Barr & Schumacher, 2004, p. 178) and encouraged dieticians to be actively involved in promoting such quality of life for their elder patients. Barr and Schumacher also remarked that "quality of life" as a concept has made numerous appearances in the nutrition literature of the past 20 years.

It should be noted that it is possible that dietary professionals might have not more fully incorporated social science perspectives into their practices not just because it was "outside" of their disciplines, as might be assumed, but also because of perceptions of the usefulness of social research, as indicated by Coveney's (2002) assessment of social research regarding food:

> Socially-based research can be of limited use to practitioners, especially when sociological perspectives are over-theorised and abstract. A key premise should be that theories serve as explanations of phenomena. A limitation of some social and cultural research is that theories become ends in themselves. (p. 113)

It is a valid critique and Coveney's criticism occurred just after expounding upon the importance of social context in research and how a social, "real-world" understanding can better inform dietary professionals' practice, a point re-emphasized in Coveney's conclusions regarding the need for more research in natural social settings. Social scientists, who want to have an impact on practices and who claim their research can better inform practice, would do well to attempt to make their research more accessible to others beyond their disciplinary boundaries. In turn, it should be recognized that socially-based theoretical development is needed in this area. So although it might appear that, in some research, theories become ends in themselves, this is a needed emphasis of social research in order to advance explanation and overall understanding of dietary behavior.

Reflections

On a final note, conducting this research was a process of discovery that was personal as well as academic. I learned much about the topic and what it can contribute to our understandings of older women's food and eating experiences. I obtained practical knowledge about working with older women and using a retirement community as a research site. I also learned some things about myself.

Interviewing the women in particular forced me to confront my own assumptions, biases, and moralities regarding food and eating. For example, I realized I had always assumed that older women learned to cook at very young ages, but the finding that some did not learn until they became married challenged this assumption and debunked it. I had also assumed that older women generally enjoyed cooking, part of a grandmotherly stereotype. This is also not accurate, and no longer in my personal assumptions inventory.

I realized I have particular biases in my notions about food. One participant shared that she loved anything made with ground beef, because ground beef was one of her favorite foods. I am not a particular fan of ground beef, but accepted that someone could rate it as a top food preference. However, when she went on to describe how she used to pinch off a bit of raw beef to taste when she made meatloaf, I was somewhat incredulous. She continued, relating a story about how a few years ago she went to a local grocery store, and at the meat counter, asked if she could have a taste of raw beef. The man refused her request, but she went back later and found another man who gave her a bite. Although she admitted that it did not taste quite as good as she remembered, I found myself quite repulsed at the thought of someone eating raw ground beef. I was raised on well-done meat, and ventured into medium/medium rare only when I was out on my own in life, though raw beef was still out of the question. Yet, I find it perfectly acceptable to eat sushi. Had I shared my love of raw fish with this participant, she most likely would have turned up her nose at the thought of it.

Finally, the intense study of dietary practices and nutrition provided me little time to follow "recommended" dietary practices myself. I rationalized and justified the laxness in my own dietary patterns, certain that I could adjust course once I finished my project. I therefore found that I too was subject to the "should syndrome" of eating and attendant feelings of guilt. Although easy to justify the guilt away, it periodically came back and would need to be rationalized away again. Taken altogether, these issues indicate that perhaps I am in the process of becoming a culturally competent food researcher.

I greatly enjoyed talking with the participants of this study and know that some of them took pleasure in sharing their stories as much as I took pleasure in listening to them. Though they might have benefited in some small way, the study of social aspects food and eating in general and the field of gerontology in particular gained in a much larger way, as the recipients of these women's valuable insights into themselves and society. This research was a fruitful enterprise personally, produced useful academic understanding, and will be a rich source scholarship and direction in future research endeavors.

Appendix A
Interview Guide for Food History

In this interview, I would like to talk about your food and eating experiences throughout your life. I am interested in what influences you think have affected the way you eat at different times in your life.

Opening:

I would like to start with talking about the recipes that I asked you to have ready to discuss. (Talk about the recipes the participant chose to share, asking about significance, where they got it, how old it is, when they use (or used) it, why it is a favorite.)

Questions:

Over your lifetime, what do you think has influenced the way you eat? What you eat?

During different times in your life, how do you think family has affected the way you eat?

Have any traditions influenced the way you eat? How? (Listen for holidays, familial, ethnic, etc.)

Have your religious or spiritual beliefs affected the way you eat now or in the past? How?

Has your health or any physical conditions affected the way you eat now or in the past?

During your life, what influence do you think you have had on the ways others eat? (If mentions choosing foods for others, e.g. children)

210

Is there a difference in how you have chosen foods for others from how you have chosen for yourself? Why?

Tell me about the food-related responsibilities have you had throughout your life. How are they similar to the food-related responsibilities other women in your family have had? How are they different?

Tell me about how you learned what you know about food. Probes: shopping, choosing foods, and preparing foods
Tell me how you learned what you know about nutrition and health.

How do you think the way you eat has been affected by living here at Colonial Square? (Listen for where they get their food, other than the dining room.)
Do you think that where you have lived in the past affected the way you eat? How?
Tell me about other places where you eat.

Do you think the way you eat has changed over your lifetime?

Have there been times when you have bought or prepared food other than for feeding yourself or your family? Probes: charity (food drives, soup kitchens), fundraisers, entertaining, gifts (reciprocity or not)

Do you think there will be any changes in the way you eat in the future? How far into the future?

Meals: What meals and meal times were like (e.g. did the family sit down together, what was eaten at lunchtime in school), snacks and snack times, what family recipes are remembered the most, did the family have a garden, canning and preserving of food

Appendix B
Sample Weekly Menus

November 18-24, 2001

Sunday

Salad: Pineapples & Cottage Cheese

Entrees: Fried Chicken, Meat Loaf, Baked Cod

Vegetables: Mashed Potatoes, Yellow Squash with Tomato, Corn, Green Beans

Monday

Salad: Pasta Salad

Entrees: Bar-Que Chicken Breast, Italian Sausage, Fried Shrimp

Vegetables: French Fries, Sour Kraut, Fresh Blend, Peas & Carrots

Tuesday

Salad: Seafood Salad

Entrees: Chicken Crepes, Veal Parmesan, Flounder

Vegetables: Stewed Tomatoes, Spinach, Zucchini & Yellow Squash, Pasta

Wednesday

Salad: Ambrosia

Entrees: Chicken Pot Pie, Beef-A-Roni, Seafood Newburg

Vegetables: Lima Beans, Brussel Sprouts, Fresh Blend, Cauliflower

Thursday

Salad: Cranberry Delight

Entrees: Turkey, Glazed Ham, Salmon

Vegetables: Baked Sweet Potatoes, Acorn Squash, Southern Green Beans, Corn
O'Brien

Friday

Salad: Broccoli Salad

Entrees: Roast Beef, Grilled Chicken, Fried Seafood Plate

Vegetables: Roasted Garlic Potatoes, Broccoli, Fresh Blend, Peas

Saturday

Salad: Calico Bean Salad

Entrees: Pepper Steak, Chicken Monterey, Baked Tilapia

Vegetables: Rice, Beets, Mixed Vegetables, Okra & Tomatoes

November 25-December 1, 2001

Sunday

Salad: Ginger Pear Salad

Entrees: Walnut Chicken, Sesame Beef, Fried Shrimp

Vegetables: Fried Rice, Broccoli & Carrots, Sugar Snap Peas, Spaghetti Squash

Monday

Salad: Strawberry Delight

Entrees: Oven Roasted Chicken, Grilled Ham, Fried Cod

Vegetables: Red Potatoes, Mixed Vegetables, Cauliflower, Zucchini

Tuesday

Salad: Cucumber Salad

Entrees: Italian Chicken, Spaghetti with Meat Sauce, Flounder

Vegetables: Augratin Potatoes, Lima Beans, Spinach, Fresh Blend

Wednesday

Salad: Spinach Salad

Entrees: Chicken Tenders, Beef Liver, Shrimp Creole

Vegetables: Rice, Mixed Vegetables, Green Beans, Corn

Thursday

Salad: Sunshine Salad

Entrees: Herb Chicken Breast, Bar-Que Pork Chops, Sole

Vegetables: Fresh Blend, Baked Potatoes, Brussel Sprouts, Stewed Tomatoes

Friday

Salad: Shrimp & Rice Salad

Entrees: Chicken Oscar, French Dip, Trout

Vegetables: Mixed Vegetables, Roasted Garlic Potatoes, Pinto Beans, Peas

Saturday

Salad: Cole Slaw

Entrees: Baked Catfish, Swiss Mushroom Burgers, Hot Dogs with Sour Kraut

Vegetables: French Fries, Baked Beans, Corn on the Cob, Fresh Blend

January 6-12, 2002

Sunday

Salad: Spinach Salad

Entrees: Roasted Chicken, Grilled Ham & Pineapples, Sole

Vegetables: Sweet Potato Casserole, Lima Beans, Corn, Fried Okra

Monday

Salad: Carri Fruit Salad

Entrees: Grilled Chicken & Mushrooms, Ground Sirloin, Fried Shrimp

Vegetables: Garlic Roasted Potatoes, Peas, Yellow Squash & Tomatoes, Mixed Vegetables

Tuesday

Salad: Seafood Salad

Entrees: Pepper Steak, Italian Chicken, Fried Cod

Vegetables: Rice, Spinach, Mixed Vegetables, Butter Beans

Wednesday

Salad: Three Bean Salad

Entrees: Chicken Monterey, Beef Liver & Onions, Tilapia

Vegetables: Sautéed Mushrooms, Onion Rings, Macaroni & Cheese, Mixed Vegetables

Thursday

Salad: Peaches & Cottage Cheese

214

Entrees: Garlic Chicken, Ham & Cheese Soufflé, Mahi-Mahi

Vegetables: Red Potatoes, Brussel Sprouts, Fresh Blend, Carrots

Friday

Salad: Strawberry Delight

Entrees: Country Fried Steak, Chicken Pacatia, Trout

Vegetables: Baked Potatoes, Vegetables Casserole, Pinto Beans, Stewed Tomatoes

Saturday

Salad: Pasta Salad

Entrees: Grilled Hamburgers, Hot Dogs & Sour Kraut, Fried Catfish

Vegetables: Baked Beans, French Fries, Mixed Vegetables, Zucchini

January 20-26, 2002

Sunday

Salad: Cole Slaw

Entrees: Fried Chicken, Meat Loaf, Baked Cod

Vegetables: Green beans, Mashed Potatoes, Stewed Tomatoes, Mixed Vegetables

Monday

Salad: Ginger Pear Salad

Entrees: Pork Loin, Sesame Chicken, Garlic Shrimp

Vegetables: Vegetables Rice Pilaf, Cabbage, Carrots, Peas

Tuesday

Salad: Spinach

Entrees: Chicken Casserole, Baked Ziti, Blackened Catfish

Vegetables: Fried Mushrooms, Zucchini, Fresh Blend, Pasta

Wednesday

Salad: Marinated Vegetables

Entrees: Chicken Tenders, Lasagna, Tuna Melt

Vegetables: French Fries, Brussel Sprouts, Yellow Squash & Tomatoes, Mixed Vegetables

Thursday

Salad: Sun Shine Salad

Entrees: Chicken Livers, Salisbury Steak, Flounder

Vegetables: Pinto Beans, Macaroni & Cheese, Onion Rings, Mixed Vegetables

Friday

Salad: Anti-Pasta Salad

Entrees: Beef Pot Pie, Veal Parmesan, Lemon Scrod

Vegetables: Rice, Corn, Broccoli, Cauliflower

Saturday

Salad: Broccoli Salad

Entrees: French Dip, Sweet & Sour Chicken, Fried Shrimp

Vegetables: Mixed Vegetables, Spinach Soufflé, Baked Potatoes, Baked Tomatoes

February 3-9, 2002

Sunday

Salad: Deviled Eggs

Entrees: Fried Chicken, Pork Loin, Baked Scrod

Vegetables: Mixed Vegetables, Mashed Potatoes, Lima Beans, Fried Okra

Monday

Salad: Cole Slaw

Entrees: Hamburgers, Hot Dogs & Kraut, Tilapia

Vegetables: French Fries, Corn on the Cob, Baked Beans, Peas & Carrots

Tuesday

Salad: Marinated Tomatoes

Entrees: Chicken Marsala, Spaghetti & Meat Sauce, Flounder

Vegetables: Yellow Squash, Baked Apples, Spinach, Italian Green Beans

Wednesday

Salad: Sunshine Salad

Entrees: Grilled Chicken, Skillet Pork Chops, Fried Shrimp

Vegetables: Rice, Black Eyed Peas, Brussel Sprouts, Mixed Vegetables

Thursday

Salad: Three Bean Salad

Entrees: Chicken Burrito, Pepper Beef, Blackened Catfish

Vegetables: Rice, Black Beans, Corn, Fresh Blend

Friday

Salad: Peaches & Cottage Cheese

Entrees: Roasted Chicken, Grilled Ham, Fried Seafood Plate

Vegetables: Stewed Tomatoes, Sweet Potatoes, Southern Green Beans, Mixed Vegetables

Saturday

Salad: Spinach Salad

Entrees: Barbeque Ribs, Hawaiian Chicken, Fried Cod

Vegetables: Zucchini, Baked Potatoes, Vegetable Casserole, Pinto Beans

May 13-19, 2002 HAPPY MOTHERS DAY

Sunday

Salad: Carrot Raisin

Entrees: Cornish Hen, Sliced Beef, Stuffed Salmon

Vegetables: Asparagus, Mashed Potatoes, Corn, Baked Apples

Monday

Salad: Cottage Cheese & Peaches

Entrees: Hot Dogs & Sauerkraut, Chicken Pasta Sauté, Swordfish

Vegetables: Fresh Blend, Scalloped Apples, French Fries, Baked Beans

Tuesday

Salad: Ambrosia

Entrees: Veal Parmesan, Chicken Picatta, Baked Trout

Vegetables: Augratin Potatoes, Buttered Pasta, Spinach Soufflé, Yellow Squash

Wednesday

Salad: Marinated Vegetables

Entrees: Vegetable Omelet, Chicken Oscar, Shrimp Creole

Vegetables: Broccoli, Potato Lyonnaise, Stewed Tomatoes, Rice

Thursday

Salad: Tomato Aspic

Entrees: Roast Beef and Cheddar Wrap, Grilled Halibut, Chicken Strips

Vegetables: Fried Zucchini, Pinto Beans, Dilled Carrots, Macaroni & Cheese

Friday

Salad: Artichoke Salad

Entrees: Spaghetti & Meat Sauce, Chicken Fajitas, Blackened Catfish

Vegetables: Peas, Black Beans, Fiesta Rice, Fresh Blend

Saturday

Salad: Marinated Carrots

Entrees: Chicken Salad Croissant, Cabbage Rolls, Fried Oysters

Vegetables: Spinach, Zucchini and Mushrooms, Scalloped Potatoes, Corn O'Brien

Menus subject to change based on availability and quality

Appendix C
Participants' Life Course Outlines

Mrs. Adams

1914	Born in the Northeast
1932	Graduated from high school; started college
1936	Graduated from college; worked for girls organization in the South
1937	Worked in children's hospital in Northeast
1942	Graduated library school; worked as librarian in Washington, D.C. area
1943	Married; moved to Florida
1945	Daughter born; full-time homemaker
1946 (?)	Moved to Washington, D.C. suburb
1948 (?)	Moved to Northeast; bought house
1950	Back to library work part-time
1963	Husband died; full-time librarian
1984	Retired
1988	Moved to Lexington; lived in an apartment
2000	Moved to Colonial Square

Mrs. Brown

1911	Born in the South
1929	Graduated from high school; started college
1931	Left college; director of girl's organization
1933	Started teaching elementary school
1936	Married; became full-time homemaker
1938	1st son born; moved to the Midwest
1941	2nd son born
1945	Husband returned; moved to different Midwestern state
1946	3rd son born
1947	4th son born
1953	Moved to Lexington; secretary for healthcare organization
1973(?)	Retired
1976(?)	Husband retired
1998	Husband died
2000	Moved to Colonial Square

220

Mrs. Burkholt

1915	Born in Kentucky
1927	Moved to another town in Kentucky
1933 (?)	Graduated from high school; started college
1935	Graduated from junior college; moved back home
1936 (?)	Moved to a large city with friends; worked in an office
1938	Moved back home
1943	Married; full-time homemaker; lived with parents while husband in the war
1944	Moved to the Midwest; 1st daughter born
1949	2nd daughter born
1960	Moved to Lexington
1962	Bought business; became office manager for business
1982 (?)	Quit working
1986	Mother died; Husband retired (?); started wintering in FL (?)
1997 (?)	Stopped wintering in FL
1999	Moved to Colonial Square

Ms. Carr

1929	Born in Lexington
1936	Family moved to rural area outside of town
1937	In bad accident (hit by car)
1941 (?)	Family moved back to city
1943	Mother died
1947	Graduated from high school; started college
1951	Graduated from college; taught secondary school
1952	Taught elementary school
1952-54	Camp director part time
1960	Graduated from graduate school
1961-63	Taught special education
1963	Full-time state consultant in special education
1968	Father died
1972	Brother died
1980	Retired
1981 (?)	Moved to a retirement village apartment
1983	Car accident
1984	Lived in nursing home
1986	Moved to Colonial Square
1992	Diagnosed as diabetic
2001	Car accident

Mrs. Donovan

1913	Born in Kentucky; family lived on a farm
1931	Graduated from high school
1936 (?)	Moved to Midwest; job as bookkeeper
1943	Married
1947	Mother-in-law died; moved back to Kentucky to live on farm with father-in-law
1949	Started college
1953	Daughter born
1954	Graduated from college
1957 (?)	Started teaching elementary school
1965	Father-in-law died
1970	Husband retired; started wintering in Florida
1974 (?)	Retired; moved to condo in Florida
1994	Moved to Colonial Square
1998	Husband died

Mrs. Faust

1924(?)	Born in Kentucky; family lived on farm
1927(?)	Moved to town
1929	Moved back to farm
1941(?)	Father died
1942	Graduated from high school
1942	Attended college where sister taught
1943-1945	Attended college in Lexington; job as lab assistant
1946	Married, lived with another couple; worked at research center
1947	Moved into own house
1949	1st daughter born; became homemaker; office manager for husband's business
1950(?)	Moved to a bigger house
1951	1st son born
1953(?)	Moved to a different house
1954	2nd daughter born
1954(?)	Moved to final house before Colonial Square
1956	2nd son born
1959	3rd daughter born
1977-1987(?)	Real estate work
1987-1990(?)	Church bookkeeper
1995(?)	Husband (and she) retired
1999	Moved to Colonial Square

Mrs. Florsheim

1912	Born in Kentucky
1918	Moved to father's homeplace in a different county
1930	Graduated from high school; started college in Lexington
1931	Taught elementary school in home county
1938	Married; moved to apartment in husband's home county; 1st daughter born
1941	Started back to college part-time
1944	Returned to part-time elementary teaching
1946	Bought house
1947	2nd daughter born
1963	Graduated from college
1968	Mother died
1972	Retired
1978	Husband retired
1998	Moved to Colonial Square

Mrs. Ford

1917	Born the Northeast
1933	Graduated from high school
1937	Graduated from college; worked for extension agency
1939	Married; started teaching secondary school
1946	Son born; resigned from teaching
1947	1st daughter born
1949	2nd daughter born
1950	3rd daughter born
1955 (?)	She and husband ran a greenhouse
1962	Back to teaching
1975	Husband retired
1977	Retired; wintered in Florida
1978	Sister moved in
1986	Husband died
1988	Stroke; broke vertebrae
1998	Moved to Colonial Square; summered in North
1999	Broke back
2001	Broke hip

Mrs. Jergens

1915	Born in Kentucky
1916	Family moved to the Midwest
1918	Family moved back to Kentucky
1932	Graduated from high school
1936	Graduated from college; married; rented apartment; began substitute teaching & tutoring
1938	Quit working; built duplex
1944	Daughter born; husband in the war; lived in duplex with parents on the other side
1946	Husband back home
1950	Built house; rented out their side of duplex
1952	Father died
1953	Moved back to duplex where Mother still lived
1969	Moved to a house (mother moved with them)
1976	Husband retired
1984	Husband died
1988	Mother in nursing home
1989	Moved to a townhouse closer to mother
1990	Mother died
2000	Fall; moved to Colonial Square
2001	2nd fall

224

Mrs. Michaels

1912	Born in Kentucky
1918(?)	Family moved in with grandmother, on farm
1920(?)	Grandmother died; moved back to own farm
1930(?)	Graduated from high school
1931	Started college in Lexington
1934	Left college to teach elementary school
1936	Back to college
1937	Graduated from college; started teaching in a rural secondary school
1939	Married; had house built; taught secondary school in Lexington
1940	Husband in war; worked in occupational therapy; father died
1942	Husband returned home; returned to teaching
1947	1st son born; full-time homemaker
1951	2nd son born
1957	Taught elementary and special education
1962	Mother died
1963	Retired from teaching
1972	Husband retired
1979	2nd son died
1988	Wintered in FL
1998	Husband died
2000	Moved to Colonial Square; sold house to grandson
2001	Hip fracture

Mrs. Monroe

1912	Born in the Northeast
1918	Family moved to a new town
1930	Graduated from high school
1931	Married
1934	1st son born
1939/40	2nd son born; parents and brother lived with them briefly
1944	Daughter born
1953	Began working as a clerk
1957	Husband started with same company; transferred to Lexington; bought house
1967 (?)	Husband retired, worked as manufacturing representative
1977	Retired; wintered in Florida
1982	Husband died
1991	Moved to Colonial Square
1995 (?)	2nd son died
1999	Sold house

Mrs. Nichols

1915	Born in the Midwest
1923	Family moved from city to suburb
1927	Father died
1932	Graduated from high school Started junior college
1934	Transferred to four-year college in Kentucky
1936	Graduated college; worked for local government office in Lexington
1939	Mother moved to Lexington
1940	Married; started traveling with husband and his job around Kentucky
1944	1st daughter born
1945	Moved in with mother-in-law
1947	2nd daughter born
1949	1st son born
1951	2nd son born
1952 (?)	Husband started job as stockbroker
1957	Mother-in-law died; bought house in Lexington
1980	Husband retired
1992	Mother died
1996	Broke hip
1997	Moved to Colonial Square

Mrs. Provost

1907	Born in Kentucky
1922	Looked after Mom & home instead of high school
1926	Started high school
1931(?)	Graduated from high school; attended beauty school
1932(?)	Began work as a beautician
1935	Married; became full-time homemaker
1935-1960	Moved often with husband's job in various states of the South
1958	Graduated from junior college in Kentucky
1961	Graduated from a four-year college in Kentucky; father died
1962	Mother died
1964	Finished graduate school; began work as a college librarian
1967	Husband died
1977	Married 2nd husband
1978	Retired
1980	Divorced; moved to large city in Kentucky
1994	Moved to Colonial Square
1999	Fell and broke arm
2001	Hurt back

Mrs. Randall

1928	Born in the Midwest
1933(?)	Family moved to a new town
1943	Started working part time jobs after school and on Saturdays
1946	Graduated from high school
1948	Graduated from college; worked in health care
1949	Married; moved to Washington, D.C.; lived with in-laws (6 months), then rented an apartment
1950	Moved to suburb of Washington, D.C.
1952	Moved to Europe
1954	1st son is born
1955	Moved to West coast; lived in military quarters
1958	Moved to Texas; lived in military quarters
1959	2nd son is born
1962	Daughter born
1965	Moved to Hawaii; lived in military quarters
1968	Moved to Washington, D.C.
1969	Moved to Lexington; husband took job as a professor
1971-1976	Worked as research assistant
1984	Moved to Colonial Square
1985	Mother-in-law moved to Colonial Square
1986	Parents moved to Colonial Square
1989(?)	Husband retired
1990	Mother-in-law died
1992	Parents moved to assisted living
1994	Mother died
1996	Father died
1997	Both hips replaced

Mrs. Richardson

1917	Born in the South
1935	Graduated from high school; married
1936	1st son born
1940	Daughter born
1941	Husband in the service
1943	Husband returned home
1946	2nd son born
1950s	Worked for federal government program; very ill, in hospital in the Mid-Atlantic for several years
1965 (?)	Moved to Atlantic coast in the South
1975 (?)	Husband died
1997	Moved to Colonial Square

Mrs. Stokes

1913	Born in the Midwest
1931	Graduated from high school; started laundry job
1934	Married; became full-time homemaker; lived with father-in-law
1936	Moved to own house
1937	Daughter born; father died; mother moved in
1940	1st son born
1941	Bought house
1945	2nd son born
1945-1948	Various retail sales jobs
1950	Mother died
1955(?)	Newspaper job
1958(?)	Bookkeeper
1959(?)	Billing
1964	Card company job
1965	Husband retired; moved to Florida
1970	Office manager/bookkeeper
1976(?)	Diagnosed as diabetic
1980	Retired
1989	Husband died
1990	1st son died
1992	Moved to Colonial Square; suffered stroke
1993	Broke hip
2001	Heart problems

228

Mrs. Vossler

1916	Born in the Midwest
1934 (?)	Graduated from high school
1935	Married
1936	Son born
1939/40	House built
1954	Daughter born; son married and moved out
1957	Moved in with mother-in-law; father died
1965	Mother-in-law died
1979	Husband retired; moved to the Southwest; bought house
1985	Husband died
1986/87	Married 2nd husband
1992	2nd husband died
2000	Moved to Colonial Square

Mrs. Wilson

1922	Born in the South
1939	Graduated from high school; mother died; started business school; worked as nanny
1940	Worked as secretary
1941	Entered civil service in Washington, D.C.
1942	Married 1st husband; lived on a boat
1944	Moved to house in suburb of Washington, D.C.
1945	1st son born
1950	2nd son born
1951	Traveled around Europe and Scandinavia
1953	Moved to Northeast
1954	Trip around the world with 1st son
1959	Divorced; she and 2nd son move into new house
1963	Started college
1968	Graduated from college; married 2nd husband; moved into husband's house
1977	Husband retired; moved to Kentucky
1988	Moved to Lexington; had retirement house built
2000	Moved to Colonial Square

Appendix D
Participants' Recipes

Abbreviations used in recipes: lb. = pound

t. = teaspoon

T. = tablespoon

Mrs. Adams:

Dump Jello Salad

1 cup boiling hot water   1 packet lime jello

1 container fat free yogurt   1 can crushed pineapple

¾ cup walnuts, chopped (the size of peas)

Dissolve lime jello in boiling water. Stir jello, dump in yogurt and stir. Dump in pineapple and stir. Dump in walnuts and stir. Let congeal. Unmold on a plate garnished with lettuce leaf and parsley.

Butterscotch Brownies

¼ cup corn oil   1 cup light brown sugar (packed)

1 egg   ¾ cup sifted flour

1 t. baking powder   ½ t. salt

½ t. vanilla   ½ cup walnuts, coarsely chopped

Heat oven to 350°. Grease and 8"x8"x2" pan. Blend oil and brown sugar. Stir in egg. Sift dry ingredients and stir in. Stir in vanilla and nuts. Spread in prepared pan. Bake 25 minutes. Do not over bake. When slightly cool, cut into 18 bars. Can be easily doubled, tripled, or even quadrupled.

Mrs. Brown:

Chili

1 lb. ground beef	1 medium onion chopped
1 can condensed tomato soup	Chili pepper
½ can water	1 large or 2 medium cans red kidney beans
Catsup	

Brown beef and chopped onions. Season with chili pepper. Add tomato soup and water. When well mixed, add kidney beans – including liquid – add 2 or 3 dashes catsup – (add another ½ can water if needed).

Oatmeal Squares

Butter   Brown sugar

Oatmeal

Melt butter and brown sugar. Stir in instant oatmeal. Pour into buttered pan – Let set until firm and cut in squares. (Can add marshmallows or peanuts if desired)

Ms. Carr:

Chili

1 package of pasta (e.g., elbows)	1 T. chili powder
1 big green pepper, chopped	1 medium onion, chopped
2 cans red kidney beans	2 small cans tomato sauce
1 large can diced tomatoes	1½ lb. ground sirloin steak (or other beef)

Cook pasta, set aside. Cook onion in a large skillet, then add pepper and cook. Cook meat, and add beans. Stir only with a wooden spoon. Stir in tomato sauce and diced tomatoes. Add chili powder. Stir in pasta slowly. Cover and simmer on low for a half hour or so.

Mrs. Donovan:

Applesauce Muffins

2/3 cup soft oleo (margarine)	1 ½ cups sugar
4 eggs	2 t. vanilla
2 2/3 cups flour	2 t. baking powder
1 t. soda	1 t. salt
2 t. cinnamon	1 t. nutmeg
¼ t. cloves	1 ½ cup applesauce
1 cup nuts	1 cup raisins

Cream the oleo and sugar. Mix in the eggs and vanilla. Add the next 7 ingredients alternately with the applesauce. Fold in the nuts and raisins. Bake at 350° for 25 minutes. Makes 24.

Zucchini Muffins

3 eggs	2 cups sugar
1 cup oil	1 T. vanilla
2 cups flour	1 t. zest
1 t. cinnamon	¼ t. baking powder
¼ t. soda	1 t. salt
1 cup nuts	

Beat the eggs well and add sugar, oil and vanilla. Mix in the next 6 ingredients. Add the nuts. Bake at 350° for 27 minutes. Makes 24.

Coconut Pie

Baked pie crust	1 cup sugar
¼ cup cornstarch	2 cups milk
3 egg yolks	1 t. vanilla
½ stick oleo (margarine)	1 cup coconut

Meringue:

3 egg whites, 3 T. water, 3 heaping t. sugar

Combine sugar and cornstarch in a saucepan and add a little milk to moisten. Stir in egg yolks, and then add rest of the milk. Cook until thick. Add vanilla, oleo and coconut. Pour into a baked pie shell.

To make meringue: beat egg whites until frothy and add water. Continue beating egg whites until they form firm peaks but are not dry. Gradually add sugar. Beat until whites are thick and glossy. Spread meringue on top of pie filling. With the back of a spoon, spread the meringue to cover the filling completely. Bake at 325° until golden brown.

Butterscotch Pie

Baked pie crust	1 cup firmly packed brown sugar
¼ cup cornstarch	½ t. salt
1 ½ cups milk	3 egg yolks
3 T. butter	1 t. vanilla
¼ t. maple flavoring	

Meringue:

3 egg whites, 3 T. water, 3 heaping t. sugar

Combine sugar and cornstarch in a saucepan and add a little milk to moisten. Stir in egg yolks, and then add rest of the milk. Cook until thick. Add butter, vanilla and maple flavoring. Pour into a baked pie shell.

To make meringue: beat egg whites until frothy and add water. Continue beating egg whites until they form firm peaks but are not dry. Gradually add sugar. Beat until whites are thick and glossy. Spread meringue on top of pie filling. With the back of a spoon, spread the meringue to cover the filling completely. Bake at 325° until golden brown.

Raisin Pie

2 ½ cups raisins (1 box)	1 ½ cups water
1 T. cornstarch (in a little water)	¼ cup oleo (margarine)
4 packets of Sweet-n-Low	Unbaked pie crust

In a saucepan, boil the raisins and water for 10 minutes. Add the cornstarch, oleo and artificial sweetener. Place in an unbaked pie crust. Bake at 325° for 30 minutes.

Strawberry Pie

Baked pie crust   1 cup sugar

2 T. cornstarch   1 ¾ cups water

1 package strawberry jello   1 T. butter

Strawberries

Combine sugar, cornstarch and water in a saucepan. Cook until thick. Add the jello and butter. Let it almost gel. Pour over berries in a baked crust.

Blue Grass Pie

½ stick butter   ¼ cup brown sugar

½ cup white sugar   2 T. flour

½ cup corn syrup   1 t. vanilla

¼ cup bourbon   1 cup chopped English walnuts

1 cup chocolate chips

Cream the butter and sugar. Add eggs one at a time and mix well after each. Add the syrup, vanilla and bourbon. Flour the nuts and chips. Fold in the floured nuts and chips. Pour into an unbaked pie crust. Bake at 375° for 35 minutes.

Mrs. Faust:

Chicken Judy

1 (4-oz.) jar of dried beef   6 boned chicken breasts

1 can cream of mushroom soup   1 cup sour cream

Wrap dried beef around each breast, and put in a shallow casserole. Blend the soup, sour cream and some black pepper. Pour over the chicken. Bake for 3 hours at 275°. Serving suggestion: Serve over rice.

Ruby Sue's Lime Cheese Jello

1 large package lime jello	1 cup miniature marshmallows
2 cups boiling water	2 (8-oz.) packages cream cheese
4 T. lemon juice	1 large can crushed pineapple
8 oz. whipping cream	1 cup chopped nuts

Mix the first three ingredients and let thicken some. Then add the next three ingredients. When that begins to thicken, add whipping cream and one cup chopped nuts.

Mrs. Florsheim:

Yummy Oatmeal Cookies

1 cup margarine or butter, softened	1 cup granulated sugar
1 cup brown sugar, firmly packed	2 eggs
1 t. vanilla	2 cups all purpose flour
1 ½ t. cinnamon	1 t. baking soda
1 t. salt	3 cups quick oats
1 cup nuts or raisins	

Cream butter or margarine and sugars until smooth. Beat in eggs and vanilla. Combine and blend thoroughly flour, cinnamon, baking soda and salt, beat into creamed mixture. Stir in oatmeal and raisins. Drop by rounded teaspoonfuls onto greased baking sheet.

Preheat oven to 375 degrees. Bake 12 to 14 minutes. Makes 6 dozen cookies. Batter very thick.

Corn Pudding

2 cups of fresh or canned corn	2 T. flour
1 t. salt	3 T. butter
3 beaten eggs	2 T. sugar
1 ¾ cups milk	

Blend butter, sugar, flour, salt. Add eggs, stir in corn and milk. Pour into a buttered casserole. Bake 45 minutes at 325°. Stir once while cooking. Pudding should be a nice warm brown, and should be done when a silver knife inserted in it comes out clean.

Turkey Hash

½ cup butter	½ cup flour
4 cups milk or broth from turkey bones	3 cups diced cooked turkey
½ cup diced cooked potatoes	½ cup diced cooked carrots
½ cup diced cooked celery	Salt
Pepper	Parmesan cheese topping (optional)

Melt butter. Add flour and milk slowly. Mix in the turkey, vegetables, salt, pepper and cheese, and bake at 350° until bubbly.

Sweet Potatoes in Orange Shells

1 (15 oz.) can of sweet potatoes, mashed	Brown sugar
Spices	Butter
Orange juice	Marshmallows
Orange shells (rinds of oranges)	

To the sweet potatoes, add brown sugar and spices to taste, also a little butter and orange juice. Top with marshmallows and bake until very hot. Serves 12 in ½ orange shell. Use very small oranges.

Mrs. Ford:

Anzac Biscuits

1 cup quick oats	¾ cup coconut
1 cup flour	1 t. baking soda
1 cup sugar	½ cup margarine
1 T. light corn syrup	2 T. boiling water

Combine oats, flour, coconut and sugar. Melt syrup and margarine together. Mix baking soda with water. Add to mix. Mix into dry ingredients. Place by tablespoon on well-greased sheet. Bake at 325° for 20 minutes.

Cranberries Goodin' Pudding

1 cup cranberries	¼ cup chopped nuts
1 egg	½ cup sugar
¼ cup sugar	½ cup flour

¼ cup melted butter or margarine

Grease well an 8" pie plate. Spread cranberries over the bottom of the plate. Sprinkle ¼ cup sugar with nuts thoroughly mixed in. Beat egg well and add gradually to sugar. Add flour and melted butter or margarine to the egg-sugar mixture. Pour batter over the cranberries and nuts. Bake 45 minutes at 325° until golden brown. Cut like a pie. Serve warm or cold.

Raisin Roughs

1 cup sifted flour	1 ¾ t. salt
¾ t. baking soda	2 t. cinnamon
1 cup shortening	½ c. peanut butter
2 cups sugar	3 eggs
¼ cup milk	2 t. vanilla
3 ½ cups quick cooking oats	2 cups raisins

Sift flour, salt, baking soda and cinnamon together. Cream shortening and peanut butter, gradually add sugar. Cream thoroughly. Add eggs, milk, and vanilla. Bet well. Add sifted dry ingredients. Beat. Add oats and raisins. Mix well. Drop by teaspoon on greased sheets. Bake at 375° for 10 to 12 minutes. Makes 5 dozen.

Mrs. Jergens:

Hot Chicken Salad

2 cups chopped cooked chicken	2 cups (or 1 ½ c.) celery
2 T. chopped pimento	½ cup toasted almonds
1/3 cup chopped green pepper	1 can mushroom soup
3 T. chopped onion	½ t. salt
2 T. lemon juice	½ cup mayonnaise
1/3 cup grated sharp cheese	

Blend chicken, celery, nuts, pimento, green pepper, soup, onion, salt, lemon juice, and mayonnaise. Put in 2 quart casserole. Top with cheese and Ritz cracker crumbs that have been stirred in butter. Bake at 350° about 25-30 minutes. Serves 6.

Cranberry Salad

2 (3 oz.) packages of raspberry jello

1 ¾ cups boiling water

1 (16 oz.) can of whole (or jellied) cranberry sauce

1 (20 oz.) can of crushed pineapple (in own juice), undrained

1 c. sour cream (room temperature), whipped up

Dissolve jello in boiling water; stir in cranberry sauce and undrained pineapple until sauce melts (about 3 cups plus mixture). Put half in 9x13 pan and congeal. Leave other half at room temperature. Stir sour cream well and spread over congealed gelatin gently. Gently spoon remaining jello mixture on top of sour cream. Let stand in refrigerator overnight.

Coconut Torte

1 cup coconut	¼ t. salt
4 egg whites	1 cup crushed graham crackers
½ cup chopped pecans	1 t. vanilla
1 cup sugar	

238

Beat egg whites with salt and vanilla until foamy. Gradually add sugar until whites are stiff peaks. Add graham crackers and nuts. Fold into greased pie pan and bake at 350° for 30 minutes (325° if using Pyrex). Put pecan or caramel ice cream on each serving.

Pecan Pie

1 cup sugar	½ cup corn syrup
¼ c. butter, melted	3 eggs, well beaten
1 cup pecans	1 unbaked 9" pie shell

Combine sugar, syrup and melted butter. Add beaten eggs and pecans to syrup mixture, mixing thoroughly. Pour filling into pie shell. Bake in 375° oven for 40 to 45 minutes. Cool.

Mrs. Michaels:

Oatmeal Chocolate Chip Cookies

1 cup butter or oleo	¾ cup brown sugar
¾ cup white sugar	2 eggs
2 cups oatmeal	1 ½ cups flour
1 t. salt	1 t. soda dissolved in tap water
1 t. vanilla	1 (12 oz.) package chocolate chips (I often halve this)
1 cup nuts – optional	

Mix in order given. Bake on an ungreased cookie sheet at 375° for 10 minutes.

Asparagus Casserole

1 ½ cups cracker crumbs	1 stick oleo (margarine), melted
½ cup slivered almonds	

1 (no. 2) can cut asparagus or 1 package frozen, cooked until tender

Sauce:

4 T. butter	3 T. flour
1 t. salt	1 ½ cups milk

15 oz. glass old English cheese

Combine cracker crumbs and butter. Place ¾ cup on bottom. Place cut asparagus on top. Sprinkle with almonds. Pour on cheese sauce. Top with crumbs. Bake 12 minutes in preheated oven at 450°.

Mrs. Monroe:

Speedy Pie

1 cup flour, self-rising	1 cup sugar
1 cup milk	1 stick butter, melted

Beat all together. Pour in 8-inch square or 9-inch round greased pan. Put drained canned fruit or fresh fruit or berries on top. Bake at 400°. Can also make this with vegetables instead of fruit.

Lemon Squares

½ cup xxxx sugar	1 cup margarine
2 cups flour	

Blend together and spread in 9"x13" pan. Pat down with fingers, making ½" side crust. Bake in a 350° oven for 15 minutes.

4 eggs	2 cups sugar
1 t. baking powder	¼ t. salt
2 t. grated lemon peel	¼ cup fresh lemon juice

In meantime, beat eggs and set aside. Do not over beat. Mix sugar, baking powder, salt, grated lemon peel, and lemon juice. Fold this into eggs. Pour over hot crust and bake 20-25 minutes more in 350° oven. Cool in pan. While hot, sift powdered sugar over top. Do not cut until thoroughly cold. You can score while warm if desired.

Mrs. Nichols:

Chicken Mexicaine

4 lbs. chicken breasts	3 cups water
1 T. salt	1 T. butter
1 medium onion, chopped fine	1 green pepper, chopped
1 clove of garlic, minced	1 lb. can of stewed tomatoes
2 small cans mushrooms, drained	4 T. parsley, chopped
1 t. pepper	1 t. chili powder
½ t. oregano	2 T. cornstarch

Put chicken in 3 cups of water with 1 tablespoon of salt. Cover and bring to a boil. Simmer until tender. Cool in broth. Remove from broth and remove bones. Boil broth to 2 cups; strain. Melt 1 tablespoon butter in a skillet, add 1 medium onion chopped fine, 1 green pepper chopped, 1 minced clove of garlic, and sauté. Add 1 pound can of stewed tomatoes, 2 small cans drained mushrooms, 4 tablespoons chopped parsley, 1 teaspoon pepper, 1 teaspoon chili powder, ½ teaspoon oregano and chicken broth. Cook uncovered 15 minutes. Mix 2 tablespoons cornstarch with cold water, add and cook 1 minute, stirring constantly.

Divide chicken in casserole, add sauce, cover with foil and store in the refrigerator. Use the next day. Set casserole at room temperature for 2 hours before placing in a 400° oven for half an hour before serving. Serves 8 of you have potatoes and vegetables.

Charlotte Russe

1 package unflavored gelatin	¼ cup cold water
2 eggs	½ cup sugar
1 t. vanilla	Bourbon to taste (3+ T.)
Salt	1 pint whipping cream

2 packages ladyfingers (one is enough if it has 8 ladyfingers in the package)

Pour gelatin in cold water and set container in a pan of hot/warm water. Separate eggs. Beat yolks. Add sugar, vanilla, bourbon and a little salt. Beat. Beat egg whites until stiff. Whip cream (not too stiff). Pour gelatin mixture into yolks and stir to incorporate thoroughly. Fold in whipped cream and stir to incorporate thoroughly. Fold in egg whites and stir. Pour into bowl lined with lady fingers. Scatter pieces of ladyfingers through the Charlotte.

Serves 8. Recipe can be doubled. Will keep for several days in the refrigerator.

Mrs. Provost:

Spoon Bread

2 cups sweet milk, scalded	½ t. salt
1 T. sugar	1 cup cornmeal, added slowly
1 stick butter or margarine	3 large egg yolks, well-beaten

3 large egg whites, beaten until stiff

Mix the first 5 ingredients and when thick, add the egg yolks. When mixture is cool, fold in egg whites. Pour into a well-greased casserole. Bake for 35 minutes in a 350° oven. Serve immediately, for it falls as soon as air hits it.

Good September Relish

4 apples	4 medium onions
4 sweet green peppers	2 quarts ripe tomatoes, peeled
1 cup cider vinegar	¼ t. black pepper
Bit of cayenne pepper (or red hot pepper)	2 cups brown sugar
½ t. ground cloves	1 t. cinnamon

Bit of salt

Chop apples, tomatoes, onions and peppers. Add vinegar, sugar, black pepper, cloves and spices. Cook, stirring occasionally, until thick – about 2 hours. Can in sterilized jars.

Apple Pudding

1 cup sugar	¼ cup butter
1 egg	2 or 3 apples, chopped
1 cup flour	1 t. baking soda
1 t. cinnamon	¼ t. cloves
Dab of salt	½ cup nut meats

Cream the sugar and butter. Add the egg and apples. Add mixed together the flour, soda, cinnamon, cloves and salt. Add the nuts. Bake in 350° oven for 30 minutes in a square pan. Serve warm with whipped cream or vanilla ice cream.

Mrs. Randall:

On-the-Wing Appetizers

30 (about 2 ½ lbs.) chicken wing drums or small legs

½ t. salt	¼ cup soy sauce
¼ cup spiced peach or apricot syrup	2 T. honey
¼ t. Accent	½ t. ground ginger
1 T. lemon juice	5 drops Tabasco
1 clove garlic	

Marinate for about 8 hours (or overnight). Roast at 350° for 1 hour on a flat pan. Baste twice with marinade during roasting. Can be frozen. Can be doubled or tripled.

Mystery Slaw

3 cups shredded turnips (2 lbs)	1 ½ cups shredded carrots
½ cup raisins	½ to ¾ cup mayonnaise
1 T. lemon juice	

Combine all ingredients in a large bowl. Stir well. Cover and chill. 6 to 8 servings.

Brunch Casserole

12 slices white bread – crusts trimmed, buttered on both sides, cubed

1 lb. cooked sausage, crumbled   ½ lb. shredded cheddar cheese

4 to 6 eggs, lightly beaten   3 cups milk

½ t. salt – pepper

Butter 9x13 baking pan or dish. Sprinkle sausage and cheese over bread cubes. Combine remaining ingredients. Pour over bread cubes. Cover and refrigerate overnight. Bake covered for 45 minutes to 1 hour at 350°. Serve immediately.

English Shortbread

4 cups all purpose flour   2 cups butter, softened

1 ¼ cup 10X sugar   1 t. baking powder

¼ t. salt

Preheat oven 325°. In a large bowl, measure all ingredients. With hand, knead ingredients until well blended. (Good to beat butter before adding other ingredients). Pat dough into two 9-inch round or square cake pans. Prick dough in many places with prongs of fork. Bake 35 to 45 minutes or until golden. While warm, with sharp knife, cut into small pieces. This is very rich. Cool in pans or wire racks. Store in tightly covered containers. Lasts for weeks. Can also be baked in a 9x13 pan.

Roasted Pecan Clusters

3 T. butter or margarine   3 cups pecan pieces

12 (1 oz.) squares chocolate flavored candy coating

Melt butter in 15x10x1 jelly roll pan. Spread pecans evenly in pan. Bake at 300° for 30 minutes; stirring 3 times. Place candy coating in top of double boiler. Bring water to boil. Reduce heat to low and cook coating till melts. Cool 2 minutes. Add pecans and stir until coated. Drop by rounded teaspoon onto wax paper. Let cool completely. Yields 4 dozen.

Mrs. Richardson:

Sourdough Bread

1 cup starter	1 ½ cups water
½ cup oil	2 T. sugar
2 T. salt	5-6 cups bread flour

To the first 5 ingredients, add 4 c. flour and mix with a spoon. Add one more cup of flour. Knead 10 minutes. Add flour as needed. Put in an ungreased bowl, cover lightly overnight or until double in size.

Next day, pound down and divide into3 loaves. Let rise for 5 hours. Then bake at 350° for 35 to 40 minutes in a greased pan.

You need to re-feed the starter every 5 to 8 days. Take 1 cup hot water and dissolve in it 2 tablespoons of potato flakes, ½ cup of sugar and 1 cup of bread flour. Add to the starter, cover lightly, let stand overnight, and then refrigerate.

Mrs. Stokes:

Diabetic Pumpkin Pie

1 (no. 2) can of pumpkin	2 eggs
1 can condensed milk	1 t. vanilla

4 packets Sweet-n-Low (more if you like it sweeter)

1 t. pumpkin pie spice (a little more if you like it spicier)

Mix all the ingredients together. Pour into a pie shell. Put it in the microwave on high for 45 minutes. Test it with a knife to see if it comes out clean.

Smothered Chicken

Chicken thighs, cooked (can use breasts)

1 can cream of chicken soup, diluted with half of a liquid (usually milk, can use water)

1 cup peas and onions, chopped up	1 cup green beans
1 cup carrots	1 cup potatoes

Put the chicken and vegetables in a casserole and pour the soup mixture over it. Put it in the microwave on high for 45-50 minutes. You have to test it.

Mrs. Vossler:

Bean Salad

1 can kidney beans	1 can green beans
1 can wax beans	1 can garbanzo beans
1 large onion, sliced	1 red or green pepper, chopped
1 bunch celery, cut up	½ cup salad or olive oil
1 t. salt – pepper	½ cup cider vinegar

Mix and let sit. Lasts one month or 6 weeks.

Old Fashioned Apple Crisp

½ to ¾ cup sugar	1 t. cinnamon

4 cups Jonathan apples, cut and sliced

Topping:

½ cup sugar	½ cup flour
½ cup butter	½ cup uncooked oatmeal

Combine sugar and cinnamon with apples and place in a 9 x 9 pan. Blend together sugar, flour, butter and oatmeal until mixture resembles small peas. Sprinkle on apples. Bake at 350° for 30-45 minutes or until apples are tender and top is lightly browned.

Serve hot with ice cream, whipped cream or sharp cheddar cheese slices. Delicious as it comes plain from the oven. Makes 6 – 8 servings.

Mrs. Wilson:

Third Church Chicken

First cook, bone and cut up chicken in chunks (she cooks a whole fryer with peppercorns, cabbage, celery, and carrots until tender – takes the skin off)

246

1 small container sour cream   1 can mushroom soup

1 can sliced mushrooms   1 can sliced water chestnuts

4 cups of chopped chicken

Mix first four ingredients and then mix chicken in.

8 oz. pkg. Pepperidge Farm stuffing   ½ stick of margarine

Put in 1 cup of broth   Add 1 cup of pecans (optional)

In buttered casserole, put in mix and top with stuffing mix. Bake uncovered at 325° for 30 minutes or 350° and watch it, if in a hurry.

Freezes and reheats well. If using white meat only, 3 big chicken breasts will work.

Granola

1 cup raw wheat germ   2 cups rolled oats

1 cup oat bran   ¼ cup sesame seed

½ cup sunflower seed   1 cup chopped nuts (not fine)

Mix together. In a separate bowl, mix:

¼ cup oil (safflower)   ¾ cup honey

Work throughout the dry ingredients. Bake in 300° oven in roaster sprayed with Pam - for 1 ½ hour – need to stir every 15 minutes. After cooled, put in plastic bag. Should be a light tan color – don't over do it, but it needs enough. Towards the end of baking, may want to taste a teaspoon to make sure it is crunchy.

Bibliography

References

Adams, F. (1988). Fluid intake: how much do elders drink? *Geriatric Nursing, 9*(4), 218-221.

Alford, D. M. (1986). Behavioral response of the institutionalized elderly to eating and food services. *Nursing Homes, 35*(1), 20-24.

Alonzo, A. A., & Reynolds, N. R. (1994). Care-seeking during acute myocardial infarction: A model for intervention. Paper presented at the American Sociological Association.

Altus, D. E., Engelman, K. K., & Mathews, R. M. (2002). Using family-style meals to increase participation and communication in persons with dementia. *Journal of Gerontological Nursing, 28*(9), 47-53.

Amarantos, E., Martinez, A., & Dwyer, J. (2001). Nutrition and quality of life in older adults. *Journals of Gerontology Series A: Biological Sciences and Medical Sciences, 56A*(Special Issue II), 54-64.

Amella, E. J. (1999). Factors influencing the proportion of food consumed by nursing home residents with dementia. *Journal of the American Geriatrics Society, 47*(7), 879-885.

Asato, K. T. (1992). Retirement community residents and their use of kitchen appliances. *Spectrum: National Association for Senior Living Industries, 6*(12), 8-11.

Backett, K. C., & Davison, C. (1995). Lifecourse and lifestyle: The social and cultural location of health behaviours. *Social Science and Medicine, 40*(5), 629-638.

Ball, M. M., Whittington, F. J., Perkins, M. M., Patterson, V. L., Hollingsworth, C., King, S. V., et al. (2000). Quality of life in assisted living facilities: Viewpoints of residents. *Journal of Applied Gerontology, 19*(3), 304-325.

Bandura, A. (1986). *Social Foundations of Thought and Action: A Social Cognitive Theory.* Englewood Cliffs, NJ: Prentice Hall.

Baranowski, T. (1997). Families and health actions. In D. S. Gochman (Ed.), *Handbook of Health Behavior Research I: Personal and Social Determinants* (pp. 179-206). New York: Plenum Press.

Baranowski, T., Perry, C., & Parcel, G. (1997). How individuals, environments, and health behavior interact: Social cognitive theory. In K. Glanz, F. Lewis, & B. Rimer (Eds.), *Health Behavior and Health Education: Theory, Research and Practice* (2nd ed., pp. 153-178). San Francisco: Jossey-Bass.

248

Barnes, P. M., Powell-Griner, E., McFann, K., & Nahin, R. L. (2004). *Complementary and alternative medicine use among adults: United States, 2002* (Advance data from vital and health statistics, no. 343). Hyattsville, MD: National Center for Health Statistics.

Barr, J. T., & Schumacher, G. E. (2003). The need for a nutrition-related quality-of-life measure. *Journal of the American Dietetic Association, 103*(2), 177-180.

Bartali, B., Salvini, S., Turrini, A., Laurentani, F., Russo, C. R., Corsi, A. M., et al. (2003). Age and disability affect dietary intake. *Journal of Nutrition, 133*(9), 2868-2873.

Beardsworth, A., & Keil, T. (1997). *Sociology on the Menu: An Invitation to the Study of Food and Society.* New York: Routledge.

Beattie, E. R. A., Algase, D. L., & Song, J. (2004). Keeping wandering nursing homes residents at the table: improving food intake using a behavioral communication intervention. *Aging and Mental Health, 8*(2), 109-116.

Beck, A. M., & Ovensen, L. (2003). Influence of social engagement and dining location on nutritional intake and body mass index of old nursing home residents. *Journal of Nutrition for the Elderly, 22*(4), 1-11.

Bell, R., Quandt, S. A., Arcury, T. A., McDonald, J., & Vitolins, M. Z. (2002). Health locus of control among rural older adults: associations with demographic, health and preventive health characteristics. *Gerontology and Geriatrics Education, 22*(4), 69-89.

Bengtson, V. L., Burgess, E. O., & Parrott, T. M. (1997). Theory, explanation and a third generation of theoretical development in social gerontology. *The Journals of Gerontology Series B: Psychological Sciences and Social Sciences, 52B*(2), S72-S88.

Bennett, P., & Murphy, S. (1997). Cognitive mediators of health-related behaviours. *Psychology and Health Promotion* (pp. 25-44). Philadelphia: Open University Press.

Berkman, L., & Breslow, L. (1983). *Health and Ways of Living: The Alameda County Study.* New York: Oxford University Press.

Bermudez, O. I., & Tucker, K. L. (2004). Cultural aspects of food choices in various communities of elders. *Generations, 28*(3), 22-27.

Bisogni, C. A., Connors, M., Devine, C. M., & Sobal, J. (2002). Who we are and how we eat: A qualitative study of identities in food choice. *Journal of Nutrition Education and Behavior, 34*(3), 128-139.

Bonnel, W. B. (1999). Meal management strategies of older adult women. *Journal of Gerontological Nursing, 25*(1), 41-47.

Bovbjerg, V. E., McCann, B. S., Brief, D. J., Follette, W. C., Retzlaff, B. M., Dowdy, A. A., et al. (1995). Spouse support and long-term adherence to lipid-lowering diets. *American Journal of Epidemiology, 141*(5), 451-460.

Bowers, D. E. (2000). Cooking trends echo changing roles of women. *Food Review, 23*(1), 23-29.

Briley, M. E. (1994). Food preferences of the elderly. *Nutrition Reviews, 52*(8), S21-S23.

Brombach, C. H. (2001a). The EVA-Study: Meal patterns of women over 65 years. *Journal of Nutrition, Health and Aging, 5*(4), 263-265.

Brombach, C. H. (2001b). The EVA-Study: Nutrition behaviour in the life course of elderly women. *Journal of Nutrition, Health and Aging, 5*(4), 261-262.

Brown, S. A., Harris, R. B., Villagomez, E. T., Segura, M., Barton, S. A., & Hanis, C. L. (2000). Gender and treatment differences in knowledge, health beliefs, and metabolic control in Mexican Americans with type 2 diabetes. *The Diabetes Educator, 26*(3), 425-438.

Brown, J. L., & Miller, D. (2001). Gender role preference and family food chores. *Journal of Nutrition Education, 33*(5), 1-9.

Brownie, S., & Myers, S. (2003). Dietary and health supplement use among older Australians: results from a national survey. *Australasian Journal on Ageing, 22*(4), 171-178.

Burton, R. P. D., & Hudson, T. (2001). Achieving individually sustained commitment to treatment through self-constructed models of medical adherence. *Sociological Spectrum, 21*(3), 393-422.

Burton, L., Schulz, R., German, P. Hirsch, C., & Mittlemark, M. (1994). Effects of caregiving on life-style health behaviors and preventive health seeking: A multi-site national caregiving health effects study, an ancillary study of the cardiovascular health study. Paper presented at the annual meeting of the Gerontological Society of America, Atlanta.

Callen, B. L., & Wells, T. J. (2003). Views of community-dwelling, old-old people on barriers and aids to nutritional health. *Journal of Nursing Scholarship, 35*(3), 257-262.

Charles, N., & Kerr, M. (1988). *Women, Food and Families.* Manchester, England: Manchester University Press.

Cheang, M. (2002). Older adults' frequent visits to a fast-food restaurant: nonobligatory social interaction and the significance of play in a "third place". *Journal of Aging Studies, 16*(3), 303-321.

Chernoff, R. (2001). Nutrition and health promotion in older adults. *Journals of Gerontology Series A: Biological Sciences and Medical Sciences, 56A*(Special Issue II), 47-53.

Clark, P., Nigg, C., Greene, G., Riebe, D., & Saunders, S. (2002). Study of Exercise and Nutrition in Older Rhode Islanders (SENIOR): translating theory into research. *Health Education Research, 17*(5), 552-561.

Clarke, L. H. (2002). Older women's perceptions of ideal body weights: the tensions between health and appearance. *Ageing and Society, 22*(6), 751-773.

Clipp, E. C., Elder, G. H., George, L. K., & Pieper, C. F. (1998). Trajectories of health in aging populations. In W. M. Gesler, D. J. Rabiner, & G. H. DeFriese (Eds.), *Rural Health and Aging Research: Theory, Methods and*

250

Practical Applications (pp. 177-198). Amityville, NY: Baywood Publishing.

Cluskey, M. (2001a). Offering three-meal options in continuing care retirement communities may improve intake of residents. *Journal of Nutrition for the Elderly, 20*(3), 57-62.

Cluskey, M. (2001b). Preliminary investigation of the food intake patterns and beliefs among independent living elderly residents in a continuing care retirement community. *Journal of Nutrition for the Elderly, 20*(3), 29-38.

Cohen, R. Y., Brownell, K. D., & Felix, M. R. (1990). Age and sex differences in health habits and beliefs of schoolchildren. *Health Psychology, 9*, 208-224.

Cohen, S. J., Weinberger, M. H., Fineberg, N. S., Miller, J. Z., Grim, C. E., & Luft, F. C. (1991). The effect of a household partner and home urine monitoring on adherence to a sodium restricted diet. *Social Science and Medicine, 32*(9), 1057-1061.

Cohen, M. J., Werner, P., Weinfield, M., Braun, J., & Kraft, G. (1995). Autonomy for nursing home residents: The role of regulations. *Behavioral Sciences and the Law, 13*(3), 415-423.

Conn, V. S. (1997). Older women: social cognitive theory correlates of health behavior. *Women and Health, 26*(3), 71-85.

Conn, V. S., & Armer, J. S. (1995). Older spouses: Similarity of health promotion behaviors. *Journal of Family Nursing, 1*(4), 397.

Connell, C. M. (1994). Impact of spouse caregiving on health behaviors and physical and mental health status. *American Journal of Alzheimer's Care and Related Disorders and Research, 9*(1), 26-36.

Connell, C. M., & Schulenberg, J. (1990). Daily variations in physical and mental health impact of caregiving. Paper presented at the annual meeting of the Gerontological Society of America, Boston.

Connors, M., Bisogni, C. A., Sobal, J., & Devine, C. M. (2001). Managing values in personal food systems. *Appetite, 36*(3), 189-200.

Coreil, J., Bryant, C., & Henderson, J. N. (2001). The social environment and health. In J. Coreil, C. Bryant, & J. N. Henderson (Eds.), *Social and Behavioral Foundations of Public Health* (pp. 103-126). Thousand Oaks, CA: Sage.

Courtenay, W. H. (2000). Construction of masculinity and their influence on men's well-being: A theory of gender and health. *Social Science and Medicine, 50*(10), 1385-1402.

Coveney, J. (2002). What does research on family and food tell us? Implications for nutrition and dietetic practice. *Nutrition & Dietetics, 59*(2), 113-119.

Cowell, J. M., & Marks, B. A. (1997). Health behavior in adolescents. In D. S. Gochman (Ed.), *Handbook of Health Behavior Research III: Demography, Development and Diversity* (pp. 73-96). New York: Plenum Press.

Dangour, A. D., Sibson, V. L., & Fletcher, A. E. (2004). Micronutrient supplementation in later life: limited evidence for benefit. *Journals of Gerontology Series A: Biological Sciences and Medical Sciences, 59A*(7), 659-673.

Daniel, T. D., Houston, D. K., & Johnson, M. A. (1995). Vitamin and mineral supplement use among the elderly. In B. J. Vellas et al. (Eds.) *Facts and Research in Gerontology* (Supplement: Nutrition, pp. 163-179). New York: Springer.

Davis, C., & Saltos, E. (1999). Dietary recommendations and how they have changed over time. In E. Frazão (Ed.), *America's Eating Habits: Changes and Consequences* (ABI-750, pp. 33-50). Washington D.C.: U.S. Department of Agriculture/Economic Research Service.

Davis, M. A., Murphy, S. P., & Neuhaus, J. M. (1988). Living arrangements and eating behaviors of older adults in the United States. *Journals of Gerontology Series B: Psychological Sciences and Social Sciences, 43*(3), S96-S98.

de Groot, L. C. P. M. G., Verheijden, M. W., de Henauw, S., Schroll, M., & van Staveren, W. A. (2004). Lifestyle, nutritional status, health, and mortality in elderly people across Europe: a review of the longitudinal results of the SENECA Study. *Journals of Gerontology Series A: Biological Sciences and Medical Sciences, 59A*(12), 1277-1284.

DeVault, M. (1991). *Feeding the Family: The Social Organization of Caring and Gendered Work*. Chicago: University of Chicago Press.

Devine, C. M. (2005). A life course perspective: Understanding food choices in time, social location, and history. *Journal of Nutrition Education and Behavior, 37*(3), 121-128.

Devine, C. M., Connors, M., Bisogni, C. A., & Sobal, J. (1998). Life-course influences on fruit and vegetable trajectories: Qualitative analysis of food choices. *Journal of Nutrition Education, 30*(6), 361-370.

Devine, C. M., & Olson, C. M. (1991). Women's dietary prevention motives: Life stage influences. *Journal of Nutrition Education, 23*, 269-274.

Devine, C. M., & Olson, C. M. (1992). Women's perceptions about the way social roles promote or constrain personal nutrition care. *Women's Health, 18*, 79-95.

Devine, C. M., & Sandström, B. (1996). Relationship of social roles and nutrition beliefs to fat avoidance practices: Investigation of a U.S. model among Danish women. *Journal of the American Dietetic Association, 96*(6), 580-584.

Devine, C. M., Wolfe, W. S., Frongillo, E. A., & Bisogni, C. A. (1999). Life-course events and experiences: Associations with fruit and vegetable consumption in 3 ethnic groups. *Journal of the American Dietetic Association, 99*(3), 309-314.

Donini, L. M., Savina, C., & Cannella, C. (2003). Eating habits and appetite control in the elderly: the anorexia of aging. *International Psychogeriatrics, 15*(1), 73-87.

Douglas, M. (1984). Standard social uses of food: Introduction. In M. Douglas (Ed.), *Food in the Social Order* (pp. 1-39). New York: Russell Sage Foundation.

Douglas, M., & Isherwood, B. (1979). *The World of Goods: Towards an Anthropology of Consumption*. London: Routledge.

Douglas-Steele, D. (1995). 'Don't Drink All the Milk Esther': The interactive production of identity and hierarchy in a nursing home. *Semiotica, 103*(1-2), 69-95.

Doyle, V. (1994). *It's My Turn Now: The Choice of Older Women to Live Alone.* Vancouver: Gerontology Research Center at Simon Frasier University.

Drewnowski, A., & Evans, W. J. (2001). Nutrition, physical activity, and quality of life in adults: Summary. *Journals of Gerontology Series A: Biological Sciences and Medical Sciences, 56A*(Special Issue II), 89-94.

Duncan, H. H., Travis, S. S., & McAuley, W. J. (1995). An emergent theoretical model for interventions encouraging physical activity (mall walking) among older adults. *Journal of Applied Gerontology, 14*(1), 64-78.

Edstrom, K. M., & Devine, C. M. (2001). Consistency in women's orientations to food and nutrition in midlife and older age: A 10-year qualitative follow-up. *Journal of Nutrition Education, 33*(4), 215-223.

Elder, G. H. (1985). Perspectives on the life course. In G. H. Elder (Ed.), *Life Course Dynamics: Trajectories and Transitions, 1968-1980* (pp. 23-49). Ithaca, NY: Cornell University Press.

Elder, G. H. (1995). The life course paradigm: Social change and individual development. In P. Moen, G. Elder, & K. Luscher (Eds.), *Examining Lives in Context: Perspectives on the Ecology of Human Development* (pp. 101-139). Washington D.C.: American Psychological Association.

Elder, G. H., Shanahan, M. J., & Clipp, E. C. (1994). When war comes to men's lives: Life-course patterns in family, work and health. *Psychology of Aging, 9*(1), 5-16.

Elsner, R. J. F. (2002). Changes in eating behavior during the aging process. *Eating Behaviors, 3*(1), 15-43.

Evans, B. C., & Crogan, N. L. (2005). Using the FoodEx-LTC to assess institutional food service practices through nursing home residents' perspectives on nutrition care. *Journals of Gerontology Series A: Biological Sciences and Medical Sciences, 60A*(1), 125-128.

Evans, B. C., Crogan, N. L., & Shultz, J. A. (2003). Quality dining in the nursing home: the residents' perspectives. *Journal of Nutrition for the Elderly, 22*(3), 1-17.

Evans, B. C., Crogan, N. L., & Shultz, J. A. (2005). Meaning of mealtimes: connection to the social world of the nursing home. *Journal of Gerontological Nursing, 31*(2), 11-17.

Evans, W. J., & Cyr-Campbell, D. (1997). Nutrition, exercise and healthy aging. *Journal of the American Dietetic Association, 97*(6), 632-638.

Farrand, L. L., & Cox, C. L. (1993). Determinants of positive health behaviors in middle childhood. *Nursing Research, 42*(4), 208-213.

Ferraro, K. F., Farmer, M. M., & Wynbraniec, J. A. (1997). Health trajectories: Long-term dynamics among Black and White adults. *Journal of Health and Social Behavior, 38*(1), 38-54.

Fetto, J. (2000). Drink plenty of fluids. *American Demographics, 22*(8), 8-9.

Finkelstein, J. (1985). Dining out: The self in search of civility. *Studies in Symbolic Interaction, 6*, 183-212.

Fischer, J. G., Johnson, M. A., Poon, L. W., & Martin, P. (1995). Dairy product intake of the oldest old. *Journal of the American Dietetic Association, 95*(8), 918-921.

Ford, E., Ahluwalia, I., & Galuska, D. (2000). Social relationships and cardiovascular disease risk factors: Findings from the third National Health and Nutrition Examination Survey. *Preventive Medicine, 30*(2), 83-92.

Frazão, E. (1999). High costs of poor eating patterns in the United States. In E. Frazão (Ed.), *America's Eating Habits: Changes and Consequences* (ABI-750, pp. 5-32). Washington, D.C.: U.S. Department of Agriculture/Economic Research Service.

Frazier, S. K., & Garvin, B. J. (1996). Cardiac patients' conversation and the process of establishing meaning. *Progressive Cardiovascular Nursing, 11*(4), 25-34.

Fries, J. F. (2000). Compression of morbidity in the elderly. *Vaccine, 18*(16), 1584-1589.

Furst, T., Connors, M., Bisogni, C. A., Sobal, J., & Falk, L. W. (1996). Food choice: A conceptual model of the process. *Appetite, 26*(3), 247-266.

Geersten, R. (1997). Social attachments, group structures, and health behavior. In D. S. Gochman (Ed.), *Handbook of Health Behavior Research I: Personal and Social Determinants* (pp. 267-288). New York: Plenum Press.

Giele, J. Z., & Elder, G. H. (1998). Life course research: Development of a field. In J. Z. Giele, & G. H. Elder, (Eds.), *Methods of Life Course Research: Qualitative and Quantitative Approaches* (pp. 5-27). Thousand Oaks, CA: Sage.

Gilani, S. (1995). Tempting the tastes of seniors. *Spectrum: National Association for Senior Living Industries, 9*(3), 20-22.

Gillette, F. L., & Ziemann, H. (1887). *The White House Cook Book*. Chicago: The Werner Company.

Glanz, K., Lewis, F. M., & Rimer, B. (Eds.). (1997). *Health Behavior and Health Education: Theory, Research and Practice* (2nd ed.). San Francisco: Jossey-Bass.

Glik, D. C., & Kronenfeld, J. J. (1989). Well roles: An approach to reincorporate role theory into medical sociology. In J. J. Kronenfeld, & D. C. Weitz

254

(Eds.), *Research in the Sociology of Health Care, Volume 8* (pp. 289-309). Stamford, CT: JAI Press.

Gochman, D. S. (Ed.). (1997). *Handbook of Health Behavior Research I: Personal and Social Determinants.* New York: Plenum Press.

Gochman, D. S. (1997). Health behavior research: Definitions and diversity. In D. S. Gochman (Ed.), *Handbook of Health Behavior Research I: Personal and Social Determinants* (pp. 3-20). New York: Plenum Press.

Greaney, M. L., Lees, F., Greene, G., & Clark, P. (2004). What older adults find useful for maintaining healthy eating and exercise habits. *Journal of Nutrition for the Elderly, 24*(2), 19-35.

Grembowski, D., Patrick, D., Durham, M., Beresford, S., Kay, E., & Hecht, J. (1993). Self-efficacy and health behaviors of older adults. *Journal of Health and Social Behavior, 34*(2), 89-104.

Grzywacz, J. G., & Marks, N. F. (1999). Family solidarity and health behaviors. *Journal of Family Issues, 20*(2), 243-268.

Gubrium, J. F. (1997). *Living and Dying at Murray Manor* (expanded paperback ed.). Charlottesville, VA: University Press of Virginia.

Gustafsson, K., Andersson, I., Andersson, J., Fjellstrom, C., & Sidenvall, B. (2003). Older women's perceptions of independence versus dependence in food-related work. *Public Health Nursing, 20*(3), 237-247.

Haines, P. S. (1996). Food consumption patterns in women. In D. A. Krummel, & P. M. Kris-Etherton (Eds.), *Nutrition in Women's Health* (pp. 103-140). Gaithersburg, MD: Aspen Publishers.

Harper, D. (2000). Reservations about dinner. *Assisted Living Today, 7*(9), 36-38.

Hatch, L. R. (2000). *Beyond Gender Differences: Adaptation to Aging in Life Course Perspective.* Amityville, NY: Baywood Publishing Co.

Hayaki, J., & Brownell, K. D. (1996). Behaviour change in practice: Group approaches. *International Journal of Obesity and Related Metabolic Disorders, 20*(Supplement 1), S27-S30.

Heaney, C., & Israel, B. (1997). Social networks and social support. In K. Glanz, F. Lewis, & B. Rimer (Eds.), *Health Behavior and Health Education: Theory, Research and Practice* (2nd ed., pp. 179-205). San Francisco: Jossey-Bass.

Hendricks, J., Calasanti, T. M., & Turner, H. B. (1988). Foodways of the elderly: Social research considerations. *American Behavioral Scientist, 32*(1), 61-83.

Hitchcock, P. B., Brantley, P. J., Jones, G. N., & McKnight, G. T. (1992). Stress and social support as predictors of dietary compliance in hemodialysis patients. *Behavioral Medicine, 18*(1), 13-20.

Hogan, D. B., Maxwell, C. J., & Ebly, E. M. (2003). Use of complementary and alternative medicines by older individuals: results from the Canadian Study of Health and Aging. *Geriatrics Today, 6*(1), 21-25.

Holmes, T. S., & Gates, G. E. (2003). Influences on fruit, vegetable, and grain intake of older men. *Journal of Nutrition for the Elderly, 22*(3), 43-61.

Horwath, C. C. (1989). Marriage and diet in elderly Australians: Results from a large random survey. *Journal of Human Nutrition and Dietetics, 2,* 185-193.

Houston, D. K., Daniel, T. D., Johnson, M. A., & Poon, L. W. (1998). Demographic characteristics of supplement users in an elderly population. *Journal of Applied Gerontology, 17*(1), 79-96.

Hover, S., & Gaffney, L. (1988). Factors associated with smoking behavior in adolescent girls. *Addictive Behaviors, 13*(2), 139-145.

Howarth, G. (1993). Food consumption, social roles and personal identity. In S. Arber, & M. Evandrou (Eds.), *Ageing, Independence and the Life Course* (pp. 65-77). London: Jessica Kingsley Publishers.

Huck, D. M., & Armer, J. M. (1996). Health perceptions and health-promoting behaviors among elderly Catholic nuns. *Family and Community Health, 18*(4), 81-91.

Institute of Medicine. (2000). *The Role of Nutrition in Maintaining Health in the Nation's Elderly.* Washington D.C.: National Academy Press.

International Food Information Council. (2001). Exploring the food and health attitudes of older Americans. *Journal of Nutrition for the Elderly, 20*(3), 39-43.

International Longevity Center-USA. (2000). *Maintaining Healthy Lifestyles: A Lifetime of Choices.* New York: International Longevity Center-USA.

Jacobs, J. (1975). *Older Persons and Retirement Communities: Case Studies in Gerontology.* Springfield, IL: Charles C. Thomas.

Johnson, A. E., Donkin, A. J., Morgan, K., Neale, R. J., Page, R. M., & Silburn, R. L. (1998). Fruit and vegetable consumption in later life. *Age and Ageing, 27*(6), 723-728.

Johnson, C. S. (2002). Nutritional considerations for bereavement and coping with grief. *Journal of Nutrition, Health and Aging, 6*(3), 171-176.

Kant, A. K., Graubard, B. I., & Schatzkin, A. (2004). Dietary patterns predict mortality in a national cohort: The National Health Interview Surveys, 1987 and 1992. *Journal of Nutrition, 134*(7), 1793-1799.

Kaplan, G. A. (1992). Health and aging in the Alameda County Study. In K. W. Schaie, D. Blazer, & J. House (Eds.), *Aging, Health Behaviors and Health Outcomes* (pp. 69-95). Hillsdale, NJ: Lawrence Earlbaum Associates.

Kaplan, G. A., & Strawbridge, W. J. (1994). Behavioral and social factors in healthy aging. In R. P. Abeles, H. C. Gift, & M. G. Ory (Eds.), *Aging and Quality of Life* (pp. 57-78). New York: Springer.

Kayser-Jones, J. (1996). Mealtime in nursing homes: The importance of individualized care. *Journal of Gerontological Nursing, 22*(3), 26-31.

Kayser-Jones, J. (2000). Improving the nutritional care of nursing home residents. *Nursing Homes: Long Term Care Management, 49*(10), 56-58.

Kayser-Jones, J., & Schell, E. S. (1997). Staffing and mealtime experience of nursing home residents on a special care unit. *American Journal of Alzheimer's Disease, 12*(2), 67-72.

Kelsey, K., Earp, J. A. L., & Kirkley, B. G. (1997). Is social support beneficial for dietary change? A review of the literature. *Family and Community Health, 20*(3), 70-82.

Keith Ross, J. (1977). *Old People, New Lives: Community Creation in a Retirement Residence.* Chicago: University of Chicago Press.

King, M. O. B., & Pettigrew, A. C. (2004). Complementary and alternative therapy use by older adults in three ethnically diverse populations: a pilot study. *Geriatric Nursing, 25*(1), 30-37.

Kremmer, D., Anderson, A. S., & Marshall, D. W. (1998). Living together and eating together: Changes in food choice and eating habits during the transition from single to married/cohabiting. *The Sociological Review, 46*(1), 48-72.

Lancaster, K. J. (2004). Characteristics influencing daily consumption of fruits and vegetables and low-fat dairy products in older adults with hypertension. *Journal of Nutrition for the Elderly, 23*(4), 21-33.

LaRossa, R., & Reitzes, D. C. (1993). Symbolic interactionism and family studies. In P. G. Boss, W. J. Doherty, R. LaRossa, W. R. Schumm, & S. K. Steinmetz (Eds.), *Sourcebook of Family Theories and Methods: A Contextual Approach* (pp. 135-163). New York: Plenum Press.

Lau, R., Quadrel, M. J., & Hartman, K. A. (1990). Development and change of young adults' preventive health beliefs and behavior: Influence from parents and peers. *Journal of Health and Social Behavior, 31*(3), 240-259.

Lauque, S., Soleilhavoup, C., Faisant, C., Ghisolfi-Marque, A., Bertiere, M. C., Sachet, P. et al. (1995). Prospective study of the consequences of retiring on nutritional intake: Preliminary study. In B. J. Vellas et al. (Eds.) *Facts and Research in Gerontology* (Supplement: Nutrition, pp. 133-141). New York: Springer.

Law, J. (1984). How much of society can the sociologist digest at one sitting? The 'macro' and the 'micro' revisited. *Studies in Symbolic Interaction, 5*, 171-196.

Leigh, J. P., & Fries, J. F. (1992). Health habits, health care use and costs in a sample of retirees. *Inquiry Chicago, 29*(1), 44-54.

Leininger, M. M. (1985). Life health-care history: Purposes, methods, and techniques. In M. M. Leininger (Ed.), *Qualitative Research Methods in Nursing* (pp. 119-132). Orlando: Grune & Stratton.

Levenstein, H. (2003). *Paradox of Plenty: A Social History of Eating in Modern America* (Revised ed.). Berkeley, CA: University of California Press.

Leventhal, E. (2000). Aging women, getting older, getting better? In S. B. Manuck, R. Jennings, B. S. Rabin, & A. Baum (Eds.), *Behavior, Health and Aging* (pp. 27-42). Mahwah, NJ: Lawrence Earlbaum Associates.

Lévi-Strauss, C. (1970). *The Raw and the Cooked.* London: Jonathon Cape.

Levy, S. (1981). Personal narratives: A key to interpreting consumer behavior. *Western Folklore, 40*(1), 94-106.

Lewin, K. (1943). Forces behind food habits and methods of change. In National Research Council (Ed.), *The Problem of Changing Food Habits* (pp. 35-65). Washington, D.C.: National Academy Press.

Louk, K. R., Schafer, E., Schafer, R. B., & Keith, P. (1999). Comparison of dietary intakes of husbands and wives. *Journal of Nutrition Education, 31*(3), 145-152.

Luborsky, M. R. (1994). The identification and analysis of themes and patterns. In J. F. Gubrium, & A. Sankar (Eds.), *Qualitative Methods in Aging Research* (pp. 189-210). Thousand Oaks, CA: Sage.

Lupton, D. (1994). Food, memory and meaning: The symbolic and social nature of food events. *The Sociological Review, 42*(4), 664-685.

Lupton, D. (1996). *Food, the Body and the Self.* London: Sage Publications.

Lupton, D. (2000). The heart of the meal: Food preferences and habits among rural Australian couples. *Sociology of Health and Illness, 22*(1), 94-109.

Lynch, J. W., Kaplan, G. A., & Salonen, J. T. (1997). Why do poor people behave poorly? Variation in adult health behaviours and psychosocial characteristics by stages of the socioeconomic lifecourse. *Social Science and Medicine, 44*(6), 809-819.

Manton, C. (1999). *Fed Up: Women and Food in America.* Westport, CT: Bergin & Garvey.

Marken, D. (2004). Enhancing the dining experience in long-term care: Dining With Dignity program. *Journal of Nutrition for the Elderly, 23*(3), 99-109.

Matheson, D. M., Woolcott, D. M., Matthews, A. M., & Roth, V. (1991). Evaluation of a theoretical model predicting self-efficacy toward nutrition behaviors. *Journal of Nutrition Education, 23*(1), 3-9.

Matthews, L. E. (1987). Perceptions of elderly residents - geriatric not pediatric. *Journal of Nutrition for the Elderly, 6*(3), 57-60.

McDaniel, J. H., Hunt, A., Hackes, B., & Pope, J. F. (2001). Impact of the dining room environment on nutritional intake of Alzheimer's residents: A case study. *American Journal of Alzheimer's Disease and Other Dementias, 16*(5), 297-302.

McDonald, J., Quandt, S. A., Arcury, T. A., Bell, R. A., & Vitolins, M. Z. (2000). On their own: Nutritional self-management strategies of rural widowers. *The Gerontologist, 40*(4), 480-491.

McGinnis, J. M., & Meyers, L. D. (1995). Dietary change and health: policy implications. *Behavioral Medicine, 20*(4), 165-169.

McIntosh, W. A., & Shifflett, P. A. (1984). The influence of social support systems on dietary intake of the elderly. *Journal of Nutrition of the Elderly, 4*(1), 5-18.

McIntosh, W. A., & Zey, M. (1998). Women as gatekeepers of food consumption: A sociological critique. In C. Counihan, & S. Kaplan (Eds.), *Food and Gender: Identity and Power* (pp. 125-144). Amsterdam: Harwood Academic Publishers.

McKenzie, J., & Keller, H. H. (2003). Who are the users of vitamin-mineral and herbal preparations among community-living older adults? *Canadian Journal of Aging, 22*(2), 167-175.

McKie, L., MacInnes, A., Hendry, J., Donald, S., & Peace, H. (2000). The food consumption patterns and perceptions of dietary advice of older people. *Journal of Human Nutrition and Dietetics, 13*(3), 173-183.

Medeiros, L. C., Shipp, R., & Taylor, D. T. (1993). Dietary practices and nutrition beliefs through the adult life cycle. *Journal of Nutrition Education, 25*(4), 201-204.

Mennell, S. (1996). *All Manners of Food: Eating and Taste in England and France from the Middle Ages to the Present* (2nd ed.). Champaign, IL: University of Illinois Press.

Mennell, S., Murcott, A., & van Otterloo, A. H. (1992). The sociology of food: eating, diet and culture. *Current Sociology, 40*(2), 1-46.

Michels, K. B., & Wolk, A. (2002). A prospective study of variety of healthy foods and mortality in women. *International Journal of Epidemiology, 31*(4), 847-854.

Miles, M. B., & Huberman, A. M. (1994). *Qualitative Data Analysis: An Expanded Sourcebook* (2nd ed.). Thousand Oaks, CA: Sage.

Mitchell, J. (1999). California residents measure quality. *Assisted Living Today, 6*(3), 50-53.

Moen, P., Dempster-McClain, D., & Williams, R. M. (1992). Successful aging: A life course perspective on women's multiple roles and health. *American Journal of Sociology, 97*(6), 1612-1638.

Morgan, K. J., Zabik, M. E., & Stampley, G. L. (1986). Breakfast consumption patterns of older Americans. *Journal of Nutrition for the Elderly, 5*(4), 19-44.

Morley, J. E. (1993). Nutrition and the older female: A review. *Journal of the American College of Nutrition, 12*(4), 337-343.

Murcott, A. (1982). On the social significance of the cooked dinner in South Wales. *Social Science Information, 21*(4/5), 677-696.

Nickels, A. (2000). Eating habits. *Assisted Living Today, 7*(9), 55-56.

Niewind, A. C., Krondl, M., & Lau, D. (1988). Relative impact of selected factors on food choices of elderly individuals. *Canadian Journal on Aging, 7*(1), 32-47.

Nolan, B. A., & Mathews, R. M. (2004). Facilitating resident information seeking regarding meals in a special care unit: an environmental design intervention. *Journal of Gerontological Nursing, 30*(10), 12-16.

Nowicki, J. S. (1996). Health behaviors and the Great Depression. *Geriatric Nursing, 17*(5), 247-250.

O'Brien, R. W., & Bush, P. J. (1997). Health behavior in children. In D. S. Gochman (Ed.), *Handbook of Health Behavior Research III: Demography, Development and Diversity* (pp. 49-72). New York: Plenum Press.

O'Brien Cousins, S. (2000). "My heart couldn't take it": Older women's beliefs about exercise benefits and risks. *Journals of Gerontology Series B: Psychological Sciences and Social Sciences, 55B*(5), P283-P294.

Oka, M., & Chaboyer, W. (1999). Dietary behaviors and sources of support in hemodialysis patients. *Clinical Nursing Research, 8*(4), 302-314.

Olson, C. M. (2005). Tracking of food choices across the transition to motherhood. *Journal of Nutrition Education and Behavior, 37*(3), 129-136.

O'Rand, A. M., & Krecker, M. L. (1990). Concepts of the life cycle: Their history, meanings and uses in the social sciences. *Annual Review of Sociology, 16*(1), 241-262.

Ory, M. G., Abeles, R. P., & Lipman, P. D. (1992). Introduction: An overview of research on aging, health, and behavior. In M. G. Ory, R. P. Abeles, & P. D. Lipman (Eds.), *Aging, Health and Behavior* (pp. 1-23). Newbury Park, CA: Sage.

Padula, C. A., Rossi, S., Nigg, C., Lees, F., Fey-Yensan, N., Greene, G., et al. (2003). Using focus groups for instrument development: application of the transtheoretical model to fruit and vegetable behaviors of older adults. *Journal of Nutrition for the Elderly, 22*(4), 13-33.

Paisley, J., Sheeshka, J., & Daly, K. (2001). Qualitative investigation of the meanings of eating fruits and vegetables for adult couples. *Journal of Nutrition Education, 33*(4), 199-207.

Parham, E. S. (1993). Enhancing social support in weight loss management groups. *Journal of the American Dietetic Association, 93*(10), 1152-1156.

Patterson, B. H., Block, G., Rosenberger, W. F., Pee, D., & Kahle, L. L. (1990). Fruit and vegetables in the American diet: Data from the NHANES II Survey. *American Journal of Public Health, 80*(12), 1443-1449.

Paulin, G. D. (2000). Let's do lunch: Expenditures on meals away from home. *Monthly Labor Review, 123*(5), 36-45.

Pavis, S., Cunningham-Burley, S., & Amos, A. (1998). Health-related behavioral change in context: Young people in transition. *Social Science and Medicine, 47*(10), 1407-1418.

Pearson, A., Fitzgerald, M., & Nay, R. (2003). Mealtimes in nursing homes: the role of nursing staff. *Journal of Gerontological Nursing, 29*(6), 41-47.

Percival, J. (2002). Domestic spaces: uses and meanings in the daily lives of older people. *Ageing and Society, 22*(6), 729-749.

Pestello, F. P. (1995). Committed selves, epiphany, and behavioral consistency: A study of commitment to 'natural' dieting. *Studies in Symbolic Interaction, 17*, 185-205.

Pezza, P. E. (1990-1991). Efforts to promote lifestyle change and better health: Whither symbolic interactionism? *International Quarterly of Community Health Education, 10*(4), 273-283.

260

Pierce, M., Sheehan, N., & Ferris, A. M. (2002). Nutrition concerns of low-income elderly women and related social support. *Journal of Nutrition for the Elderly, 21*(3), 37-53.

Potts, M., Hurwicz, M., Goldstein, M., & Berkanovic, E. (1992). Social support, health-promotive beliefs and preventive health behaviors among the elderly. *Journal of Applied Gerontology, 11*(4), 425-440.

Prohaska, T. R., & Clark, M. A. (1997). Health behavior and the human life cycle. In D. S. Gochman (Ed.), *Handbook of Health Behavior Research III: Demography, Development, and Diversity* (pp. 29-37). New York: Plenum Press.

Prohaska, T. R., Peters, K. E., & Warren, J. S. (2000). Health behavior: From research to community practice. In G. Albrecht, R. Fitzpatrick, & S. Scrimshaw (Eds.), *The Handbook of Social Studies in Health and Medicine* (pp. 359-373). Thousand Oaks, CA: Sage.

Quandt, S. A., Arcury, T. A., Bell, R. A., McDonald, J., & Vitolins, M. Z. (2001). The social and nutritional meaning of food sharing among older rural adults. *Journal of Aging Studies, 15*(2), 145-162.

Quandt, S. A., McDonald, J., Arcury, T. A., Bell, R. A., & Vitolins, M. Z. (2000). Nutritional self- management of elderly widows in rural communities. *The Gerontologist, 40*(1), 86-96.

Quandt, S. A., Vitolins, M. Z., DeWalt, K. M., & Roos, G. M. (1997). Meal patterns of older adults in rural communities: Life course analysis and implications for undernutrition. *Journal of Applied Gerontology, 16*(2), 152-172.

Rahkonen, O., Lahelma, E., & Huuhka, M. (1997). Past or present? Childhood living conditions and current socioeconomic status as determinants of adult health. *Social Science and Medicine, 44*(3), 327-336.

Rainey, C. J., Mayo, R. M., Haley-Zitlin, V., Kemper, K. A., & Cason, K. L. (2000). Nutritional beliefs, attitudes and practices of elderly, rural, Southern women. *Journal of Nutrition for the Elderly, 20*(2), 3-27.

Rakowski, W., & Hickey, T. (1980). Late life health behavior: Integrating health beliefs and temporal perspectives. *Research on Aging, 2*(3), 283-308.

Rakowski, W., Julius, M., Hickey, T., & Halter, J. (1987). Correlates of preventive health behavior in late life. *Research on Aging, 9*(3), 331-355.

Raynes, N. V. (1998). Involving residents in quality specification. *Ageing and Society, 18*(1), 65-78.

Read, M., & Schlenker, E. D. (1993). Food selection patterns among the aged. In E. D. Schlenker (Ed.), *Nutrition in Aging* (pp. 284-312). St. Louis: Mosby.

Reynolds, J. S., Kennon, L. R., & Kniatt, N. L. (1998). From the golden arches to the golden pond: Fast food and older adults. *Marriage and Family Review, 28*(1-2), 213-224.

Rieker, P., & Bird, C. E. (2000). Sociological explanations of gender differences in mental and physical health. In C. E. Bird, P. Conrad, & A. Fremont

(Eds.), *Handbook of Medical Sociology* (pp. 98-113). Upper Saddle River, NJ: Prentice Hall.

Riffle, K. L., Yoho, J., & Sams, J. (1989). Health-promoting behaviors, perceived social support, and self-reported health of Appalachian elderly. *Public Health Nursing, 6*(4), 204-211.

Rimal, A. P. (2002). Factors affecting meat preferences among American consumers. *Family Economics and Nutrition Review, 14*(2), 36-43.

Rimal, R. N., & Flora, J. A. (1998). Bi-directional familial influences in dietary behavior: Test of a model of campaign influences. *Human Communication Research, 24*(4), 610-638.

Roebuck, J. (1986). Sociability in a black outdoor drinking place. *Studies in Symbolic Interaction, 7*(A), 161-197.

Rose, J. H. (1991). A life course perspective on health threats in aging. *Journal of Gerontological Social Work, 17*(3-4), 85-97.

Rosenbloom, C. A., & Whittington, F. J. (1993). Effects of bereavement on eating behaviors and nutrient intakes in elderly widowed persons. *Journals of Gerontology Series B: Psychological Sciences and Social Sciences, 48*(4), S223-S229.

Russell, C., & Porter, M. (2003). Single older men in disadvantaged households: narratives of meaning around everyday life. *Ageing International, 28*(4), 359-371.

Rybarczyk, B., & Bellg, A. (1997*). Listening to Life Stories: A New Approach to Stress Intervention in Health Care*. New York: Springer.

Sallis, J. F., & Owen, N. (1997). Ecological models. In K. Glanz, F. Lewis, & B. Rimer (Eds.), *Health Behavior and Health Education: Theory, Research and Practice* (2nd ed., pp. 403-424). San Francisco: Jossey- Bass.

Schafer, R. B., & Keith, P. M. (1981). Influences on food decisions across the family life cycle. *Journal of the American Dietetic Association, 78*, 144-148.

Schafer, R. B., & Keith, P. M. (1982). Social-psychological factors in the dietary quality of married and single elderly. *Journal of the American Dietetic Association, 81*, 30-34.

Schafer, R. B., & Schafer, E. (1989). Relationship between gender and food roles in the family. *Journal of Nutrition Education, 21*(3), 119-126.

Schlettwein, G. D., & Barclay, D. (1995). Dietary habits and attitudes in healthy elderly. In J. L. C. Dall, M. Ermini, P. L. Herrling, W. Meier-Ruge, & H. B. Stahelin (Eds.), *Adaptations in Aging* (pp. 253-264). San Diego: Academic Press.

Schoenberg, N. E. (1998). The relationship between perceptions of social support and adherence to dietary recommendations among African-American elders with hypertension. *International Journal of Aging and Human Development, 47*(4), 279-297.

Schone, B. S., & Weinick, R. M. (1998). Health-related behaviors and the benefits of marriage for elderly persons. *The Gerontologist, 38*(5), 618-627.

262

Seigley, L. (1998). Effects of personal and environmental factors on health behaviors of older adults. *Nursing Connections, 11*(4), 47-58.

Shahar, D. R., Schultz, R., Shahar, A., & Wing, R. R. (2001). The effect of widowhood on weight change, dietary intake, and eating behavior in the elderly population. *Journal of Aging and Health, 13*(2), 186-199.

Sharpe, D. L., Huston, S. J., & Finke, M. S. (2003). Factors affecting nutritional adequacy among single elderly women. *Family Economics and Nutrition Review, 15*(1), 74-82.

Sharpe, P. A., & Mezoff, J. S. (1995). Beliefs about diet and health: Qualitative interviews with low income older women in the rural South. *Journal of Women and Aging, 7*(1-2), 5-18.

Shelton, A. (1993). Writing McDonald's, eating the past: McDonald's as a postmodern space. *Studies in Symbolic Interaction, 15*, 103-118.

Sidenvall, B., Nydahl, M., & Fjellstrom, C. (2000). The meal as a gift - the meaning of cooking among retired women. *Journal of Applied Gerontology, 19*(4), 405-423.

Sidenvall, B., Nydahl, M., & Fjellstrom, C. (2001). Managing food shopping and cooking: The experiences of older Swedish women. *Ageing and Society, 21*(2), 151-168.

Sigman, S. J. (1985). Conversational behavior in two health care institutions for the elderly. *International Journal of Aging and Human Development, 21*(2), 137-154.

Silverman, P., Hecht, L., & McMillin, J. D. (2002). Social support and dietary change among older adults. *Ageing and Society, 22*(1), 29-59.

Sisk, R. J. (2000). Caregiver burden and health promotion. *International Journal of Nursing Studies, 37*(1), 37-43.

Sjoberg, S., Kim, K., & Reicks, M. (2004). Applying the theory of planned behavior to fruit and vegetable consumption by older adults. *Journal of Nutrition for the Elderly, 23*(4), 35-46.

Slesinski, M. J., Subar, A. F., & Kahle, L. L. (1995). Trends in use of vitamin and mineral supplements in the United States: The 1987 and 1992 National Health Interview Surveys. *Journal of the American Dietetic Association, 95*(8), 921-923.

Smith, A. (1998). Breakfast consumption and intelligence in elderly persons. *Psychological Reports, 82*(2), 424-426.

Sobal, J., Bove, C. F., & Rauschenbach, B. S. (2002). Commensal careers at entry into marriage: Establishing commensal units and managing commensal circles. *The Sociological Review, 50*(3), 378-397.

Sobal, J., & Maurer, D. (Eds.). (2000). *Interpreting Weight: The Social Management of Fatness and Thinness*. New York: Aldine de Gruyter.

Spangler, A. A., & Pettit, R. T. (2003). Differences in preferences of entrees by elderly congregate meal participants according to age, gender, ethnicity and education and a factor analysis approach to group entree preferences. *Journal of Nutrition for the Elderly, 23*(2), 33-53.

263

Stearns, S. C., Bernard, S. L., Fasick, S. B., Schwartz, R., Konrad, R., Ory, M. G., et al.. (2000). Economic implications of self-care: The effects of lifestyle, functional adaptations, and medical self-care among a national sample of Medicare beneficiaries. *American Journal of Public Health, 90*(10), 1608-1612.

Stinnett, K. A., & Adams, E. C. (1995). Institutionalized frail older person and the dining experience. *Topics in Geriatric Rehabilitation, 11*(2), 26-34.

Strecher, V., DeVellis, B., Becker, M., & Rosenstock, I. (1986). The role of self-efficacy in achieving health behavior change. *Health Education Quarterly, 13*(1), 73-91.

Subar, A. F., & Block, G. (1990). Use of vitamin and mineral supplements: Demographics and amounts of nutrients consumed. *American Journal of Epidemiology, 132*(6), 1091-1102.

Sulander, T., Helakorpi, S., Rahkonen, O., Nissinen, A., & Uutela, A. (2003). Changes and associations in healthy diet among the Finnish elderly, 1985-2001. *Age and Ageing, 32*(4), 394-400.

Taub, D. E., & McLorg, P. A. (2001). Anorexia Nervosa. In D. L. Peck, & N. A. Dolch (Eds.), *Extraordinary Behavior: A Case Study Approach to Understanding Social Problems* (pp. 41-52). Westport, CT: Praeger.

Tomlinson, G. (1986). Thought for food: A study of written instructions. *Symbolic Interaction, 9*(2), 201-216.

Trippet, S. E. (1991). Being aware: The relationship between health and social support among older women. *Journal of Women and Aging, 3*(3), 69-80.

Trowbridge, F., & Collins, B. (1993). Measuring dietary behaviors among adolescents. *Public Health Reports, 108*(Supplement 1), 37-41.

Umberson, D. (1987). Family status and health behaviors: Social control as a dimension of social integration. *Journal of Health and Social Behavior, 28*(3), 306-319.

Umberson, D. (1992). Gender, marital status and the social control of health behavior. *Social Science and Medicine, 34*(8), 907-917.

U. S. Department of Health and Human Services. (2000). *Healthy People 2010: Understanding and Improving Health* (2nd ed.). Washington, D.C.: Government Printing Office.

Valentine, G. (1999). Eating in: Home, consumption and identity. *The Sociological Review, 47*(3), 491-524.

Vanderbilt, A. (1961). *Amy Vanderbilt's Complete Cookbook*. Garden City, NY: Doubleday & Company, Inc.

Verbrugge, L. M. (1990). The twain meet: Empirical explanations of sex differences in health and mortality. In M. Ory, & H. Warner (Eds.), *Gender, Health and Longevity: Multidisciplinary Perspectives* (pp. 159-199). New York: Springer.

Vitolins, M. Z., Quandt, S. A., Bell, R., Arcury, T. A., & Case, L. D. (2002). Quality of diets consumed by older rural adults. *Journal of Rural Health, 18*(1), 49-56.

264

Wadden, T. A., Stunkard, A. J., Rich, L., Rubin, C. J., Sweidel, G., & McKinney, S. (1990). Obesity in black adolescent girls: A controlled trial of treatment by diet, behavior modification, and parental support. *Pediatrics, 85*(3), 345-352.

Wadsworth, M. E. J. (1997). Health inequalities in life course perspective. *Social Science and Medicine, 44*(6), 859-869.

Waisbren, S. E., Rokni, H., Bailey, I., Brown, T., & Warner-Rogers, J. (1997). Social factors and the meaning of food in adherence to medical diets: results of a maternal phenylketonuria summer camp. *Journal of Inherited Metabolic Disease, 20*(1), 21-27.

Waldron, I. (1997). Changing gender roles and gender differences in health behavior. In D. S. Gochman (Ed.), *Handbook of Health Behavior Research I: Personal and Social Determinants* (pp. 303-328). New York: Plenum Press.

Walker, S. N. (1997). Promoting healthy aging. In K. Ferraro (Ed.), *Gerontology: Perspectives and Issues* (2nd ed., pp. 305-323). New York: Springer.

Walker, S. N., Volkan, K., Sechrist, K. R., & Pender, N. J. (1988). Health-promoting lifestyles of older adults: Comparisons with young and middle-aged adults, correlates and patterns. *Advances in Nursing Science, 11*(1), 76-90.

Wakimoto, P., & Block, G. (2001). Dietary intake, dietary patterns, and changes with age: An epidemiological perspective. *Journals of Gerontology Series A: Biological Sciences and Medical Sciences, 56A*(Special Issue II), 65-80.

Warde, A., & Hetherington, K. (1994). English households and routine food practices: A research note. *The Sociological Review, 42*(4), 758-778.

Wdowik, M. J., Kendall, P. A., & Harris, M. A. (1997). College students with diabetes: Using focus groups and interviews to determine psychosocial issues and barriers to control. *The Diabetes Educator, 23*(5), 558-562.

Wellman, N. S., & Johnson, M. A. (2004). Translating the science of nutrition into the art of healthy eating. *Generations, 28*(3), 6-10.

Weng, Y.-L., Raab, C., Georgiou, C., & Dunton, N. (2004). Herbal and vitamin/mineral supplement use by retirement community residents: preliminary findings. *Journal of Nutrition for the Elderly, 23*(3), 1-13.

Wethington, E. (2005). An overview of the life course perspective: Implications for health and nutrition. *Journal of Nutrition Education and Behavior, 37*(3), 115-120.

White, J., & Ham, R. J. (1999). Older adults. In G. Morrison, & L. Hark (Eds.), *Medical Nutrition and Disease* (2nd ed., pp. 134-155). Malden, MA: Blackwell Science.

Wickrama, K. A. S., Conger, R. D., Wallace, L. E., & Elder, G. H. (1999). The intergenerational transmission of health-risk behaviors: Adolescent lifestyles and gender moderating effects. *Journal of Health and Social Behavior, 40*(3), 258-272.

Wilcox, S., & King, A. C. (1999). Health behaviors and aging. In W. R. Hazzard, J. P. Blass, W. H. Ettinger, J. B. Halter, & J. G. Ouslander (Eds.), *Principles of Geriatric Medicine and Gerontology* (4th ed., pp. 287-302). New York: McGraw-Hill.

Wilson, D. K., & Ampey-Thornhill, G. (2001). The role of gender and family support on dietary compliance in an African American adolescent hypertension prevention study. *Annuals of Behavioral Medicine, 23*(1), 59-67.

Wing, R. R., & Jeffrey, R. W. (1999). Benefits of recruiting participants with friends and increasing social support for weight loss and maintenance. *Journal of Consulting and Clinical Psychology, 67*(1), 132-138.

Yen, P. K. (1995). What elders think about food. *Geriatric Nursing, 16*(4), 187-188.

Yoon, S. L., & Home, C. H. (2004). Perceived health promotion practice by older women: use of herbal products. *Journal of Gerontological Nursing, 30*(7), 9-15.

Yu, B. P. (2002). Nutrition as modulator of aging, disease, and longevity. *Journal of Food Science and Nutrition, 7*(1), 108-112.

Additional Sources

Aaronson, L. S. (1989). Perceived and received support: Effects on health behavior during pregnancy. *Nursing Research, 38*, 4-9.

Adler, T. A. (1981). Making pancakes on Sunday: The male cook in family tradition. *Western Folklore, 40*(1), 45-54.

Alibrio, T. (1991). Food: An important focus for nursing home residents. *Nursing Homes, 40*(2), 9-10.

Alpert, B., Field, T., Goldstein, S., & Perry, S. (1990). Aerobics enhances cardiovascular fitness and agility in preschoolers. *Health Psychology, 9*, 48-56.

Andersson, I., & Sidenvall, B. (2001). Case studies of food shopping, cooking and eating habits in older women with Parkinson's disease. *Journal of Advanced Nursing, 35*(1), 69-78.

Azjen, I. (1991). The theory of planned behavior. *Organizational Behavior and Human Decision Processes, 50*(2), 179-211.

Beers, M. H., & Berkow, R (Eds.). (1999). *The Merck Manual of Diagnosis and Therapy* (17th ed., Internet ed.). Retrieved July 18, 2002, from http://www.merck.com/pubs/mmnaual/section1/chapter2/2a.htm.

Bell, R., Vitolins, M. Z., Arcury, T. A., & Quandt, S. A. (2003). Food consumption patterns of rural older African American, Native American, and white adults in North Carolina. *Journal of Nutrition for the Elderly, 23*(2), 1-16.

Bidlack, W. R., & Wang, W. (1995). Nutrition requirements of the elderly. In J. E. Morley, Z. Glick, & L. Z. Rubenstein (Eds.), *Geriatric Nutrition* (2nd ed., pp. 25-49). New York: Raven Press, Ltd.

Blake, C., & Bisogni, C. A. (2003). Personal and family food choice schemas of rural women living in upstate New York. *Journal of Nutrition Education and Behavior, 35*(6), 282-293.

Blumer, H. (1969). *Symbolic Interactionism: Perspective and Method.* Englewood Cliffs, NJ: Prentice-Hall.

Bohannan, P. (1981). Food of old people in center-city hotels. In C. Fry (Ed.), *Dimensions of Aging, Culture and Health* (pp. 185-200). Brooklyn, NY: J.F. Bergin Publishers.

Bonnel, W. B. (1995). Managing mealtime in the dependent group dining room: An educational program for nurse's aides. *Geriatric Nursing, 16*(1), 28-32.

Breitung, J. (1980). Nutrition survey of the well older adult. *Perspective on Aging, 9*(6), 19-21.

Brooks, S. (1994). Dining with dignity. *Contemporary Long Term Care, 17*(9), 43-44.

Brownell, K. D. (1984). The psychology and physiology of obesity: Implications for screening and treatment. *Journal of the American Dietetic Association, 84*(4), 406-414.

Bruss, M. B., Morris, J., & Dannison, L. (2003). Prevention of childhood obesity: sociocultural and familial factors. *Journal of the American Dietetic Association, 103*(8), 1042-1045.

Brustad, R. J. (1996). Attraction to physical activity in urban schoolchildren: parental socialization and gender influences. *Research Quarterly for Exercise and Sport, 67*(3), 316-324.

Chao, S., Hagisavas, V., Mollica, R., & Dwyer, J. (2003). Time for assessment of nutrition services in assisted living facilities. *Journal of Nutrition for the Elderly, 23*(1), 41-55.

Clarke, E. (2001). Role conflicts and coping strategies in caregiving: A symbolic interactionist perspective. *Journal of Psychosocial Nursing and Mental Health Services, 39*(1), 28-37.

Clipp, E. C., Pavalko, E. K., & Elder, G. H. (1992). Trajectories of health: In concept and empirical pattern. *Behavior, Health, and Aging, 2*(3), 159-179.

Cohen, S., Lichtenstein, E., Mermelstein, R., Kingsolver, K., Baer, J. S., & Kamarck, T. W. (1988). Social support interventions for smoking cessation. In B. H. Gottlieb (Ed.), *Marshaling Social Support: Formats, Processes and Effects* (pp. 211-240). Newbury Park, CA: Sage.

Conner, M. (1994). Accounting for gender, age and socioeconomic differences in food choice. *Appetite, 23*(2), 195.

Dabbenigno, P. (1998). Dining experience. *Assisted Living Today, 5*(6), 36-41.

Dannefer, D., & Uhlenberg, P. (1999). Paths of the life course: A typology. In V. Bengtson, & K. W. Schaie (Eds.), *Handbook of Theories of Aging* (pp. 306-326). New York: Springer.

Devine, C. M., Connors, M., Sobal, J., & Bisogni, C. A. (2003). Sandwiching it in: spillover of work onto food choices and family roles in low- and moderate-income urban households. *Social Science and Medicine, 56*(3), 617-630.

Dinsmore, B. D., & Stormshak, E. A. (2003). Family functioning and eating attitudes and behaviors in at-risk early adolescent girls: The mediating role of intra-personal competencies. *Current Psychology, 22*(2), 100-116.

Edwards, K. A. (1979). Dining experiences in the institutional setting. *Nursing Homes, 28*(2), 6-17.

Fetto, J. (2003). Meals that heal. *American Demographics, 25*(6), 48.

Fiatarone Singh, M. A., & Rosenberg, I. H. (1999). Nutrition and aging. In W. R. Hazzard, J. P. Blass, W. H. Ettinger, J. B. Halter, & J. G. Ouslander (Eds.), *Principles of Geriatric Medicine and Gerontology* (4th ed., pp. 81-96). New York: McGraw-Hill.

Fife, B. L. (1994). The conceptualization of meaning in illness. *Social Science and Medicine, 38*(2), 309-316.

Fishbein, M. (Ed.). (1967). *Readings in Attitude Theory and Measurement*. New York: Wiley.

Foltz-Gray, D. (1996). Pleasing the palate. *Contemporary Long Term Care, 19*(8), 54-56.

Foltz-Gray, D. (1998). Let them eat cake. *Contemporary Long Term Care, 21*(7), 60-64.

Ford, E. S., Ahluwalia, I. B., & Galuska, D. A. (2000). Social relationships and cardiovascular disease risk factors: Findings from the third National Health and Nutrition Examination Survey. *Preventive Medicine, 30*(2), 83-92.

Frank, A. W. (2000). Illness and interactionist vocation. *Symbolic Interaction, 23*(4), 321-332.

Gallo, A., & Boehm, W. T. (1978). Food purchasing patterns of senior citizens. *National Food Review, 75*, 42-45.

Garay-Sevilla, M. E., Nava, L. E., Malacara, J. M., Huerta, R., Diaz de Leon, J., Mena, A., et al. (1995). Adherence to treatment and social support in patients with non-insulin dependent diabetes mellitus. *Journal of Diabetes and Its Complications, 9*(2), 81-86.

Gettings, M. A., & Kiernan, N. E. (2001). Practices and perceptions of food safety among seniors who prepare meals at home. *Journal of Nutrition Education, 33*(3), 148-154.

Glaser, B., & Strauss, A. (1967). *The Discovery of Grounded Theory: Strategies for Qualitative Research*. Chicago: Aldine.

268

268

Guigoz, Y. (1995). Recommended dietary allowances (RDA) for the elderly. In B. J. Vellas et al. (Eds.) *Facts and Research in Gerontology* (Supplement: Nutrition, pp. 205-208). New York: Springer.

Hanson, B. S., Matisson, I., & Steen, B. (1987). Dietary intake and psychosocial factors in 68 year-old men: A population study. *Comprehensive Gerontology, 1*(2), 62-67.

Hart, J., Einav, C., Weingarten, M. A., & Stein, M. (1990). The importance of family support in a behavior modification weight loss program. *Journal of the American Dietetic Association, 90*(9), 1270-1271.

Hawley, P. J., & Klauber, M. R. (1988). Health practices and perceptions of social support in persons over age sixty. *Journal of Applied Gerontology, 7*(2), 205-230.

Haveman-Nies, A., de Groot, L. C. P. M. G., & van Staveren, W. A. (2003). Relation of dietary quality, physical activity, and smoking habits to 10-year changes in health status in older Europeans in the SENECA study. *American Journal of Public Health, 93*(2), 318-323.

Hays, N. P., Bathalon, G. P., Roubenoff, R., Lipmann, R., & Roberts, S. B. (2002). The association of eating behavior with risk for morbidity in older women. *Journals of Gerontology Series A: Biological Sciences and Medical Sciences, 57*(2), M128-M133.

Hiatt, L. G. (1981). Designing therapeutic dining. *Nursing Homes, 30*(2), 33-39.

Janzen, W., & O'Brien Cousins, S. (1995). "I do" or don't: Marriage, women, and physical activity throughout the lifespan. *Journal of Women and Aging, 7*(1/2), 55-70.

Kaplan, G. A., Seeman, T. E., Cohen, R. D., Knudsen, L. P., & Guralnik, J. (1987). Mortality among the elderly in the Alameda County Study: Behavioral and demographic risk factors. *American Journal of Public Health, 77*(3), 307-312.

Kaplan, R. M., & Hartwell, S. L. (1987). Differential effects of social support and social network on physiological and social outcomes in men and women with type II diabetes mellitus. *Health Psychology, 6*(5), 387-398.

Kim, K. H., & Sobal, J. (2004). Religion, social support, fat intake, and physical activity. *Public Health Nutrition, 7*(6), 773-781.

Kimiecik, J. C., & Horn, T. S. (1998). Parental beliefs and children's moderate-to-vigorous physical activity. *Research Quarterly for Exercise and Sport, 69*(2), 163-176.

Lutz, B. (2001). Restaurateur's approach. *Contemporary Long Term Care, 24*(6), 15.

Maddux, J. E., & DuCharme, K. A. (1997). Behavioral intentions in theories of health behavior. In D. S. Gochman (Ed.), *Handbook of Health Behavior Research I: Personal and Social Determinants* (pp. 133-151). New York: Plenum Press.

Mai, V., Kant, A. K., Flood, A., Lacey, J. V., Schairer, C., & Schatzkin, A. (2005). Diet quality and subsequent cancer incidence and mortality in a prospective cohort of women. *International Journal of Epidemiology, 34*(1), 54-60.

Manthorpe, J., & Watson, R. (2003). Poorly served? Eating and dementia. *Journal of Advanced Nursing, 41*(2), 162-169.

Martikainen, P., Brunner, E., & Marmot, M. (2003). Socioeconomic differences in dietary patterns among middle-aged men and women. *Social Science and Medicine, 56*(7), 1397-1410.

Mayo, R. M., & Rainey, C. J. (2001). What we think they think: Health professionals' views of nutritional beliefs and practices of low income older women. *Journal of Nutrition for the Elderly, 20*(4), 19-41.

McIntosh, W. A., Shifflett, P. A., & Picou, J. S. (1989). Social support, stressful events, strain, dietary intake, and the elderly. *Medical Care, 27*(2), 140-153.

Misra, R., & Aguillon, S. (1999). Health behaviors in rural adolescents. *International Journal of Sociology and Social Policy, 19*(12), 1-20.

Molis, D. B. (1993). Classic cuisine: Innovations in food service. *Provider, 19*(4), 18-25.

Morgan, C. F., McKenzie, T. L., Sallis, J. S., Broyles, S. A., Nader, P. R., & Zive, M. M. (2001). Gender and ethnic differences among psychological, social, and environmental correlates of physical activity in adolescents. *Research Quarterly for Exercise and Sport, 72*(1), A-89.

Morley, J. E. (1995). The role of nutrition in the prevention of age-associated diseases. In J. E. Morley, Z. Glick, & L. Z. Rubenstein (Eds.), *Geriatric Nutrition* (2nd ed., pp. 63-73). New York: Raven Press, Ltd.

Murphy, P. A., Prewitt, T. E., Boté, E., West, B., & Iber, F. L. (2001). Internal locus of control and social support associated with some dietary changes by elderly participants in a diet intervention trial. *Journal of the American Dietetic Association, 101*(2), 203-208.

National Policy and Resource Center on Nutrition and Aging. (2001, December 18). Table 1: Dietary Reference Intakes for Older Adults. Miami: Florida International University. Retrieved March 20, 2002: http://www.fiu.edu/~nutreldr/Resources/DRIs/DRI_ Table1.pdf

National Research Council. (1989). *Recommended Dietary Allowances* (10th ed.). Washington, D.C.: National Academy Press.

O'Brien Cousins, S. (1998). *Exercise, Aging and Health: Overcoming Barriers to an Active Old Age.* Philadelphia: Brunner/ Mazel.

O'Brien Cousins, S., & Keating, N. (1995). Life cycle patterns of physical activity among sedentary and active older women. *Journal of Aging and Physical Activity, 3*, 340-359.

O'Neill, C., & Sorenson, E. S. (1991). Home care of the elderly: A family perspective. *Advances in Nursing Science, 13*(4), 28-37.

O'Reilly, P., & Thomas, H. E. (1989). Role of support networks in maintenance of improved cardiovascular health status. *Social Science and Medicine, 28*(3), 249-260.

Paffenbarger, R. S., Kampert, J. B., Lee, I. M., Hyde, R. T., Leung, R. W., & Wing, A. L. (1994). Changes in physical activity and other lifeway patterns influencing longevity. *Medicine and Science in Sports and Exercise, 26,* 857-865.

Pagan, J. (2001). Satisfaction guaranteed. *Contemporary Long Term Care, 24*(8), 33.

Paisley, J., & Skrzypczyk, S. (2005). Qualitative investigation of differences in benefits and challenges of eating fruits versus vegetables as perceived by Canadian women. *Journal of Nutrition Education and Behavior, 37*(2), 77-82.

Pate, R. R., Trost, S. G., Felton, G. M., Ward, D. S., Dowda, M., & Saunders, R. (1997). Correlates of physical activity behavior in rural youth. *Research Quarterly for Exercise and Sport, 68*(3), 241-249.

Pham, D. T., Fortin, F., & Thibaudeau, M. F. (1996). The role of the Health Belief Model in amputees' self-evaluation of adherence to diabetes self-care behaviors. *The Diabetes Educator, 22*(2), 126-132.

Pierce, M. B., Sheehan, N. W., & Ferris, A. M. (2001). Older women living in subsidized housing report low levels of nutrition support. *Journal of the American Dietetic Association, 101*(2), 251-254.

Pliner, P. (1983). Family resemblance in food preferences. *Journal of Nutrition Education, 15*(4), 137-140.

Pratt, L. (1973). Child-rearing methods and children's health behavior. *Journal of Health and Social Behavior, 14*(1), 61-69.

Pratt, L. (1976). *Family Structure and Effective Health Behavior: The Energized Family.* Boston: Houghton Mifflin.

Prochaska, J. O. (1979). *Systems of Psychotherapy: A Transtheoretical Analysis.* Pacific Grove, CA: Brooks-Cole.

Prochaska, J., Redding, C., & Evers, K. (1997). The transtheoretical model and stages of change. In K. Glanz, F. Lewis, & B. Rimer (Eds.), *Health Behavior and Health Education: Theory, Research and Practice* (2nd ed., pp. 60-84). San Francisco: Jossey-Bass.

Prout, A. (1989). Sickness as a dominant symbol in life course transitions: An illustrated theoretical framework. *Sociology of Health and Illness, 11*(4), 336-359.

Rakowski, W. (1988). Age cohorts and personal health behavior in adulthood. *Research on Aging, 10*(1), 3-35.

Resnick, B. (2000). Health promotion practices of the older adult. *Public Health Nursing, 17*(3), 160-168.

Robert, S. A., & House, J. S. (1994). Socioeconomic status and health over the life course. In R. P. Abeles, H. C. Gift, & M. G. Ory (Eds.), *Aging and Quality of Life* (pp. 253-274). New York: Springer.

Rogers, K. R. (1987). Nature of spousal supportive behaviors that influence heart transplant patient compliance. *Journal of Heart Transplantation, 6*(2), 90-95.

Rogers, R. (1975). A protection motivation theory of fear appeals and attitude change. *Journal of Psychology, 91*(1), 93-114.

Rogers, R. W., & Prentice-Dunn, S. (1997). Protection motivation theory. In D. S. Gochman (Ed.), *Handbook of Health Behavior Research I: Personal and Social Determinants* (pp. 113-132). New York: Plenum Press.

Rolfes, S. R., DeBruyne, L. K., & Whitney, E. R. (1998). *Life Span Nutrition: Conception Through Life.* Belmont, CA: West/Wadsworth.

Rosenstock, I. M. (1960). What research in motivation suggests for public health. *American Journal of Public Health, 50,* 295-301.

Ruggiero, L., Spirito, A., Bond, A., Coustan, D., & McGarvey, S. (1990). Impact of social support and stress on compliance in women with gestational diabetes. *Diabetes Care, 13*(4), 441-443.

Sallis, J. F., Alcarz, J. E., McKenzie, T. L., Hovell, M. F., Kolody, B., & Nader, P. R. (1993). Parental behavior in relation to physical activity and fitness in 9-year-old children. *American Journal of Diseases in Children, 146,* 1383-1388.

Sallis, J. F., Hovell, M. F., Hofstetter, R., & Barrington, E. (1992). Explanation of vigorous physical activity during two years using social learning variables. *Social Science and Medicine, 34*(1), 25-32.

Sallis, J. F., Taylor, W. C., Prochaska, J. J., Hill, J. O., & Geraci, J. C. (1999). Correlates of physical activity in a national sample of girls and boys in grades 4 through 12. *Health Psychology, 18*(4), 410-415.

Schoenberg, N. E. (2000). Patterns, factors, and pathways contributing to nutritional risk among rural African American elders. *Human Organization, 59*(2), 234-244.

Schumacher, K. L. (1995). Family caregiver role acquisition: Role-making through situated interaction. *Scholarly Inquiry for Nursing Practice, 9*(3), 211-226.

Sharkey, J. F. (2002). Interrelationship of nutritional risk factors, indicators of nutritional risk, and severity of disability among home-delivered meal participants. *The Gerontologist, 42*(3), 373-380.

Sharkey, J. F., & Branch, L. G. (2004). Gender differences in physical performance, body composition, and dietary intake in homebound elders. *Journal of Women and Aging, 16*(3-4), 71-90.

Shifflett, P. A. (1987). Future time perspective, past experiences, and negotiation of food use patterns among the aged. *Gerontologist, 27*(5), 611-615.

Shifflett, P. A., & McIntosh, W. A. (1986-1987). Food habits and future time: An exploratory study of age-appropriate food habits among the elderly. *International Journal of Aging and Human Development, 24*(1), 1-17.

Sobal, J. (2005). Men, meat, and marriage: Models of masculinity. *Food & Foodways, 13*(1-2), 135-158.

Soltesz, K. S., & Dayton, J. H. (1995). Effects of menu modification to increase dietary intake and maintain the weight of Alzheimer residents. *American Journal of Alzheimer's Disease and Other Dementias, 10*(6), 20-23.

272

Stokes, R., & Frederick-Recascino, C. (2003). Women's perceived body image: relations with personal happiness. *Journal of Women and Aging, 15*(1), 17-29.

Story, M., Neumark-Sztainer, D., & French, S. (2002). Individual and environmental influences on adolescent eating behaviors. *Journal of the American Dietetic Association, 102*(3, Supplement 1), S40-S51.

Tayback, M., Kumanyaki, S., & Chu, E. (1990). Body weight as a risk factor in the elderly. *Archives of Internal Medicine, 150*(1065-1072).

Taylor, D., & Polan, E. (1998). *Journey Across the Life Span: Human Development and Health Promotion.* Philadelphia: F.A. Davis Co.

Tinsley, B. J. (1997). Maternal influences on children's health behavior. In D. S. Gochman (Ed.), *Handbook of Health Behavior Research I: Personal and Social Determinants* (pp. 223-240). New York: Plenum Press.

Torres, C. C., McIntosh, W. A., & Kubena, K. S. (1992). Social network and social background characteristics of elderly who live and eat alone. *Journal of Aging and Health, 4*(4), 564-578.

Tucker, K. L., Hallfrisch, J., Qiao, N., Muller, D., Andres, R., & Fleg, J. L. (2005). The combination of high fruit and vegetable and low saturated fat intakes is more protective against mortality in aging men than is either alone: The Baltimore Longitudinal Study of Aging. *Journal of Nutrition, 135*(3), 556-561.

Vailas, L. I., Nitzke, S. A., Becker, M., & Gast, J. (1998). Risk indicators for malnutrition are associated inversely with quality of life for participants in meal programs for older adults. *Journal of the American Dietetic Association, 98*(5), 548-553.

Vellas, B. J., Guigoz, Y., Garry, P. J., & Albarede, J. L. (Eds.). (1997). *The Mini-Nutritional Assessment: MNA* (Nutrition in the Elderly, 3rd ed.). New York: Springer.

Vereecken, C. A., Van Damme, W., & Maes, L. (2005). Measuring attitudes, self-efficacy, and social and environmental influences on fruit and vegetable consumption of 11- and 12-year-old children: reliability and validity. *Journal of the American Dietetic Association, 105*(2), 257-261.

Walker, D., & Beauchene, R. E. (1991). The relationship of loneliness, social isolation, and physical health to dietary adequacy of independently living elderly. *Journal of the American Dietetic Association, 91*(3), 300-304.

Wallston, B. S., Wallston, K. A., Kaplan, G. D., & Maides, S. A. (1976). The development and validation of the health related locus of control (HLC) construct. *Journal of Consulting and Clinical Psychology, 44*, 580-585.

Walsh, N. (2001). Elderly immunity can be compromised by poor nutrition. *Family Practice News, 31*(4), 12.

Wardle, J., Carnell, S., & Cooke, L. (2005). Parental control over feeding and children's fruit and vegetable intake: How are they related? *Journal of the American Dietetic Association, 105*(2), 227-232.

Weddle, D. O., Wellman, N. S., & L. R. Shoaf. (1996). Position of the American Dietetic Association: Nutrition, aging, and the continuum of care. *Journal of the American Dietetic Association, 96*(10): 1048-1052.

Wellman, N. S., & Johnson, M. A. (Eds.). (2004). Food and nutrition for healthier aging. *Generations, 28*(3).

Wells, Y. D., & Kendig, H. L. (1997). Health and well-being of spouse caregivers and the widowed. *The Gerontologist, 37*, 666-674.

Wilson, M. M. G., & Kaiser, F. E. (1995). Nutrition in women. In Vellas et al. (Eds.) *Facts and Research in Gerontology* (Supplement: Nutrition, pp. 181-205). New York: Springer.

Wright, J. R. (1999). Food service by the book. *Nursing Homes: Long Term Care Management, 48*(6), 45-46.

Wylie, C., Copeman, J., & Kirk, S. (1999). Health and social factors affecting the food choice and nutritional intake of elderly people with restricted mobility. *Journal of Human Nutrition and Dietetics, 12*(5), 375-389.

Yang, X., Telama, R., & Laakso, L. (1996). Parents' physical activity, socioeconomic status and education as predictors of physical activity and sport among children and youths - A 12 year follow-up study. *International Review for the Sociology of Sport, 31*(3), 273-294.

Zgola, J., & Bordillon, G. (2001). *Bon Appetit! The Joy of Dining in Long-term Care.* Baltimore, MD: Health Professions Press.

Zimmerman, R. S., & Connor, C. (1989). Health promotion in context: The effects of significant others on health behavior change. *Health Education Quarterly, 16*, 57-75.

Index

276

dietary wellness, 138–49
early life experiences, 168, 169–70
environment. *See* environmental and spatial factors, living arrangements, and physical environment
family relationships, 29–38, 48, 99–100, 147, 170–71, 173
food and dining services, 9, 46, 75, 178, 179, 181, 183, 204
health issues, 98, 112, 132, 136, 148, 183, 185
health professionals, 37, 147, 171, 205, 206
life course perspective, 54–56
life course transitions, 175–78
lifestyle changes, 142
marital status, 36, 102, 175, 174–75
meals. *See* meals
meaning, 187
moderation, 43, 48, 135, 145
nutritional awareness, 148
older adults, 15–24, 36, 187
   racial and ethnic differences, 20
   rural, 20
   social support, 42
personal factors, 95–98
politics and economics, 122
social aspects, 24–48, 168–75, 178
social interaction, 98–105
   residents, 102–4, 172
social relationships, 29–38, 171–72
social roles, 105–7, 173–75, 177–78
social support, 43
supplementation. *See* vitamin and mineral supplementation
symbolic interactionism, 58
theory, 189–96, 199

dietary recommendations, 20, 53, 135, 143, 144, 169, 173, 205
dietary rules, 126–38, 176, 186, 187, 198, 199
dietary supplements. *See* vitamin and mineral supplementation
dieting, 26, *See* weight management
disability, 6, 29, 184
dress code, 78, 119, 120, 184, 186
duty, 3, 80, 125, 151, 152, 158, 162, 163, 165, 166, 173, 178, 180, 187
eating out, 22–23, 58, 116–18, 156, 164, 189
ecological models, 60
economics, 7, 127, 129, 175, 198, 200, *See* political and economic forces
   health care, 7
entertaining, 45, 111, 150, 151, 155, 156, 160, 173, 180, 182, 183
environmental and spatial factors, 44–47
ethnicity, 20, 55, 93, 94, 117, 200, 202, 204
family life course, 34, 177
family solidarity, 34
farms, 145
fast food, 22, 23, 58, 117, 189, 201, 202
food acquisition, 16–18, 101, 187
food and families. *See* dietary behavior, family
food bank, 152, 155, 157
food consumption, 20, 19–23, 39, 56, 126, 165, 169, 171, 184, 197
   beverages, 21
food history interview, 11, 209
food preparation, 18–19, 30, 39, 105, 135, 150, 158, 160, 163, 165, 172, 173, 176, 182, 184, 188, 197
food security, 17, 180, 181
food sharing, 17–18, 157
food shopping, 16–17, 28, 101, 174, 187